ClimateSkin

Gerhard Hausladen
Michael de Saldanha
Petra Liedl

ClimateSkin

Building-skin Concepts that Can Do More with Less Energy

with contributions from
Hermann Kaufmann
Gerd Hauser
Klaus Fitzner
Christian Bartenbach
Winfried Nerdinger
Winfried Heusler

Birkhäuser
Basel · Boston · Berlin

Table of contents

1006584709

Foreword

The facade plays a key role in the planning of buildings with optimised energy use and room climate. A holistic design begins with an analysis of the usage requirements and local conditions and a determination of the users' needs. This is followed by the concept design, in which the functional and physical characteristics are established, and which leads eventually to the detailed design, where the final decisions on the functional elements and materials are made. Today, the building industry operates with ever-shorter project planning times and is always striving to minimise design costs. In contrast to this trend, greater effort is being placed into designing concepts for buildings which provide improved comfort whilst reducing the costs of energy and technical systems. Additional design methods and tools to help with decision-making in the concept phase are needed to cope with these contradictory developments. In this early planning stage, the high degree of detail upon which the currently available simulation software is based means that it is only of limited benefit. This book is intended to support architects and engineers in producing energy-efficient concepts for administration buildings.

To present the multilayered aspects of facade design in the sequential arrangement of a book, the subject has been divided into five main chapters: "Building skins", "Facade functions", "Facade concepts", "Facade technology" and "Interactions". Some aspects of design feature in more than one chapter, always considered from a different angle and in different degrees of detail.

"Building skins" is an introduction to the theme of the facade and sets the building in an overall context. "Facade functions" quantifies the energetic and indoor climatic characteristics of facades in summer and in winter and illustrates some aspects of ventilation and use of natural light. The effects of decisions at the concept stage can be seen from graphs, charts and diagrams. "Facade concepts" shows the basic principles of facades and associates the most important facade types with their characteristic properties and technical data. Graphics and tables help the designer in his choice of concept. "Technology" gives a compact account of the properties, parameters and scopes of use of the important materials and functional elements in facades. Schematics and tables provide the designer with a source of reference for information on the energetic and indoor climatic properties of various types of facade technology. "Interactions" describes the influence of comfort-related requirements on the complexity of technical systems in buildings. The interactions of the facade, daylight, indoor climate, building technical systems and energy generation are related to one another in an interaction matrix. The room climate conditions for various standard cases can be simply interpreted from this matrix. The design guidelines offer a compact summary to allow the facade designer to assess the effects of design decisions.

The book is based on extensive practical design experience and scientific knowledge. Special analyses and simulations were carried out for many of the design charts and diagrams. Facade design does not just follow technical and physical premises, it also stands in a historical, cultural and sociological context. These aspects are covered in particular in the introductions to each chapter and in the contributions by the guest authors. Project examples create the link to practice.

The book is oriented towards architects and engineers who, in addition to exploiting the architectural potential of the facade, wish to make the most of its energetic and indoor climatic possibilities and use the building skin as an important component of a comprehensive climatic and technical concept. Students will find the way the book combines the themes of building form, energy, indoor climate and technology allows them to take an interdisciplinary view early in their studies. Clients, investors and everyone with an interest in buildings will gain knowledge of the principles required to make informed judgements on building skins and assess the technical and commercial consequences.

This book about the complex and multilayered subject of facades is the work of a team. The first chapter evolved out of a research project undertaken by Friedemann Jung on energy-efficient building concepts for different climatic regions. We would like to thank Christiane Kirschbaum, Friedemann Jung, Michael Kehr, Moritz Selinger, Michael Smola and Martina Thurner for their great commitment and their expert and creative input.

We hope everyone who reads this book will enjoy this comprehensive view of the facade.

Munich, Buchenberg, Hammamet 2006

Gerhard Hausladen,
Michael de Saldanha,
Petra Liedl

Essay

Thermal storage capacity

The mass of large, solid building components serves to smooth out the extremes of indoor climate. The thermal dynamic decreases and high summer temperatures are suppressed. In winter, greater use can be made of solar and internal heat gains.

Location

The less well matched a building is to the climate and its use, the greater is the complexity of its technical systems. The more compatible the building concept and required building services technology are with one another, the smaller the system space requirement and the shorter the lengths of system pipework or ducts. Short pipework lengths reduce initial investment costs and the energy requirement to drive the technical systems.

User influence

Depending on their cultural background, an increasing number of building users are "techno-savvy", especially nowadays with technology becoming more and more fascinating. Even with automatic systems, the user must be able to have some influence over his environment. The systems must have easily comprehended user interfaces.

Ventilation

Every facade should have opening lights for ventilation. The user can then immediately satisfy his need for fresh air and a direct view out. An appropriately designed facade can provide good air quality from window ventilation throughout the year.

Variability

Facades must be able to react and vary themselves in response to the dynamic outdoor climate and ever-changing indoor climatic conditions. This applies to the amount of radiation passing through them, the entry of daylight and the rate of air change. Solar screening must be efficient without blocking out daylight. Ventilation openings must allow supply air to be introduced comfortably into the room under all climatic conditions. The more adaptable the facade is, the less complex the building technical systems need to be and the lower the associated energy demand is.

Transparency

The trend for as much transparency as possible in architecture embraces the wish to dissolve the outer skin and make the building appear light and open. From the outside, fully glazed buildings only appear transparent when they are backlit, for example in twilight or with the sun shining through them. Although the user enjoys more of a view out, there is an increased risk of glare and of overheating in summer.

Comprehensibility

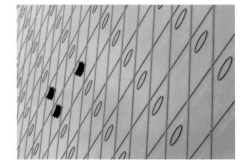

For users to accept a technical system, they must be able to understand its functions and receive feedback as directly as possible about its operational state. If this is not the case, user confidence is eroded, which limits the feeling of well-being.

Permeability

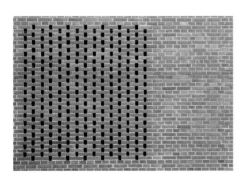

If facades were hermetically sealed, this would certainly result in the objective comfort parameters being fulfilled but many subjective aspects of comfort would be ignored. Our perception of the environment in the form of odours, sounds, air movements, fluctuations in moisture and temperature would be lost. Our consciousness of the seasons and time of day would be much reduced.

Homogeneity

Glass is one of the best construction materials for giving a building a homogenous appearance. This look is associated with dynamism, precision, prestige and progress.

Image

In addition to acting as a skin, facades have considerable influence on the external appearance of a building. They can be used to provide information or project an image to the public.

Building skins

"The key
is light

and light
illuminates forms

And these forms have
the power to excite

Through the play of proportions
Through the play of relationships
of the unexpected, of the amazing.

But also through spiritual play
of its reason to be:
its honest birth,
its ability to last,
structure,
mobility, boldness,
yes daring, play
– of creations, which
are the important creations –
the basis of architecture."

Le Corbusier

Source: Ronchamp, Stuttgart 1957, p. 8

Human skin

The skin is the largest organ of the human body. It is a layer only a few millimetres thick, which separates us from the outside world. With an adult, the skin covers an area of 1.5 to 2 m² and weighs a sixth of our bodyweight, on average 10 to 12 kg. If a person loses 20% of his skin, for example by being burned, his life is in danger. The skin protects the body against bacteria, chemicals and physical influences. It serves as an excretory organ, regulates the body's moisture balance and temperature and gives off odours through glands. It is one of the most important organs of the human body in terms of our immune system, sensory perception and touch. The skin is often described as the mirror of the soul. The closeness of this association is expressed in various ways: When something gets under your skin, you want to get rid of it. Reddening or heavy sweating of the hands indicates shame or the awkwardness of a situation. Our largest organ can also betray us when we lie or feel guilty: Stress causes changes in the composition of the skin's water-fat film, which can be measured with a lie detector. The colour of this multifunctional protective skin can signal physical illness. The human skin is an extremely elastic organ which can expand and contract. The signs of aging are first seen on the skin. It becomes thin and dry and hence less elastic.

How strongly the skin is linked with the brain is shown in the development of the human embryo. The nervous system and the top layer of skin develop from the same layer of cells. In the first months of life the skin plays a crucial role: Bodily contact with parents has a great influence on the further development of the newborn. In the 13th century some children who, on the orders of Fredrick II, were fed and cleaned by their wet nurses but received no tender affection did not survive. Frequent bodily contact is important to healthy development not only in the first few months of life.

The three main layers of this multifunctional protective skin are the thin epidermis, the thicker dermis and the subcutis, connective and subcutaneous fatty tissue. The whole skin surface is renewed every month and the body is able to quickly repair damage to its enclosing outer tissues.

The skin performs an important function in the body's response to a range of climatic information and regulates its emission of heat with the help of heat and cold receptors, blood vessels, sweat glands and hairs. The thermal conductivity of the skin is changed by its temperature-controlled blood supply. When it is hot, the blood vessels close to the skin's surface receive their maximum supply of blood to increase the rate of heat emission. When it is cold, the blood supply and hence the heat loss are reduced.

Clothing

Clothing forms an artificial skin next to the natural skin of our bodies. It is often described as a "second skin" which can be put on and taken off. Clothing has a wide variety of functions. Clothing offers protection from the weather or other external influences. It warms or cools, soaks up sweat and must not prevent the skin from "breathing". Organic natural materials such as wool and silk best fulfil all the requirements of clothing. The skin remains dry, well supplied with blood, evenly warmed, and unaffected by the weather or outside temperature.

The way people dress depends on climate and their cultural situation. Eskimos, for example, wear many layers one on top of the other in an attempt to protect themselves from the cold. In spite of similar climatic data, the amount and extent of this extra skin can vary greatly. Whilst the Arabs are fully enclosed by their clothing to protect themselves from dangerous solar radiation, the people of the Sudan wear almost nothing.

As well as being a physical skin, clothing also represents a spiritual skin for humans. It is an expression of cultural traditions, serves as fashion and jewellery, and contributes to a person's identity. The symbolism of clothing shows in its use in religious and cultural contexts. Christian children wear a christening gown when they are baptised and women a wedding dress when they marry. The costumes worn at carnivals reflect another significance of clothing: For a few hours the participants play other roles—their clothing serves as a mask. The states of belonging to or disassociation with particular groups are made obvious to the outside world by clothing. In the Europe of the Middle Ages, for example, there were laws on clothing which laid down how members of different social classes had to dress. Today, clothing makes it easy for us to tell the type of jobs we perform, such as police officers, doctors or ticket inspectors. Therefore our clothing is also a means of nonverbal communication. The cultural and societal aspect of clothing expresses itself in our continuously changing world of fashion: The bikini in 1950s and jeans in the 1960s were symbols of a whole generation, as were flared trousers in the 1970s. How much people in western industrialised societies are defined by their clothes is reflected in the saying "the clothes make the man". Clothing is a readily purchased image, signifying prestige. In these ways, clothing can emphasise or help the actual self in setting the scene for the ideal apparent self and therefore serves to promote reality or compensate for it.

The original purpose of buildings is to satisfy the human need for safety: a house offers protection from the weather, wild animals and other dangers. With the help of huts, tents and houses, people have adjusted to a wide range of different climatic and geographic conditions. Energy-efficient buildings of all types have developed throughout the world in response to the demands of climate and local conditions. Buildings also reflect the spirit in which they were constructed. The built environment has always been an expression of contemporary culture and society.

The need for homes arises from basic requirements essential to our social and psychological well-being. "My own four walls" symbolise safety, security and shelter – "my home is my castle" – and provide people with a place of withdrawal and refuge. In western industrialised countries they are also status symbols for their owners. Where someone lives defines the physical centre of relationships in a person's everyday life. Depending on the needs, demands and current living situation, people configure their living space in very individual ways and styles. Urban planning and residential developments face new challenges from a pluralisation of living arrangements.

As our "third skin", the outside of a building fulfils tasks similar to those of human skin or clothing. It creates an interior and an exterior; it separates but is also permeable, thus allowing exchange to take place. This can only work properly if the materials used in the building skin are able to perform the many functions of skin. The dwellings can sharpen and stimulate the senses, but can also lead to discomfort. The body and its senses must have a suitably designed room.

As people nowadays spend most of their time in rooms and hardly any time outdoors, room climate has become increasingly important to our feeling of well-being. It is not just the measurable and physical parameters such as air and surface temperatures, air speed, relative humidity and air quality that play an important role. Soft factors and subjective requirements must also be taken into account. The user would like to signal his needs and have the opportunity of influencing his immediate room climate. In addition he must be able to understand the processes going on around him in order not to feel like a helpless recipient. As the emphasis of work in office buildings shifts from routine to more critical activities, the comfort of the employees' rooms is playing an ever-greater role.

Office buildings are not only workplaces but also an important source of corporate prestige. The more authentically the company's concept is depicted by the building, the more sustainable the effect on those outside and the sense of identification of the employees inside.

Atmosphere

The Earth is surrounded by an atmosphere, which acts as its outer skin. Our weather is the result of the many physical and chemical processes at work in the atmosphere. Without the atmosphere there would be no weather on the Earth.

The composition of the gas layer around the other planets is very different from that of our atmosphere, in which the proportions of gas have changed radically over the Earth's history. In its dry state, with all the water vapour removed, the Earth's atmosphere consists of the following mixture of gases: 78.1 % nitrogen, 20.9 % oxygen, 0.9 % argon and 0.037 % carbon dioxide, 0.06 % neon, helium, methane, ozone, hydrogen, sulphur dioxide. The proportion of CO_2 varies from place to place as well as with the time of day and the season. It is also increasing rapidly at the moment. Although the water content is very low and confined almost exclusively to the lower atmosphere, without it the Earth would not have become an inhabited planet.

Different temperatures prevail in the various segments of the atmosphere. Thin boundary layers separate the segments. The troposphere is the bottom layer and mixing zone, where powerful vertical movements thoroughly mix the air. It is also described as the weather zone as this is where practically all the water vapour can be found. Ozone is present in the adjacent stratosphere and is important for the distribution of solar radiation on the Earth's surface. All the weather happens in the two lower levels of the Earth's atmosphere. Above them follow the mesosphere, thermosphere and the exosphere, the top layer. Whilst uncharged particles travelling at high speed can escape into space from the exosphere, the Earth's magnetic field holds back charged particles.

The Sun is the star at the centre of our planetary system and constitutes 99.9 % of its mass. The molten core of the Sun releases large amounts of energy. Although only a minuscule fraction of this energy reaches the outermost layers of the Earth's atmosphere some 150 million kilometres away, the amount of energy supplied is so unimaginably huge that one day's worth would be enough to cover human beings' entire energy requirement for almost 100 years. Only about half of this energy reaches the Earth's surface, as one third is scattered and reflected back into space by air particles and a sixth is absorbed by the atmosphere (accompanied by an increase in temperature).

Assumed data on the universe	
Age	$13.7 \cdot 10^9$ years (13.7 bn. years)
Size	$96 \cdot 10^9$ light years (96 bn. light years)
Mass	$8.5 \cdot 10^{52}$ to 10^{53} kg
Galaxies	10^{11} (100 bn.)
Temperature	2.725 K (−270.425 °C)

Gas	%
Nitrogen	78.08
Oxygen	20.95
Water vapour	0–5
Carbon dioxide	0.035
Argon	0.934
Neon	0.0018
Helium	0.0005
Methane	0.00017

Data on the Earth	
Diameter	12,756 km
Mass	$5.974 \cdot 10^{24}$ kg
Density	5.515 g/cm³
Time for one rotation	23 h 56 min 4 s
Time for one rotation around the Sun	365.256 days
Water surface area	70.7 %
Land surface area	29.3 %
$T_{max, surface}$	58 °C
$T_{min, surface}$	−89.6 °C
$T_{av. surface}$	15 °C

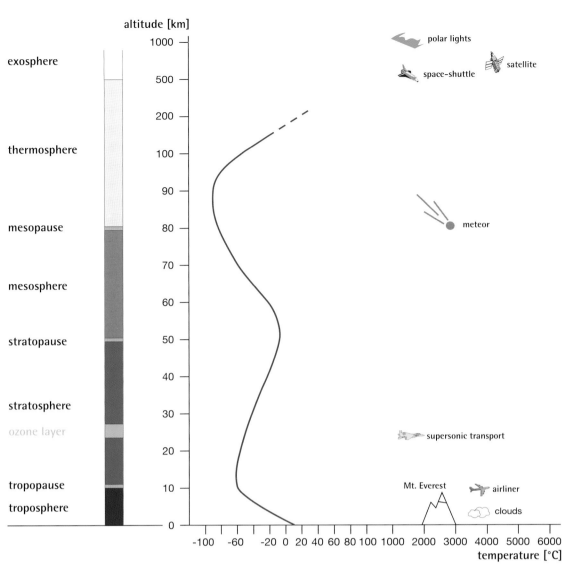

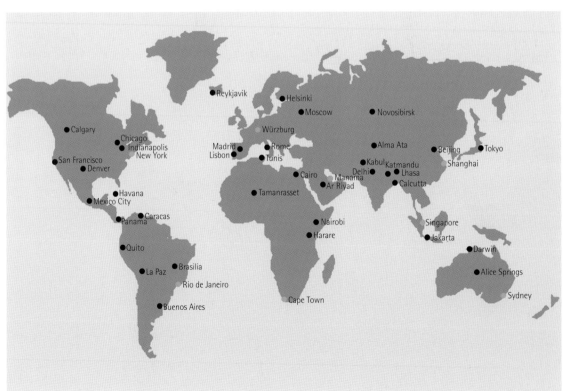

Fig. 1.1 Climate in various cities
The selected cities are listed in a table on the following pages and classified according to their location and climate. Simulations of global solar radiation, proportion of window area and room conditioning were carried out for the cities shown in yellow (p. 18ff).

Location

Low location:
Altitude above sea level: 0–200 m

Coastal location:
Distance to sea: 0–50 km

Medium high location:
Altitude above sea level: 200–1,000 m

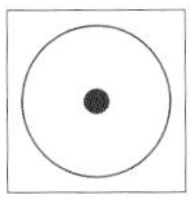

Inland location:
Distance to sea: >50 km

High location:
Altitude above sea level: > 1,000 m

Climate

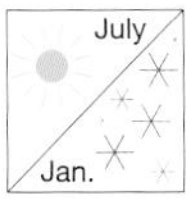

Strongly seasonal:
Difference in monthly average temperatures over the year: > 7 K

Low temperatures:
Average outdoor temperature over year: < 10 °C

Dry:
Annual total rainfall: < 200 mm

Medium temperatures:
Average outdoor temperature over year: 10–18 °C

Wet:
Annual total rainfall: 200–1,000 mm

High temperatures:
Average outdoor temperature over year: > 18 °C

Extremely wet:
Annual total rainfall: > 1,000 mm

Low global solar radiation:
Average annual global solar radiation: < 120 W/m²

Low wind speeds:
Average annual wind speed: < 2.5 m/s

Medium global solar radiation:
Average annual global solar radiation: 120–180 W/m²

Medium wind speeds:
Average annual wind speed: 2.5–3.5 m/s

High global solar radiation:
Average annual global solar radiation: > 180 W/m²

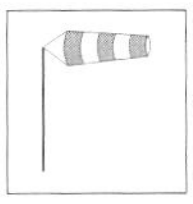

High wind speeds:
Average annual wind speed: > 3.5 m/s

Fig. 1.2 Legend for geographic and climatic aspects used to characterise the cities

City	Latitude	Longitude	Altitude [m above sea level]	Low location	Medium high location	High location	Inland location	Coastal location
Alice Springs	-23.48°	133.54°	545		+		++	
Alma Ata	43.19°	76.55°	976		+		++	
Brasilia	-15.55°	-47.40°	960		+		++	
Buenos Aires	-34.40°	-58.30°	0	+				+
Calgary	51.05°	-114.05°	1,056			+	+	
Caracas	10.32°	-66.56°	1,051			+		+
Chicago	41.50°	-87.45°	185	+			+	+
Darwin	-12.24°	130.52	31					+
Delhi	28.40°	77.14°	213		+		++	
Denver	39.45°	-105.00°	1,622			+	++	
Harare	-17.50°	31.03°	1,508			+	+	
Havana	23.08°	-82.22°	0	+				+
Helsinki	60.19°	24.58°	53	+				+
Indianapolis	39.45°	-86.10°	215		+		+	
Jakarta	-6.08°	106.45°	0	+				+
Kabul	34.30°	69.10°	2,743			++	++	
Cairo	30.03°	31.15°	84	+			+	+
Calcutta	22.30°	88.20°	0	+				+
Cape Town	-33.56°	18.28°	0					+
Katmandu	27.43°	85.19°	1,524			+	++	
La Paz	-16.3°	-68.10°	4,115			+++	+	
Lhasa	29.39°	91.06°	4,267			+++	++	
Lisbon	38.43°	-9.09°	77	+				+
Madrid	40.27°	-3.33°	582		+		+	
Manama	26.12°	50.34°	0	+				+
Mexico City	19.25°	-99.10°	2,269			++	+	
Moscow	55.50°	37.37°	156	+			++	
Nairobi	-1.17°	36.50°	1,691			+	+	
New York	40.45°	-73.59°	10	+				+
Novosibirsk	55.04°	83.05°	152	+			+++	
Panama	8.59°	-79.30°	0	+				+
Beijing	39.56°	116.24°	30	+			+	
Quito	-0.14°	-78.3°	2,438			++	+	
Reykjavik	64.08°	-21.54°	66	+				+
Ar Riyad	24.39°	46.46°	701		+		+	
Rio de Janeiro	-22.53°	-43.17°	152	+				+
Rome	41.48°	12.35°	37	+			+	
San Francisco	37.45°	-122.27°	0	+				+
Shanghai	31.14°	121.28°	8	+				+
Singapore	1.17°	103.51°	30	+				+
Sydney	-33.55°	151.10°	0					+
Tamanrasset	22.47°	5.31°	1,377			+	++	
Tokyo	35.40°	139.45°	16	+				+
Tunis	36.50°	10.13°	43	+				+
Würzburg	49.48°	9.57°	214		+		+	

T_{max} [°C]	T_{min} [°C]	T [K]	Global solar radiation max [W/m²]	Global solar radiation min [W/m²]	Relative humidity max [%]	Relative humidity min [%]	Wind speed max. [m/s]	Precipitation year [mm]	City
28.9	12.2	16.7	311	179	60	34	4.1	250.0	Alice Springs
23.0	-6.5	29.5	228	58	93	67	2.0	649.4	Alma Ata
22.4	19.0	3.4	229	195	78	53	4.1	1,532.2	Brasilia
23.9	11.8	12.1	296	90	74	65	5.2	1,086.8	Buenos Aires
16.7	-9.2	25.9	283	44	67	53	5.0	400.1	Calgary
22.1	19.1	3.0	209	171	87	80	1.8	906.7	Caracas
23.8	-5.4	29.2	261	61	72	60	5.4	909.7	Chicago
29.4	25.0	4.4	273	210	80	60	3.5	1,563.0	Darwin
33.3	14.4	18.9	299	155	75	39	2.0	715.0	Delhi
23.2	-1.3	24.5	285	89	52	43	4.7	401.6	Denver
21.6	14.1	7.5	280	201	77	54	4.6	804.0	Harare
27.7	23.0	4.7	259	134	83	71	6.2	1,189.9	Havana
16.6	-6.9	23.5	249	6	87	70	3.9	651.0	Helsinki
24.1	-3.4	27.5	269	67	76	64	5.2	1,020.7	Indianapolis
27.5	26.2	1.3	264	136	85	78	4.7	1,678.9	Jakarta
17.4	-7.4	24.8	356	107	89	59	2.6	318.5	Kabul
27.4	13.3	14.1	329	129	62	42	4.4	25.5	Cairo
29.5	20.6	8.9	277	164	85	65	4.1	1,581.0	Calcutta
20.5	13.4	7.1	343	104	77	73	8.0	475.2	Cape Town
23.0	9.1	13.9	278	182	90	76	4.1	1,393.6	Katmandu
8.7	4.8	3.9	262	195	78	55	3.3	554.7	La Paz
12.0	-5.8	17.8	288	195	87	36	2.3	415.6	Lhasa
22.8	11.4	11.4	302	78	79	62	4.1	753.0	Lisbon
24.3	5.5	18.8	310	66	77	51	2.8	414.0	Madrid
34.2	17.2	17.0	251	130	75	50	5.1	72.4	Manama
19.1	13.6	5.5	253	180	70	53	3.9	777.8	Mexico City
18.2	-9.3	27.5	218	14	82	62	1.5	691.0	Moscow
20.5	16.7	3.8	260	158	76	65	6.2	867.8	Nairobi
24.9	-1.5	26.4	250	62	69	55	4.7	1,081.5	New York
19.4	-17.0	36.4	278	15	82	61	4.6	520.8	Novosibirsk
28.8	26.9	1.9	215	176	83	66	4.7	1,847.6	Panama
26.0	-4.2	30.2	230	71	76	51	3.2	577.9	Beijing
15.0	14.3	0.7	209	174	77	65	4.1	970.8	Quito
10.6	-0.5	11.1	190	2	83	75	6.8	801.0	Reykjavik
34.8	13.3	21.4	332	171	54	17	3.6	101.1	Ar Riyad
25.9	20.2	5.7	244	134	82	80	4.1	1,217.1	Rio de Janeiro
24.4	7.2	17.2	290	67	78	67	3.5	876.0	Rome
19.4	10.2	9.2	306	82	76	63	6.0	532.1	San Francisco
28.1	2.7	25.4	222	74	83	77	2.4	1,112.2	Shanghai
27.4	25.6	1.8	214	164	86	82	2.6	2,194.2	Singapore
22.4	13.2	9.2	271	97	73	61	6.3	1,043.0	Sydney
28.9	12.8	16.1	325	191	34	27	4.3	43.0	Tamanrasset
27.2	5.5	21.6	169	86	76	50	3.7	1,405.7	Tokyo
26.6	10.2	16.4	318	101	82	63	4.3	466.7	Tunis
18.6	0.7	17.9	224	27	84	68	5.1	597.6	Würzburg

Singapore   1.17° N / 103.51° E

Manama   26.12° N / 50.34° E

Location and climate

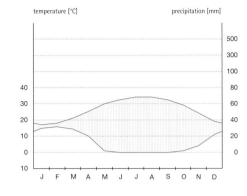

Air temperature [°C]
and rainfall [mm]

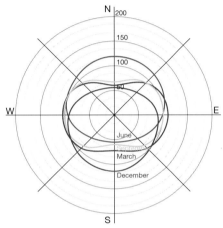

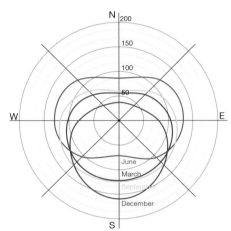

Insolation on vertical
facades [W/m²]

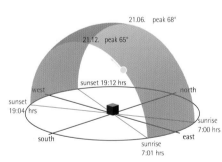

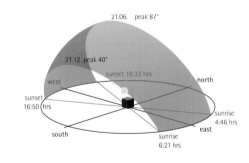

Path of the Sun

New York 40.45° N / 73.59° W

Rio de Janeiro 22.53° S / 43.17° W

Location and climate

Air temperature [°C]
and rainfall [mm]

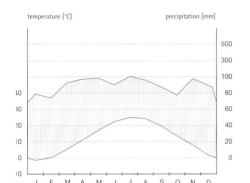

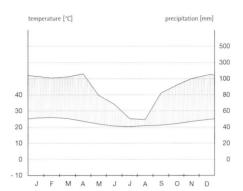

Insolation on vertical
facades [W/m²]

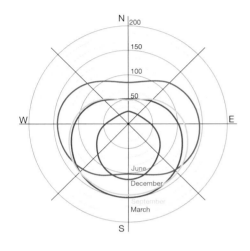

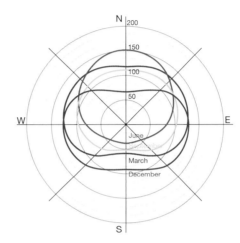

Path of the Sun

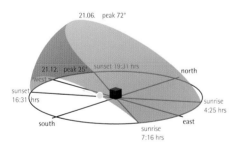

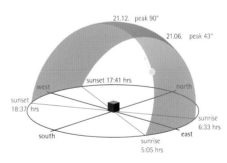

Capetown 33.56° S / 18.28° E

Shanghai 31.14° N / 121.28° E

Location and climate

**Air temperature [°C]
and rainfall [mm]**

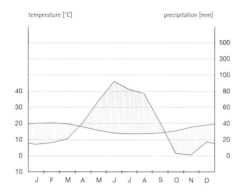

temperature [°C]   precipitation [mm]

J F M A M J J A S O N D

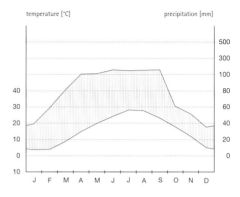

temperature [°C]   precipitation [mm]

J F M A M J J A S O N D

**Insolation on vertical
facades [W/m²]**

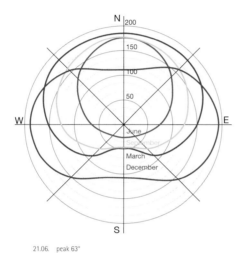

N 200
150
100
50
W   E
June
September
March
December
S

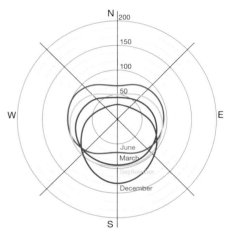

N 200
150
100
50
W   E
June
March
September
December
S

Path of the Sun

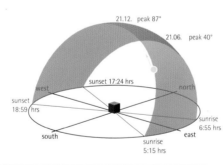

21.06. peak 63°
21.12. peak 87°
21.06. peak 40°
west   north
sunset 17:24 hrs
sunset
18:59 hrs
sunrise
6:55 hrs
south   east
sunrise
5:15 hrs

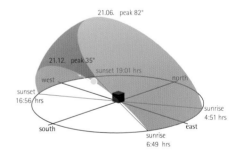

21.06. peak 82°
21.12. peak 35°
west   north
sunset 19:01 hrs
sunset
16:56 hrs
sunrise
4:51 hrs
south   east
sunrise
6:49 hrs

Sydney 33.55° S / 151.10° E

Würzburg 49.48° N / 9.57° E

Location and climate

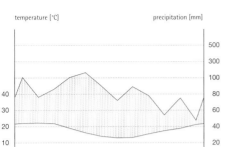

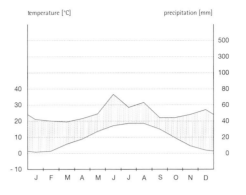

Location and climate

Air temperature [°C] and rainfall [mm]

temperature [°C]   precipitation [mm]

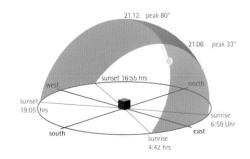

temperature [°C]   precipitation [mm]

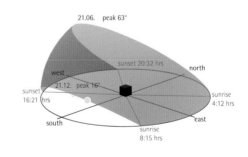

Insolation on vertical facades [W/m²]

N | 200
150
100
50
W ———————— E
June
September
March
December
S

N | 200
150
100
50
W ———————— E
December
March
June
September
S

Path of the Sun

21.12. peak 80°

21.06. peak 33°

sunset 16:55 hrs   north

sunset 19:05 hrs

south

sunrise 4:42 hrs   east   sunrise 6:59 Uhr

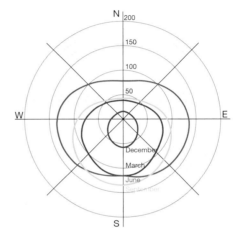

21.06. peak 63°

sunset 20:32 hrs   north

west

21.12. peak 16°

sunset 16:21 hrs

south   east   sunrise 4:12 hrs

sunrise 8:15 hrs

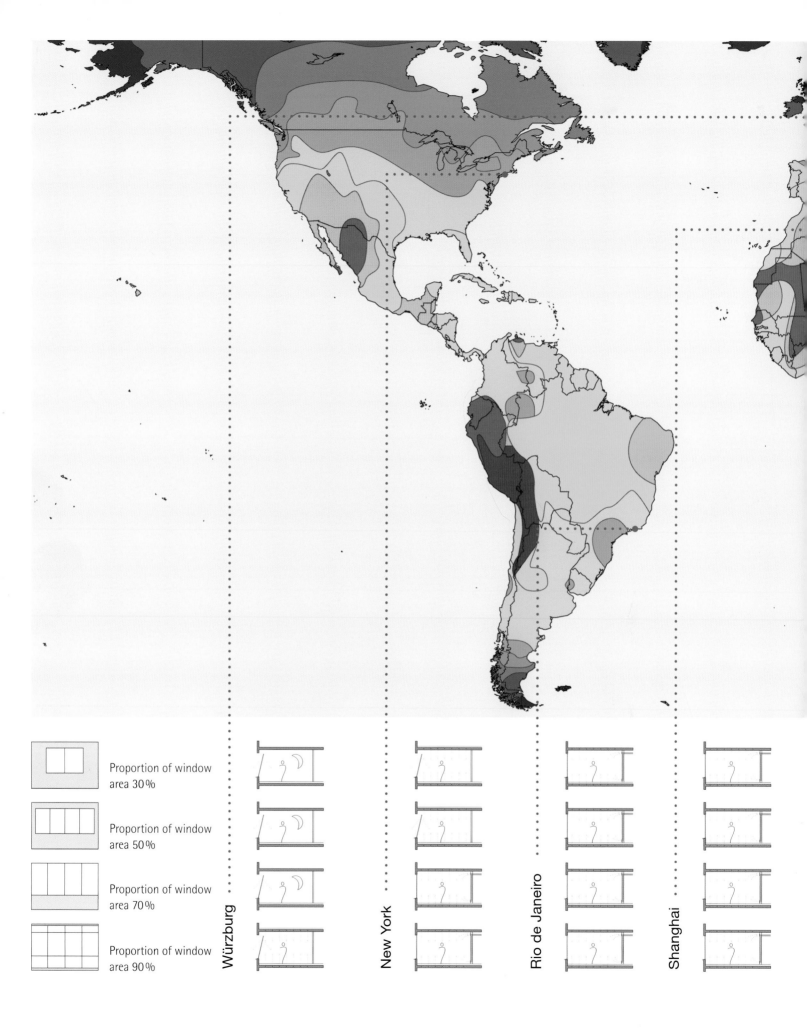

Proportion of window
area 30%

Proportion of window
area 50%

Proportion of window
area 70%

Proportion of window
area 90%

Würzburg

New York

Rio de Janeiro

Shanghai

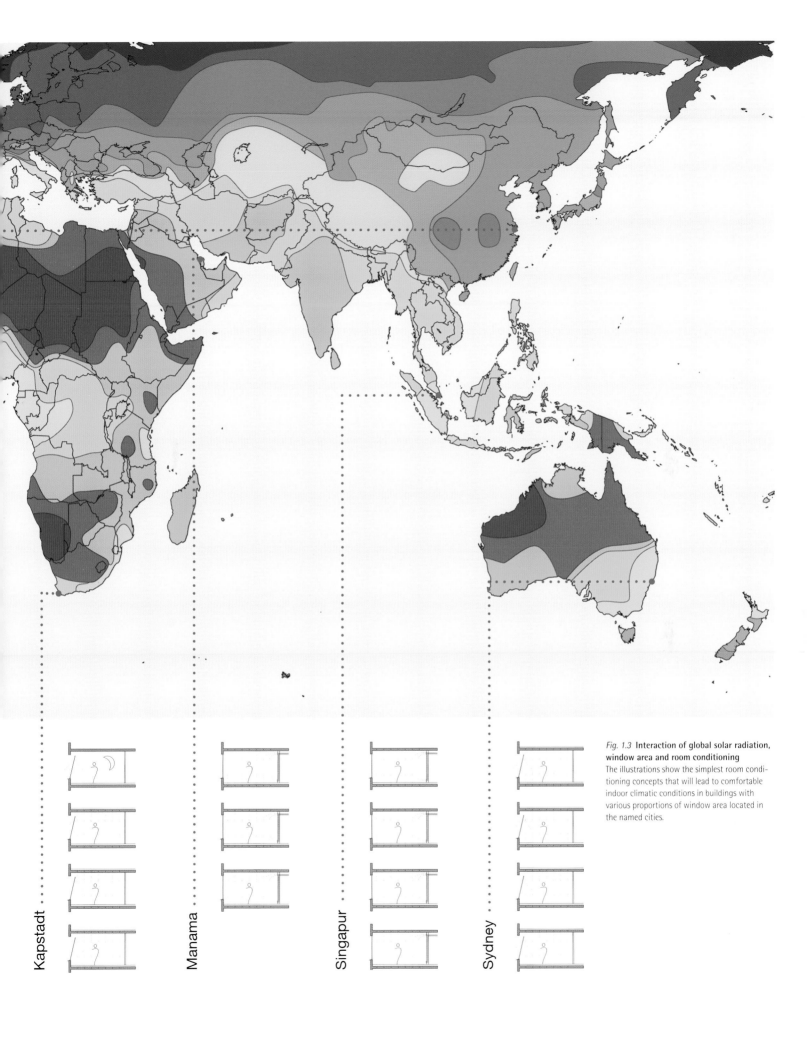

Kapstadt

Manama

Singapur

Sydney

Fig. 1.3 **Interaction of global solar radiation, window area and room conditioning**
The illustrations show the simplest room conditioning concepts that will lead to comfortable indoor climatic conditions in buildings with various proportions of window area located in the named cities.

Facade functions

"The polylingual and the multilayered are important to us in our approach to architecture. We would never allow ourselves to become fixated on any particular style. Our architecture gains expression much more from an intensive analysis of the building itself, the conditions and opportunities of the locality in which it must be realised, the available means for achieving this and from the interplay of all the project partners in the conception and realisation. The common denominator of the resulting architecture is the openness and accessibility of the building for the mind and senses and therefore its usability. The range of spatial concepts extends from buildings surrounded by other volumes to those in open landscapes—they all stand in continuous dialogue with their spatial and social environment. In this respect we view our work as a social and cultural service of a high artistic, functional and technological standard. Architectural quality and sustainability must be measured primarily by how openly and flexibly it can be interpreted in the rich variety of forms of living for which it creates a setting."

Auer+Weber+Assoziierte

Source: Auer+Weber+Assoziierte

The facade in winter

The facade in summer

Ventilation

Natural light

The heating energy balance of buildings has changed crucially over recent years. The use of materials with good insulation properties, highly effective insulation glazing and increased insulation thicknesses considerably reduces transmission heat losses. Therefore nowadays a greater proportion of heating energy is required to compensate for ventilation heat losses, which can be regulated with ventilation through the facade. Computer workstations, artificial lighting and a high occupation density in administration buildings lead to high internal heat gains. Solar gains are therefore only usable to a very limited degree.

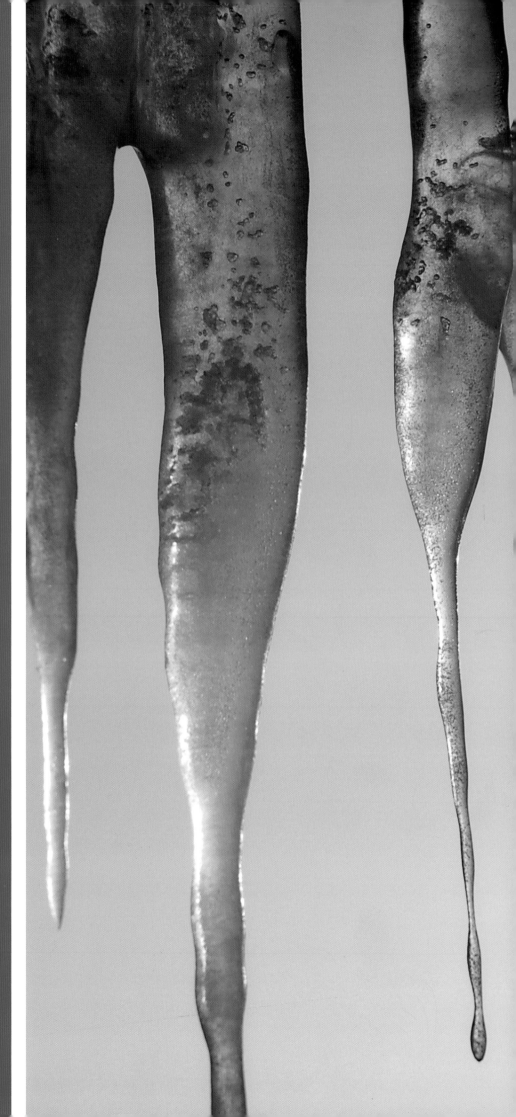

The facade in winter

The interaction between the reduction of heating energy demand and architecture

Architecture develops as the expression and reflection of what is technically and culturally possible for a society. Thus the history of human dwellings reflects not only the technological and cultural progress of civilisation but also the intelligent analysis of how to create enclosed spaces that offer people protection from nature and are as comfortable as possible. The answers were highly varied and dependent on the region, which can be explained by the wide range of applicable boundary conditions. For example, the availability of suitable construction materials and the climatic situation are important factors in the design of an interior. However, the original forms of human dwellings in all cultures have the following in common: External forms are consistently influenced by consideration of energy optimisation in terms of heating and cooling. Impressive examples include the Mongolian yurt, Eskimo igloo and the mud huts of the Middle East. In addition to forms and materials, the construction techniques used are pragmatic reactions to the climatic environment, which has a crucial influence on the architectural expression. This is just as clearly discernable from historical buildings in mountainous regions.

In a similar way, the floor layout of the German hall-kitchen house is uniquely determined by the question of heating. The oven in the centre warming all the rooms, the minimising of surface area by the square plan shape, and the closable lateral veranda are the result of centuries of refinement of the constructional answers to the questions of providing energy-efficient and comfortable houses in a harsh environment.

Only with the easy availability of cheap heating energy has construction divested itself of this question. This freedom has characterised buildings over the last one hundred years and produced a wealth of ideas and diverse architectural designs with precise answers for social and cultural challenges. The downside however is countless numbers of formless and ill-thought-out buildings which neither accord with the criteria of the construction culture nor comply with the fundamental energy efficiency rules, because they are based on short-sighted economic arguments.

Again today, we are standing at a turning point just as we did a hundred years ago. The impending energy shortage and increasingly acute environmental problems, which have arisen from our civilisation's hunger for energy, will radically change our buildings. The long-hidden question of energy efficiency will once again become a major theme in architecture. It is a matter of applying our technical knowledge and our long years of experience logically to create concepts for new and refurbished construction that will lead to low-energy buildings. This will naturally have consequences for the design of our buildings – an exciting challenge for architecture. There are already countless examples to show that these premises can produce good design and high-quality architecture. Concerning itself logically with the theme of energy will not mean a step back for architecture but should be an enrichment, provided it is tackled in a creative way.

Prof. Dipl.-Ing. Hermann Kaufmann

	2-pane glazing unit	3-pane glazing unit
U_g [W/m²K]	Down to 1.1	Down to 0.5
g [–]	0.55–0.65	0.5
τ [–]	0.8	0.7
R_w [dB]	30–31	32

Tab. 2.1 **Typical building physical properties of 2- and 3-pane insulation glazing**
Total thermal transmittance U_g, total solar energy transmittance g, light transmittance τ and sound reduction index R_w

Transmission heat losses

The insulation thickness and quality of the glazing influence the transmission heat losses and surface temperatures on the inside of the facade. The latter also have effects on ventilation heat losses, as room air temperatures must be higher where surface temperatures are lower. Surface temperatures also influence the comfort-parameters radiation asymmetry and air velocity, the latter caused by cold air drop at the facade. There is therefore an interaction between the standard of insulation and the heat transfer system. Thus with well-insulated buildings the radiators can also be fitted on the internal walls of rooms, which simplifies installation. Radiant-panel heating systems can be used without detrimentally affecting comfort. Another criterion for the level of surface temperatures is the heat output, which can be reduced by using better quality insulation. This leads to higher flexibility in the choice of heat transfer and heat generating systems.

Insulation thickness Transmission heat loss reduces with increasing insulation thickness, with the insulating effect not being directly proportional to the layer thickness. Therefore, in practice, the insulation thickness is determined by the type of construction, the available space, the amount of energy required during manufacture, the building technical services concept, building type and the proportion of window area (Tab. 2.2). A lower heat insulation may be justified for a building with high internal heat loads. Vacuum insulation may be an effective alternative where a large layer thickness is not desirable or possible.

Thermal bridges and opaque elements With the increasing improvement of insulation standards the effect of thermal bridges is considerably increased, making it important to pay particular attention to them for reasons of energy-efficiency and building physics. The construction of opaque parts of an elementalised facade and the enclosing ceilings and walls is more difficult as a high insulating effect is required in very little constructional thickness. Vacuum insulation panels can also be a solution here.

Glazing With insulation glazing the designer has a choice of two-pane and three-pane units. For approximately double the insulating effect the latter have 10 to 15 % less total solar energy transmittance and 10 % lower natural light transmittance (Tab. 2.1). Colour rendering inside buildings and when looking out through glass may be changed. The cost is higher than double glazing and the construction of the hardware is more complex. In practice the type of glazing is determined by the proportion of window area, internal heat loads and heat transfer concept. High internal loads in combination with a low proportion of window area normally justify the use of two-pane glazing. Three-pane glazing may help to save energy in buildings with a larger proportion of window area, but its main benefits are comfort and less complicated building technical services. In terms of energy, the weak point is the window frame; hence a high proportion of frame area is disadvantageous, and glazing with multiple small panes should be avoided.

Tab. 2.2 **Best practice insulation thicknesses and glazing types for various building types**
The required thermal insulation quality of the building skin is a function of the proportion of window area, building use and building technical services.

Building type	Proportion of window area	Glazing type	Insulation thickness (WLG 035)
Low-energy housing	< 30 %	2-pane insulating glazing	15–25 cm
Low-energy housing	> 30 %	3-pane insulating glazing	15–25 cm
Passive house	< 50 %	3-pane insulating glazing	25–35 cm
Office building	< 50 %	2-pane insulating glazing	> 15 cm
Office building	> 50 %	3-pane insulating glazing	> 15 cm
Office building, high internal loads	< 70 %	2-pane insulating glazing	> 10 cm
Office building, high internal loads	> 70 %	3-pane insulating glazing	> 10 cm
Office building, thermoactive ceiling	< 70 %	3-pane insulating glazing	> 15 cm

Fig. 2.1 **Effect of insulation standard on heating energy demand and heating system output**

Variation: Insulation standard
Poor U_{wall} = 0.5 W/m²K $U_{glazing}$ = 1.4 W/m²K
Medium U_{wall} = 0.3 W/m²K $U_{glazing}$ = 1.1 W/m²K
Good U_{wall} = 0.2 W/m²K $U_{glazing}$ = 0.7 W/m²K

The savings potential offered by good insulation in administration buildings being used conventionally is approximately 30 %. The required heating system output is reduced by up to 25 %, which allows the option of a simpler building technical services system.

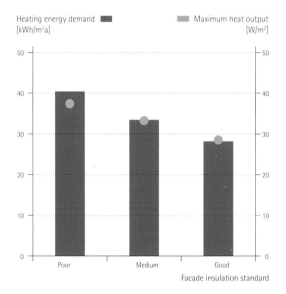

Heating energy demand ■   Maximum heat output ■
[kWh/m²a]   [W/m²]

Facade insulation standard

Fig. 2.2 **High internal heat loads: effect of insulation standard on the heating energy demand and heating system output**

Variation: Insulation standard with additional internal loads of 50 W/m²
Poor U_{wall} = 0.5 W/m²K $U_{glazing}$ = 1.4 W/m²K
Medium U_{wall} = 0.3 W/m²K $U_{glazing}$ = 1.1 W/m²K
Good U_{wall} = 0.2 W/m²K $U_{glazing}$ = 0.7 W/m²K

With additional high internal heat loads from equipment (50 W/m² whilst the building is being used), the heating energy demand is reduced by approximately 75–90 %. The effect of the loads on the heating system output is lower because of the warming-up phase.

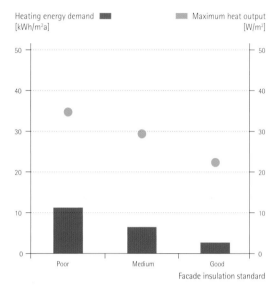

Heating energy demand ■   Maximum heat output ■
[kWh/m²a]   [W/m²]

Facade insulation standard

Boundary conditions applicable to Figs. 2.1 and 2.2, if not varied as a parameter

Office area	22.5 m²
Orientation	South
Facade area	13.5 m²
Proportion of window area	50%
U-value glazing	Varies
g-value	0.5/0.6
Solar screening	Closes at T_{room}>24 °C
U-value external wall	varies
Internal walls	Lightweight, adiabatic
Ceilings	Solid, adiabatic
Loads 8:00–18:00 hrs	Weekdays 2 pers. + 2 PCs
Lighting 8:00–10:00 hrs	Weekdays 10 W/m²
10:00–16:00 hrs	Off
16:00–18:00 hrs	10 W/m²
Ventilation weekdays 8:00–18:00 hrs	n = 1.0 h⁻¹
Ventilation other times	n = 0.5 h⁻¹
Heating	T_{room} < 20 °C
Heat-up time	t = 1.0 h
Climate	Würzburg

Fig. 2.3 **South facade: Influence of the glazing quality on the heating energy demand as a function of proportion of window area**

Variation: Glazing   Proportion of window area, south
2-pane $U_{glazing}$ = 1.1 W/m²K   30%, 50%, 70%
3-pane $U_{glazing}$ = 0.7 W/m²K   Solar screening

For administration buildings there is little advantage in specifying triple glazing if the proportion of window area is low. Triple glazing is worthwhile above all for thermal comfort where the proportion of glass is high. Higher proportions of window area are generally viewed as less favourable in energy terms as the additional solar gain is limited by the solar screening necessary to reduce the danger of overheating.

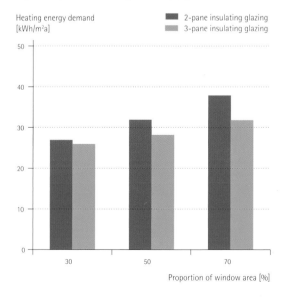

Heating energy demand   ■ 2-pane insulating glazing
[kWh/m²a]   ■ 3-pane insulating glazing

Proportion of window area [%]

Fig. 2.4 **North facade: Influence of the glazing quality on the heating energy demand as a function of proportion of window area**

Variation: Glazing   Proportion of window area, north
2-pane $U_{glazing}$ = 1.1 W/m²K   30%, 50%, 70%
3-pane $U_{glazing}$ = 0.7 W/m²K   No solar screening

Higher proportions of window area on the north-facing facades are viewed as particularly unfavourable in energy terms.

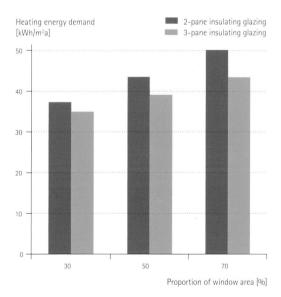

Heating energy demand   ■ 2-pane insulating glazing
[kWh/m²a]   ■ 3-pane insulating glazing

Proportion of window area [%]

Boundary conditions to Figs. 2.3 and 2.4, unless varied as a parameter

Office floor area	22.5 m²
Orientation	South, north
Facade area	13.5 m²
Proportion of window area	Varies
U-value glazing	Varies
g-value	0.5/0.6
Solar screening	Closed at T_{room}>24 °C
U-value external wall	0.2 W/m²K
Internal walls	Lightweight, adiabatic
Ceilings	Solid, adiabatic
Loads 8:00–18:00 hrs	Weekdays 2 pers. + 2 PCs
Loads 8:00–10:00 hrs	Weekdays 10 W/m²
10:00–16:00 hrs	Off
16:00–18:00 hrs	10 W/m²
Ventilation weekdays 8:00–18:00 hrs	n = 1.0 h⁻¹
Ventilation other times	n = 0.5 h⁻¹
Heating	T_{room} < 20 °C
Heat-up time	t = 1.0 h
Climate	Würzburg

Ventilation heat losses

The improved insulation standard of facades has increased the ratio of ventilation heat losses to heating energy demand in buildings. This has created the potential for saving energy by limiting air changes to the minimum required for hygiene (Fig. 2.5) and heat recovery (Fig. 2.8). The importance of ventilation heat losses lies in their interaction with internal heat loads. Where these loads are high they compensate for the ventilation heat losses (Fig. 2.6) and ventilation dissipates the loads. In this case the importance of heat recovery is reduced, unless the heat can be used in other ways, e.g. for other building components or for prewarming service water.

Air change The rate of air change has a decisive influence on ventilation energy demand. Therefore the building should contain the fewest possible number of items of furniture, construction materials and equipment that emit odour or pollutants. The airtightness of the building skin and the adjustability of the ventilation openings play a role in limiting air changes. Particular attention should be paid during construction to the airtightness of the building skin in order to prevent unintentional air changes through leaks driven by thermal currents or wind, or by pressure differences resulting from the ventilation system. The airtightness should be tested using the blower-door-test. A high degree of airtightness is also important from the point of view of building physics, for example to avoid the formation of condensation water. The commonly available window fittings used in facades

providing ventilation normally allow only two settings. The users cannot therefore adjust the ventilation opening sufficiently to balance their own needs and the outside climate. Finely adjustable ventilation elements should be provided then which may also be automatically controlled.

Supply air preheating Regenerative sources of heat such as groundwater or earth can be used to preheat the supply air. The temperature of the supply air can be raised by as much as 10°C thus reducing the effect of increased air changes on the heating energy demand (Fig. 2.7).

Heat recovery Heat can be recovered from the exhaust air by means of a heat exchanger or an exhaust air heat pump. Heat exchangers are highly efficient but require flows of supply and exhaust air. Therefore they cannot be used where the building user opts for ventilation through the facade. Exhaust air heat pumps can be integrated in a mechanical exhaust air system. They transfer the heat to a heating radiator system or make it available for heating water. Heat recovery is worthwhile in energy terms for buildings where location or use makes a supply and exhaust air system necessary (Fig. 2.8). This applies in particular if displacement ventilation is to be used, as the supply air temperature must be heated to 2 K below room temperature. If the supply air is brought into the building through the facade then the efficiency of the heat recovery system must be checked with respect to usability of the heat generated and the required drive energy.

	Window ventilation	Exhaust air systems	Exhaust air systems with heat recovery	Supply and exhaust air system with heat recovery
Tab. 2.3 **Ventilation strategies suitable for different uses in residential and administration buildings**	Single household	Low-energy house	Office building	Family household
	Individual office	Combi-office	Low-energy house with heating radiators	Passive house
		Office with atrium	Low-energy house with hot water demand	High noise load
				Multiperson office
				Open-plan office

Fig. 2.5 **Influence of air changes on the heating energy demand – and heat output**

Variation: Air change rate
n = 1.0 h⁻¹, n = 1.5 h⁻¹, n = 2.0 h⁻¹

The rate of air change has a considerable influence on the heating energy demand (increasing it by up to 50%) and on the required heating system output (increasing it by up to 65%).

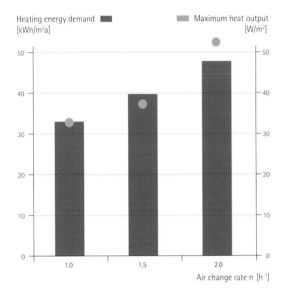

Fig. 2.6 **High internal heat loads: Influence of air changes on the heating energy demand – and heating system output**

Variation: Air changes with additional internal loads of 50 W/m²
n = 1.0 h⁻¹, n = 1.5 h⁻¹, n = 2.0 h⁻¹

The heating energy demand is reduced considerably with high internal heat loads from equipment (50 W/m² during periods of use). The influence of air changes on the heating energy demand remains. The influence on the heating system output is small as air changes and heat loads occur at the same time.

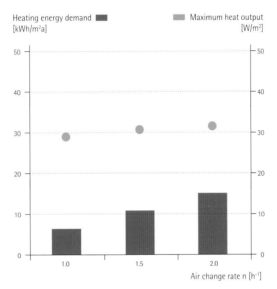

Boundary conditions to Figs. 2.5 to 2.8, unless varied as a parameter

Office floor area	22.5 m²
Orientation	South
Facade area	13.5 m²
Proportion of window area	50%
U-value glazing	1.1 W/m²K
g-value	0.6
Solar screening	Closed at T_{room} > 24 °C
U-value external wall	0.30 W/m2K
Internal walls	Lightweight, adiabatic
Ceilings	Solid, adiabatic
Loads 8:00–18:00 hrs	Weekdays 2 pers. + 2 PCs
Lighting 8:00–10:00 hrs	Weekdays 10 W/m²
10:00–16:00 hrs	Off
16:00–18:00 hrs	10 W/m²
Ventilation weekdays 8:00–18:00 hrs	Varies
Ventilation other times	n = 0.5 h⁻¹
Heating Heat-up time	T_{room} < 20 °C t = 1.0 h
Climate	Würzburg

Fig. 2.7 **Supply air preheating: Influence of air changes on heating energy demand**

Variation: Air change rate   Supply air preheating
n = 1.0 h⁻¹, n = 1.5 h⁻¹, n = 2.0 h⁻¹   during the period of use at 10°C

The heating energy demand is reduced by up to 25% with supply air preheating at 10°C, e.g. by groundwater. Heat output is scarcely increased by the higher air change rate.

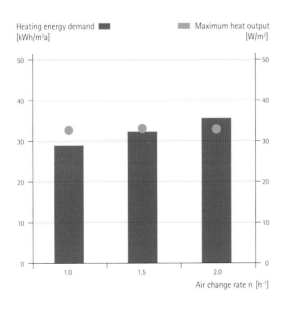

Fig. 2.8 **Heat recovery: Influence of air changes on heating energy demand**

Variation: Air change rate   Heat recovery
n = 1.0 h⁻¹, n = 1.5 h⁻¹, n = 2.0 h⁻¹   60%, 80% (excluding drive energy)

Heat recovery can reduce heating energy demand by up to 25% with low air change rates and by up to 40% with high air change rates. However the increased complexity and drive energy need to be taken into consideration.

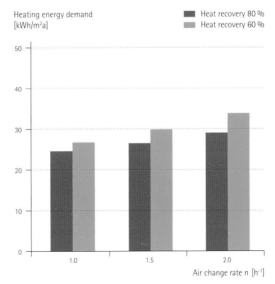

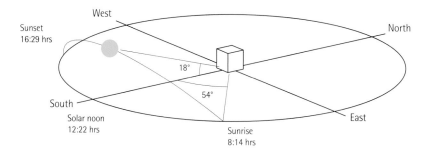

Fig. 2.9 **Course of the sun on 21 December**
(CET, Stuttgart, 48°46'N, 9°10' E)
*In winter the sun rises at an azimuth of 126°. Only
south-facing facades can generate solar gain.*

Solar gains

Solar gains inside buildings depend on the area of transparent and translucent surfaces, their orientation and energy transmittance, which are based on the g-value of the glazing and the reduction factor of the solar screening. The usability of the solar gains depends on the thermally exploitable storage masses and the internal loads, required heating energy demand and local climatic situation. Improvement in insulation has reduced the heating energy demand and the usable solar gain because heating heat is only necessary on cold winter days with little solar radiation.

Proportion of window area The amount of solar radiation entering the building increases directly in proportion to the proportion of window area. In practice however, in administration buildings over 30% of the solar gains from the proportion of window area cannot be exploited. Windows lead to increased heat losses in times of low solar radiation, which detrimentally affects total energy balance (Fig. 2.10). In summer high solar energy input may result in overheating.

Climatic aspects The usable yield from solar gain depends on local climate, which can change over just a few kilometres. Favourable conditions occur when a high heating requirement caused by low outside temperatures coincides with large amounts of solar radiation entering the building. This is often the case at altitude. Locations prone to frequent mist on the other hand are unfavourable.

Thermal storage mass Adequate thermal storage masses capable of being activated quickly are necessary to ensure that solar gain does not produce an immediate rise in room temperature. Heating energy demand is reduced by adopting massive construction (Fig. 2.12). Phase change materials (PCM) can enhance or replace the thermal storage capacity of construction components.

Functional interactions Attention needs to be paid to screening if solar gain is to be exploited. Additional internal solar screening is required because working at desks in direct sunlight can become unpleasant.

Interaction with internal heat loads Solar gain and internal heat loads usually occur at the same time, with the effect that very limited use can be made of solar gain (Fig. 2.11), especially where thermal storage mass is low.

Solar screening The exploitation of solar gain requires solar screening to be open. Room temperature rises particularly where thermal storage mass is low and this is not always considered comfortable. In practice solar screening may also need to be partially closed in winter. This ideally should depend on room temperature. Heating energy demand increases if solar screening is required to be closed in winter to avoid high room temperatures (Fig. 2.13).

Fig. 2.10 **Influence of orientation and proportion of window area on the heating energy demand**

Variation: Orientation   Proportion of window area
North, east, south, west   30%, 70%

The influence of the proportion of window area on heating energy demand is low on the south side, providing the solar screening is continuously left open. This results in considerably increased room temperatures on some occasions even during winter. For all other building orientations heating energy demand rises with increasing proportion of window area.

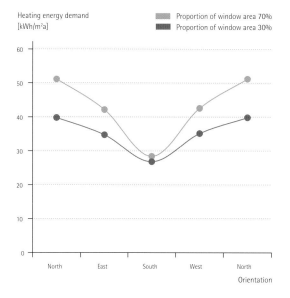

Fig. 2.11 **High internal heat loads: Influence of orientation and proportion of window area on the heating energy demand**

Variation: Orientation and proportion of window area with internal loads of 50 W/m^2 during occupancy period

Orientation has considerably less influence with additional high internal heat loads from equipment (50 W/m^2 during the occupancy period). High proportions of window area have detrimental effects on heating energy demand.

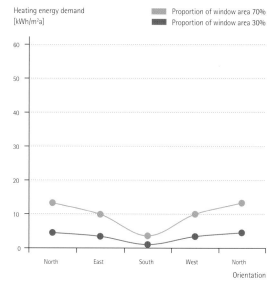

Boundary conditions to Figs. 2.10 and 2.11, unless varied as a parameter

Office floor area	22.5 m^2
Orientation	Varies
Facade area	13.5 m^2
Proportion of window area	Varies
U-value glazing	1.1 W/m^{2}K
g-value	0.6
Solar screening	Open
U-value external wall	0.30 W/m^{2}K
Internal walls	Lightweight, adiabatic
Ceilings	Solid, adiabatic
Lighting	Weekdays
8:00–18:00 hrs	2 pers. + 2 PCs
Lighting	Weekdays
8:00–10:00 hrs	10 W/m^2
10:00–16:00 hrs	Off
16:00–18:00 hrs	10 W/m^2
Ventilation weekdays	
8:00–18:00 hrs	n = 1.0 h^{-1}
Ventilation other times	n = 0.5 h^{-1}
Heating	T$_{room}$ < 20 °C
Climate	Würzburg

Fig. 2.12 **Influence of thermal storage mass on heating energy demand with solar screening control (closed at T$_{room}$ > 24 °C)**

Variation: Proportion of window area 30 %, 70 % and thermal storage mass
Light   Internal walls lightweight, double floors, suspended ceilings
Medium Internal walls lightweight, exposed ceilings
Heavy   Internal walls solid, exposed ceilings

Thermal storage mass has a considerable influence on the heating energy demand. A large proportion of window area in combination with heavy construction can give rise to a reduction of up to 40 %.

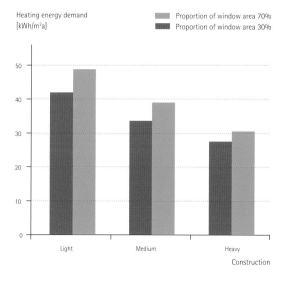

Fig. 2.13 **Influence of solar screening control on heating energy demand with medium-heavy construction**

Variation: Solar screening control

Solar screening control has a considerable influence on the heating energy demand. In practice, screening and increased room temperatures act to prevent the savings from solar gain on the south side of the building from being fully realised.

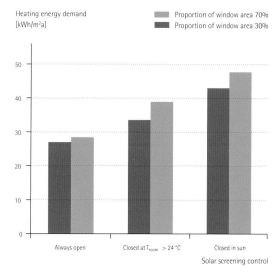

Boundary conditions to Figs. 2.12 and 2.13, unless varied as a parameter

Office floor area	22.5 m^2
Orientation	South
Facade area	13.5 m^2
Proportion of window area	Varies
U-value glazing	1.1 W/m^{2}K
g-value	0.6
Solar screening	Varies
U-value external wall	0.30 W/m^{2}K
Internal walls	Varies, adiabatic
Ceilings	Varies, adiabatic
Loads	Weekdays
8:00–18:00 hrs	2 pers. + 2 PCs
Lighting	Weekdays
8:00–10:00 hrs	10 W/m^2
10:00–16:00 hrs	off
16:00–18:00 hrs	10 W/m^2
Ventilation weekdays	
8:00–18:00 hrs	n = 1.0 h^{-1}
Ventilation other times	n = 0.5 h^{-1}
Heating	T$_{room}$ < 20 °C
Climate	Würzburg

Campo at Bornheimer Depot
Economical

The planned residential property in Bornheim, Frankfurt am Main is designed to the passive house standard. The basic idea of the passive house is to prevent heat losses and optimise usable heat gains. By combining a very well insulated building skin with insulation thicknesses of up to 40 cm with the use of solar heat gains and the heat given off by people and household equipment, it is possible to achieve an annual heating energy demand of less than 15 kWh/m²a. This project has separate ventilation and heating systems although, because of the low heating energy demand, it would have been possible to heat the building by hot air. The arrangement chosen allows the necessary air changes to be reduced to suit the number of occupants and the requirements of building physics. The average rate of air change is 0.35 h^{-1}. Further characteristic parameters for a passive house are a primary energy demand of 120 kWh/m²a and an airtightness of $c_p 50 < 0.6$ h^{-1}.

Location The residential building at Bornheimer Depot is surrounded by dense block development. Consequently it was not always possible to adhere to some of the fundamental design principles of the passive house, such as a southern orientation and little shading from neighbouring buildings. However in order to achieve passive house parameter values and to maximise residential floor area whilst minimising costs, the energy parameters were calculated and checked at every stage of the design. This allowed all design decisions to be evaluated based on the initial investment cost, operating cost and energy demand.

Building skin Design variables such as window size, glazing quality and insulation thickness can be examined to optimise the building skin of a passive house. Eliminating heat bridges and increasing airtightness also have a positive effect. Above all in the facade areas where little yield from solar gain can be expected, the requirements for adequate lighting of the room and reduction of heat losses through the window conflict with one another. Heating and primary energy demand can also be strongly influenced by factors other than optimisation of the building skin; for example the level of heat recovery and the power consumed by the ventilation equipment.

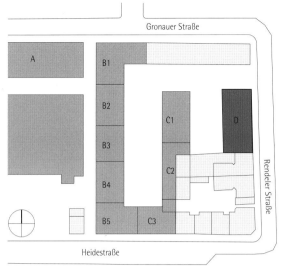

Gronauer Straße

A

B1

B2

C1

D

B3

C2

B4

Rendeler Straße

B5

C3

Heidestraße

Layout

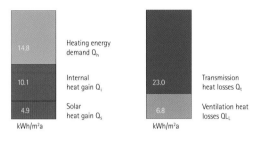

14.8	Heating energy demand Q_h
10.1	Internal heat gain Q_i
4.9	Solar heat gain Q_s
kWh/m²a	

23.0	Transmission heat losses Q_t
6.8	Ventilation heat losses QL_L
kWh/m²a	

Transmission heat losses Q_T

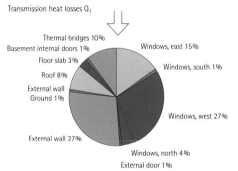

Thermal bridges 10%
Basement internal doors 1%
Floor slab 3%
Roof 8%
External wall Ground 1%
External wall 27%
Windows, east 15%
Windows, south 1%
Windows, west 27%
Windows, north 4%
External door 1%

Block D energy balance

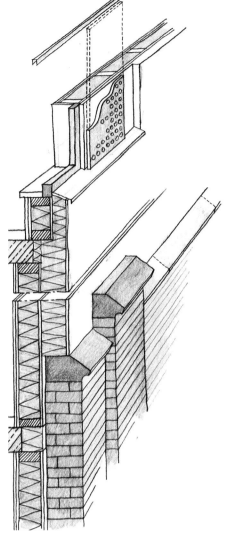

Sketch showing facade cross-section

Completion: 2007
Use: Residential and commercial
Client: ABG Frankfurt Holding, Frankfurt
Architects: Scheffler+Partner Architekten
Albert Speer & Partner GmbH,
Stefan Forster Architekten, all from Frankfurt
Project Director: Urbane Projekte GmbH
Building services: IB Hausladen, Kirchheim
Passive house consultant: IB Hausladen, Kirchheim;
Passivhaus Dienstleistungs GmbH, Darmstadt

Fig. 2.14 **Layout**
The four to six apartment blocks constructed to passive house standard are partially in strong shadow from the adjacent buildings. In addition solar gain is reduced as not all the blocks can face south. An existing clinker brick facade is integrated into block D.

Fig. 2.15 **Block D energy balance**
Heat losses are composed of transmission and ventilation heat losses. Heat losses are very small compared to ordinary new-builds thanks to large insulation thicknesses and the high levels of heat recovery of their controlled room ventilation systems. Solar and internal heat gains are matched as far as possible to heat losses so that the heating energy demand is below the maximum permissible value of 15 kWh/m2a allowed by the passive house requirements.

Fig. 2.16 **Sketch showing facade cross-section**
The walls at Campo am Bornheimer Depot were of timber stud construction with an attached external thermal insulation composite system.
Wall thickness of around 40 cm was achieved. The bulkheads were constructed in reinforced concrete with ETHICS in thicknesses of up to 40 cm. The total wall thickness is up to 60 cm with U-values of up to 0.10 W/m²K.

Fig. 2.17 **Original building**
The clinker brick wall of the "welding shop" of the former tram depot.

Fig. 2.18 **Preliminary sketch**
Despite the reduction of insulation standards, the integration of the clinker brick facade of the former welding shop resulted in a loss of floor area because of its thick wall construction. The projections in the front building exterior create additional heat bridges, which must be minimised.

The main concern for administration buildings in relation to energy consumption and technical complexity is room climate in summer. The increased use of IT equipment is accompanied by higher internal heat loads. The desire for flexibility and transparency leads to reduced thermal storage mass and increased entry of solar radiation. The room climate of buildings in summer is determined to a great extent by the orientation, proportion of window area, solar screening and construction. There are also effects on daylight provision and the reference of the building to the outside world.

The facade in summer

The potential for optimising the behaviour of buildings in summer

The thermal behaviour of buildings in summer has once more come to the fore and is now even a theme within political magazines. The increasingly hot summers of recent years in which greater amounts of solar energy have entered buildings through their facades have caused room climates to be increasingly perceived as uncomfortable. An additional factor has been the appreciably higher internal heat loads from electronic equipment. As the cooling energy demand of nonresidential buildings must be assessed in accordance with energy saving regulations, it claims more of the designer's attention and, along with the contributions to the energy demand made by heating, hot water, ventilation and lighting, exerts a much greater influence than in earlier times on the planning process and building operation.

As early as the 1970s the thermal behaviour of buildings in summer was a highly topical subject in building physics and was also embodied in the provisions of national standards. The aim was to build in such a way that a comfortable room climate was created or an air conditioning system could be operated economically. The idea was no longer to correct building design errors through the choice of an appropriate air conditioning system.

Recent years have seen the installation of more systems in which construction and plant engineering work closely together. Among these are in particular thermally activated components, mostly in the form of concrete core activation. Separate from this for the moment are trials of so-called phase change materials, or PCMs, which allow the thermal storage capacity of even quite lightweight building construction to be noticeably increased within selected temperature ranges. The adaptation of these systems for building construction is currently in the development or trial phases. In future these systems will surely see increased use in combination with thermally activated systems.

The external cooling load of a building is primarily determined by its facade, where there are often conflicting demands of architecture, natural light, visual relationships with the outside world, and cooling load.

The resulting requirements on facades, which with respect to the optimisation of the thermal behaviour of buildings in summer suggest that facades should be modifiable with respect to their use of natural light, solar radiation transmittance, luminance of surfaces, light redirection into deeper rooms, air and energy permeabilities, i.e. controllable to suit needs. This would include not only switchable glazing, which allows for a wide range of variation in its radiation transmission properties but also user-friendly solar screening devices with light redirection and glare protection that can remain in action even in high winds, as well as enclosures with variable air permeability capable of providing intensive night ventilation.

It should also be possible for facades to have integrated thermal and electrical energy generating systems. Facades today are already the most important systems for the use of renewable energy; in Germany 83.2 TWh of solar energy from facades are used in residential buildings, whilst the amounts generated from photovoltaics and wind are 1.0 and 26.5 TWh respectively. Improvements in the exploitation of solar energy through integrated systems in the facade must be the objective and will make buildings of the future into electricity generating plants.

Prof. Dr.-Ing. Gerd Hauser

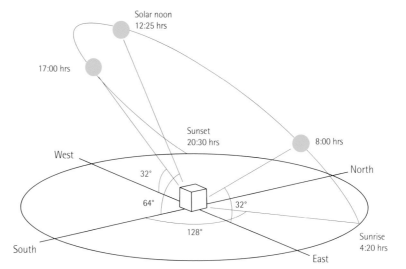

Solar noon
12:25 hrs

17:00 hrs

Sunset
20:30 hrs

8:00 hrs

West

North

32°

64°

32°

128°

Sunrise
4:20 hrs

South

East

Fig. 2.19 **Course of the sun on 21 June**
(CET, Stuttgart, 48°46'N, 9°10'O)
In summer the sun rises at an azimuth of 128°. The solar load on the east and west sides is particularly high as the sunlight in the morning and afternoon strikes the facade almost at right angles. The light reaches far into the interior of the room and produces glare. On the south side, on the contrary, the sun stands high in the sky and hence the amount of solar radiation entering the building is less.

Influence of orientation

The orientation of the building has a considerable influence on its behaviour in summer (Fig. 2.21). It determines the azimuth and altitude angles of the sun to the facade and the intensity of the solar irradiance (Fig. 2.19). For each facade orientation there will be a particular period during which it receives direct sunlight. This period interacts with the working hours of the offices and the outside temperature profile with respect to time (Fig. 2.20). During office working hours the room must be kept within thermal comfort limits, which involves taking into account internal heat loads. For reasons of hygiene the required supply fresh air must be provided whilst limiting natural light and views out as little as possible. Window ventilation can remove heat, depending on the outside air temperature. Room climate can be considerably improved at little extra cost if the characteristics of a facade arising from its orientation are taken into account in the strategies for providing solar screening and adequate ventilation.

Northern orientation The northern facade only receives direct sunlight around the summer solstice, which allows it to be extensively glazed. However the entry of diffused sunlight must be taken into account, especially against the background that normally no solar screening is provided on northern facades. room temperature controlled solar screening or solar control glazing can be provided in order to achieve a comfortable room climate in buildings with large window areas (Figs. 2.21 and 2.22). The latter option may be seen as less thermally advantageous but more worthwhile on economic and practical grounds.

Eastern orientation In summer a large amount of solar radiation enters the east facade at a shallow angle, which makes adequate shading difficult to provide, because it usually results in a reduction of daylight entry and views out. On the other hand the period of use coincides with only about 50 % of the period of direct incident sunlight. Solar screening can remain fully closed in the early morning hours as daylight and views out are not required. In the morning outside air temperatures are usually below 26°C, allowing rooms to be cooled by increased ventilation, which takes away internal and solar loads (Fig. 2.20).

Southern orientation The south facade receives its light at a steep angle. Thus the intensity of radiation on the facade is less and efficient shade can be provided with little detrimental effect on daylight entry or views out, e.g. by permanent projections or horizontal louvres. The period of direct sunlight covers the whole of the period of use, with the result that solar and internal loads coincide. Solar screening must preserve a certain amount of the view out. Heat can be removed by window ventilation for 50 % of the time of direct incident sunlight, until about 12:00 (Fig. 2.20). In the afternoons, the rate of air change can be reduced to that required for hygiene alone in order to avoid additional heat loads.

Western orientation In summer, a large amount of solar energy enters the east facade at a shallow angle. making it more difficult to design the solar screening to be highly efficient and yet allow enough daylight into the room and preserve views out. The period of direct sunlight covers about 75 % of the period of use. Solar screening can be fully closed again after the period of use and air changes minimised when outdoor air temperatures are high. Furthermore the higher room temperatures have no effect on building users. However the energy entering the building in the evening must be removed again overnight. High outdoor air temperatures in the afternoon may prevent increased radiation entering the building from being removed through window ventilation (Fig. 2.20). Therefore the west side of the building in summer is the most unfavourable (Fig. 2.23).

Evaluating the building orientation From a thermal aspect a north-south orientation is the most favourable. Only the south facade receives a significant amount of direct sunlight. The designer has to take into account the reduced amount of diffused solar radiation entering the building from the north. The disadvantage of north-south orientation is the considerable differences in room qualities, which can lessen the building's appeal.

An east-west orientation is thermally much less favourable but more attractive to users because it means all rooms receive direct sunlight. The proportion of window area must be limited in order to achieve a comfortable room climate in summer and to make full use of the potential for an optimised ventilation and solar screening strategy. Furthermore the shallow angle of incidence has particular implications for the design of solar control and anti-glare measures.

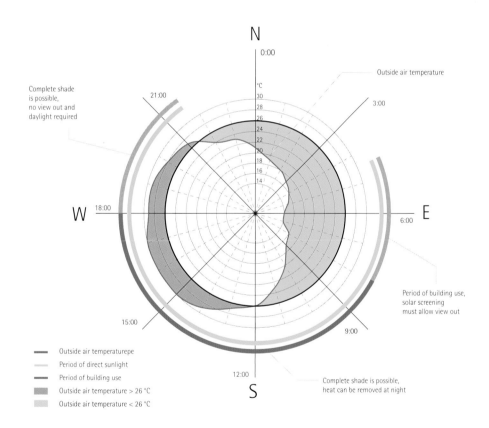

Fig. 2.20 **Interaction of functional and thermal effects depending on facade orientation**
The diagram shows the functional requirements, a plot of the outside air temperature and the period of direct sunlight on a hot summer's day [TRY Würzburg, 1 August].
In the early hours of the morning and in the evening solar screening can be completely closed as the room does not require daylight and views out. During the time the building is in use, i.e. between 8:00–18:00 (green line), the comfort limits must be observed, there must be views out and adequate provision of natural light.
During the night and up to midday on the following day (yellow area), outside air temperatures are usually below 26°C and can be used to remove heat.

Boundary conditions to Figs. 2.21 and 2.22, unless varied as a parameter

Office floor area	22.5 m²
Orientation	Varies
Facade area	13.5 m²
Proportion of window area	70%
U-value glazing	1.1 W/m²K
g-value	0.6
F_c-value	0.2
Solar screening control	Varies
U-value external wall	0.30 W/m²K
Internal walls	Lightweight, adiabatic
Ceilings	Solid, adiabatic
Loads	Weekdays
8:00–18:00 hrs	2 pers. + 2 PCs
Ventilation	Weekdays
8:00–10:00 hrs	n = 5 h⁻¹
10:00–18:00 hrs	n = 2 h⁻¹
18:00–8:00 hrs	n = 1 h⁻¹
Weekends	n = 1 h⁻¹
Lighting	None
Cooling	None
Climate	Würzburg

Fig. 2.21 **Possible proportion of window area as a function of building orientation if the operating room temperature is not to exceed 28 °C for more than 50 hours per year during the period of building use**
The graph shows the values for a solar screening strategy depending on direct sunlight and for a solar screening strategy depending on room temperature.

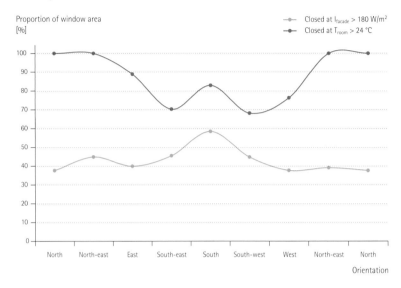

Fig. 2.22 **Over-temperature hours during the period of use and operating room temperatures on three hot days in northern rooms with different solar screening control regimes**

Variation: Solar screening control
Solar screening closed when T_{room} > 24 °C
Solar screening closed when direct irradiation I_{facade} > 180 W/m²
Solar control glass, g = 0.33
without solar screening

Diffused light has a major effect at the north facade if there is no solar screening or it is open. For functional and economic reasons, solar screening is often not provided at northern facades and therefore solar control glazing can be a simple way of improving room climate in summer.

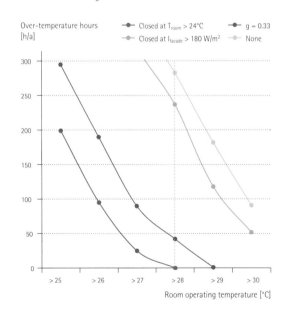

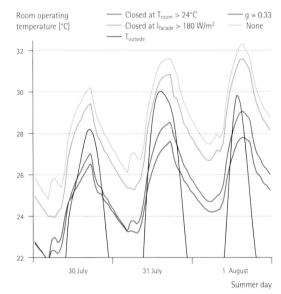

Fig. 2.23 Over-temperature hours during the period of use and operating room temperatures on three hot days in northern rooms with different orientations

Variation: Orientation
         east, south, west

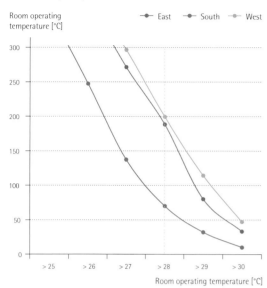

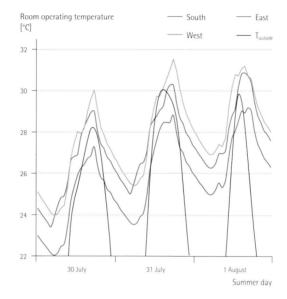

A southern orientation is more favourable in terms of room climate in summer than an east or west orientation, where there is some potential for improvement through optimisation of the solar screening control and in particular the ventilation strategy.

Boundary conditions to Figs. 2.23 and 2.24, unless varied as a parameter

Office floor area	22.5 m²
Orientation	Varies
Facade area	13.5 m²
Proportion of window area	70%
U-value glazing	1.1 W/m²K
g-value	0.6
F_c-value	0.2
Solar screening control	Closed from I_{facade}> 180 W/m²
U-value external wall	0.30 W/m²K
Internal walls	Lightweight, adiabatic
Ceilings	Solid, adiabatic
Loads	Weekdays
8:00–18:00 hrs	2 pers. + 2 PCs
Ventilation	Weekdays
8:00–10:00 hrs	n = 5 h⁻¹
10:00–18:00 hrs	n = 2 h⁻¹
18:00–8:00 hrs	n = 1 h⁻¹
Weekends	n = 1 h⁻¹
Lighting	None
Cooling	None
Climate	Würzburg

Fig. 2.24 Cooling energy demand, cooling output and room operating temperatures on three hot days for rooms with active room cooling and different orientations

Variation: Orientation   room cooling
         east, south, west   Cooling at T_{room} > 26 °C
                               during the period of use
                               Cooling off time t = 1.0 h

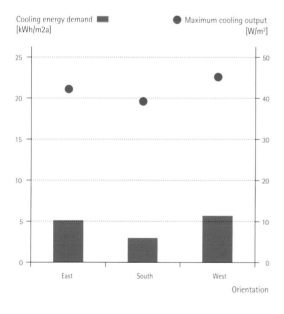

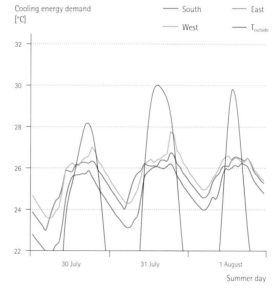

Rooms with a southern orientation have their cooling energy demand reduced by approximately 50%. The effect of orientation on cooling energy output is low. Cooling energy output can still be reduced to some extent by an optimised regulation strategy.

Influence of window area

The proportion of window area has a considerable influence on room climate in summer (Fig. 2.26). As is evident below, it is possible to consider large proportions of window area for facades exposed to sunlight. In general terms, large window areas exposed to direct sunlight are only acceptable with exterior solar screening. Large glazed areas are possible on the north side if the amount of solar radiation passing through the windows is limited. The south side allows higher transparency than the east or west sides (Fig. 2.25). The thermal dynamic of a building increases with the proportion of window area, with the result that active cooling and a considerably higher cooling output are necessary. The cooling energy demand rises almost in direct proportion to the proportion of window area (Fig. 2.27). In relation to the provision of natural light, the arrangement of the transparent areas is more crucial than their absolute size, provided that a proportion of window area of 50 % is achieved. The height of the top edge of the window plays a role here. With proportions of window area greater than 50 %, the additional solar gain in winter is scarcely usable.

Fig. 2.25 **Achievable proportions of window area for various orientations**
Possible proportions of window area for various building orientations if the room operating temperature is not to exceed 28 °C for more than 100 hours per year during the period of building use.

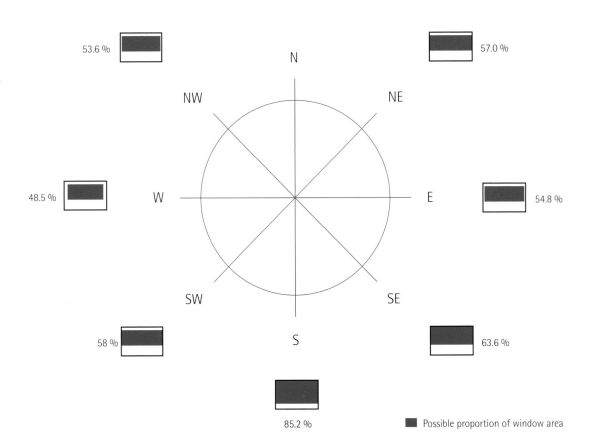

Fig. 2.26 **Over-temperature hours during the period of use and room operating temperatures on three hot days shown in relation to the proportion of window area**

Variation: Proportion of window area
30%, 50%, 70%, 90%

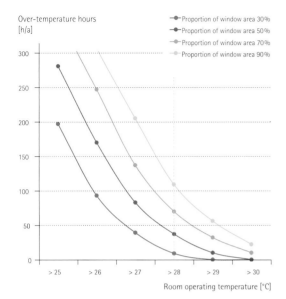

Over-temperature hours
[h/a]

- Proportion of window area 30%
- Proportion of window area 50%
- Proportion of window area 70%
- Proportion of window area 90%

Room operating temperature [°C]

The amount of solar radiation entering is directly proportional to the proportion of window area. Without active or passive cooling, acceptable conditions can only be achieved by having a proportion of window area of less than 50%, provided that there are moderate internal loads and exterior solar screening.

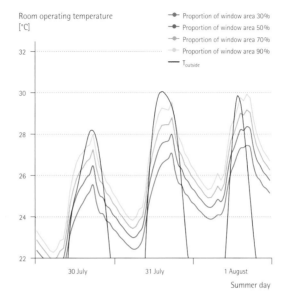

Room operating temperature
[°C]

- Proportion of window area 30%
- Proportion of window area 50%
- Proportion of window area 70%
- Proportion of window area 90%
- T$_{outside}$

30 July   31 July   1 August

Summer day

Boundary conditions to Figs. 2.26 and 2.27, unless varied as a parameter

Office floor area	22.5 m²
Orientation	South
Facade area	13.5 m²
Proportion of window area	Varies
U-value glazing	1.1 W/m²K
g-value	0.6
Fc-value	0.2
Solar screening control	Closed from I$_{facade}$ > 180 W/m²
U-value external wall	0.30 W/m²K
Internal walls	Lightweight, adiabatic
Ceilings	Solid, adiabatic
Loads 8:00–18:00 hrs	Weekdays 2 pers. + 2 PCs
Ventilation 8:00–10:00 hrs	Weekdays n = 5 h⁻¹
10:00–18:00 hrs	n = 2 h⁻¹
18:00– 8:00 hrs	n = 1 h⁻¹
Weekdays	n = 1 h⁻¹
Lighting	None
Cooling	None
Climate	Würzburg

90 %

70 %

50 %

30 %

Proportions of window area

Fig. 2.27 **Cooling energy demand, cooling output and room operating temperatures on three hot days for various proportions of window area with active room cooling**

Variation: Proportion of window area   room cooling
30%, 50%, 70%, 90%   Cooling at T$_{room}$ > 26 °C
during the period of use
Ideal cooling
Cooling off time t = 1.0 h

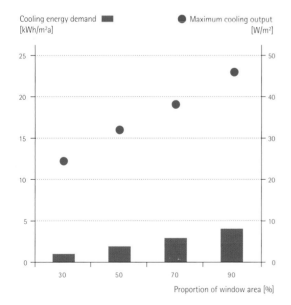

Cooling energy demand ▬   ● Maximum cooling output
[kWh/m²a]   [W/m²]

Proportion of window area [%]

Cooling energy demand and cooling output rise as the proportion of window area increases. With good solar screening, the cooling energy demand is relatively low even with large proportions of window area. Cooling energy output can be reduced to some extent by an optimised regulation strategy.

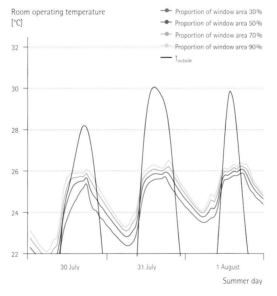

Room operating temperature
[°C]

- Proportion of window area 30%
- Proportion of window area 50%
- Proportion of window area 70%
- Proportion of window area 90%
- T$_{outside}$

30 July   31 July   1 August

Summer day

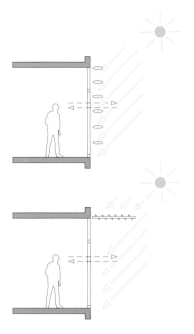

Fig. 2.28 **Solar screening on the south facade**
The high altitude of the sun to the south in summer means that horizontal screening can reduce the amount of radiation entering the building with very little effect on the view out.

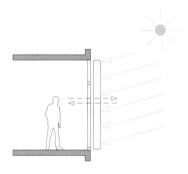

Fig. 2.29 **Solar screening on east and west facades**
The altitude of the sun in the east and west is low in summer. Horizontal screening has to be fully closed. Vertical systems can allow light to enter and retain some of the view out.

Fig. 2.30 **Practical application of solar screening systems for various orientations**
Solar control glazing and internal systems are suitable for use on all sides. Vertical louvres perform well on east and west facades. Horizontal louvres and permanent projections can be used effectively on south facades. Awnings and screens are suitable for all orientations.

Influence of solar screening

The energy entering through a facade is determined by the total solar energy transmittance g of the glazing and the shading factor F_c of the solar screening. The total solar energy transmittance can be influenced by coatings on the glass or by solar control elements in the glazing cavity. The shading factor of the solar screening depends on whether it is placed inside or outside of the building. External screening can be between three and five times as efficient, although it has to be raised in windy conditions. Internal systems are low maintenance, inexpensive and can be deployed irrespective of the weather. Inefficient systems give rise to higher surface temperatures on the inside of the facade. The associated heat emitted into occupied zones may be perceived as uncomfortable by the users. By installing the solar screening in the facade cavity of double-skinned facades or in box windows, solar screening can be highly efficient and unaffected by the weather.

Orientation The design of the solar screening system must take into account the orientation of the building (Fig. 2.30). Horizontal solar screening louvres can exclude direct sunlight on the south side with negligible effect on the view out (Fig. 2.28). Low-energy diffused natural light can enter the rooms and reduce the electricity required for lighting and the associated internal heat loads. Permanent shading features such as cantilever projections, roof overhangs or balconies (Fig. 2.28) on the south facade can be used as seasonal solar screening. In winter the low sun can penetrate deep into the room and so reduce the heating energy demand. Sunlight strikes the facade on an east-west orientated building almost at right angles, hence the amount of energy entering is high and reflection off the glass negligible. The low solar altitude requires horizontal louvres to be almost closed, which obstructs the view out and blocks natural light. The electricity required for lighting increases and the user loses his reference to the outside world. East and west facades can be screened with

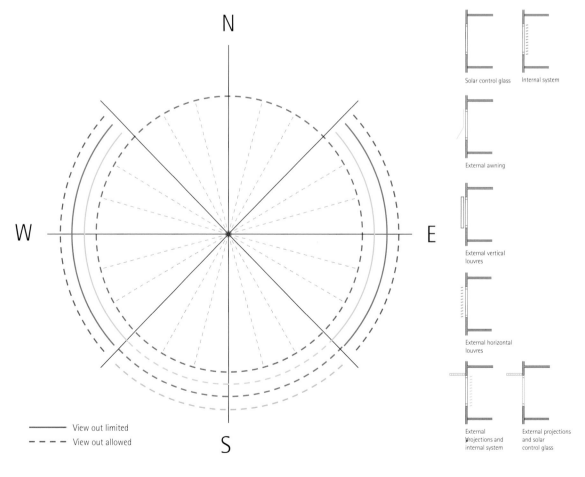

N

W   E

S

——— View out limited
- - - View out allowed

Solar control glass   Internal system

External awning

External vertical louvres

External horizontal louvres

External projections and internal system

External projections and solar control glass

guided vertical louvres (Fig. 2.29). By setting the angle of the louvers, direct sunlight can be blocked out whilst retaining some of the view out.

Influence of the control strategy
The control strategy of the solar screening has considerable influence on room climate in summer (Fig. 2.31). To prevent the entry of diffused light it is often beneficial to close the solar screening even though there is no direct light falling upon the facade. In this respect a solar screening system reacting to room temperature is more effective than one reacting to light. In practice however, this can lead to user acceptance problems because having the solar screening closed when there is no direct sunlight does not conform with user expectations. In addition the solar screening must be automated as users will not normally adjust solar screening to control room temperature in these circumstances. The influence the user can exert is consequently limited. The automatic control system also determines the period of time that the solar screening is closed. If the room air temperature limit at which the solar screening is closed is set at 24°C, then the room climate is better and the solar screening is closed for only half the time a light-controlled system would be. A temperature limit of 22°C produces an even better room climate and the period of closure of the solar screening is still shorter than that of a light-controlled system. If the limit is raised on a light-controlled system so that it admits even some direct sunlight into the room then it does not take long before a considerably more unfavourable room climate develops. A room-temperature-controlled solar screening system can create a pleasant room climate although the solar screening must be closed less often.

Interaction with the proportion of window area
The achievable proportion of window area depends greatly on the type of solar screening. The choice of system must ensure that any limitation of the view out is as little as possible whilst providing the user with the best solar screening.

Boundary conditions to Fig. 2.31, unless varied as a parameter

Office floor area	22.5 m²
Orientation	South
Facade area	13.5 m²
Proportion of window area	70%
U-value external wall	1.1 W/m²K
g-value	0.6
F_c-Value	0.2
Solar screening control	Varies
U-value external wall	0.30 W/m²K
Internal walls	Lightweight, adiabatic
Ceilings	Solid, adiabatic
Loads 8:00–18:00 hrs	Weekdays 2 pers. + 2 PCs
Ventilation	Weekdays
8:00–10:00 hrs	n = 5 h⁻¹
10:00–18:00 hrs	n = 2 h⁻¹
18:00– 8:00 hrs	n = 1 h⁻¹
Weekends	n = 1 h⁻¹
Lighting	None
Cooling	None
Climate	Würzburg

Fig. 2.31 **Over-temperature hours during the period of building use and hours of closed solar screening over the summer half-year shown in relation to the type of solar screening control**

Variation: Solar screening control
Solar screening closed when T_{room} > 22 °C
Solar screening closed when T_{room} > 24 °C
Solar screening closed when the direct radiation on the facade I_{facade} > 180 W/m²
Solar screening closed when the direct radiation on the facade I_{facade} > 270 W/m²

Solar screening control has considerable influence on room climate in summer. The ideal is a room-temperature-controlled solar screening system. This leads to a pleasant room climate despite the solar screening being closed for fewer hours during the period of building use. If solar screening is light-controlled then the threshold value should be set such that solar screening is closed as soon as direct sunlight strikes the facade.

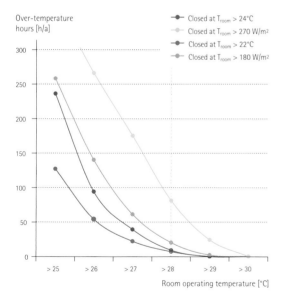

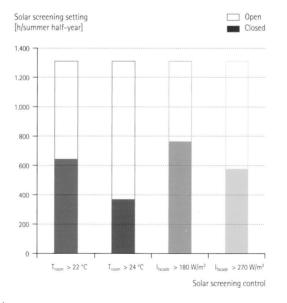

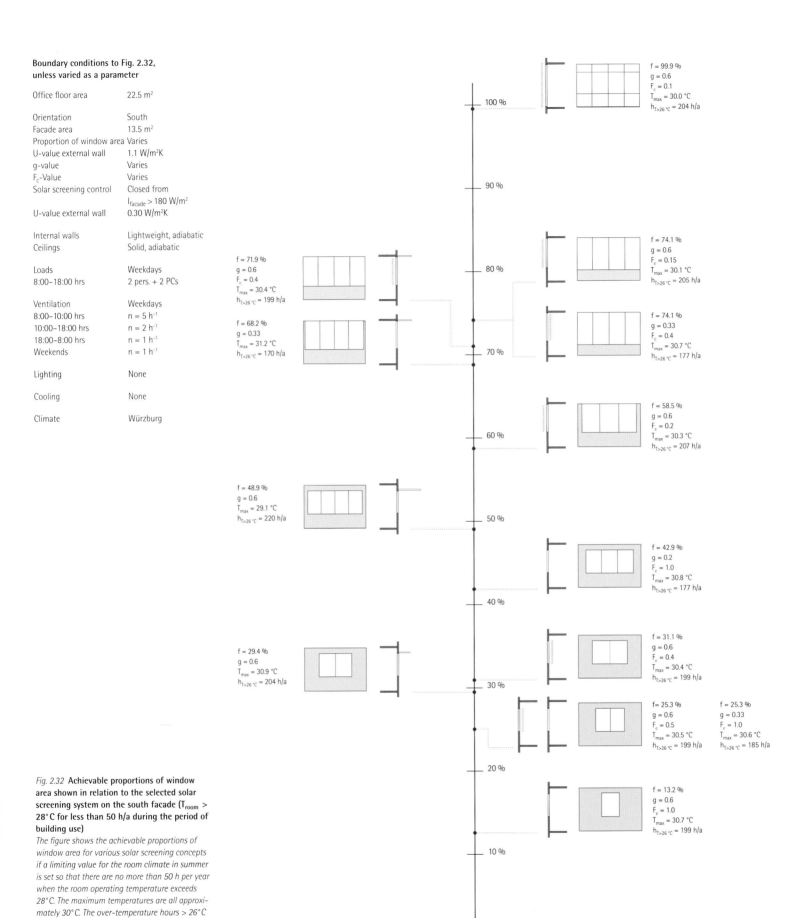

Boundary conditions to Fig. 2.32, unless varied as a parameter

Office floor area	22.5 m²
Orientation	South
Facade area	13.5 m²
Proportion of window area	Varies
U-value external wall	1.1 W/m²K
g-value	Varies
F_c-Value	Varies
Solar screening control	Closed from
	I_{facade} > 180 W/m²
U-value external wall	0.30 W/m²K
Internal walls	Lightweight, adiabatic
Ceilings	Solid, adiabatic
Loads	Weekdays
8:00–18:00 hrs	2 pers. + 2 PCs
Ventilation	Weekdays
8:00–10:00 hrs	n = 5 h⁻¹
10:00–18:00 hrs	n = 2 h⁻¹
18:00–8:00 hrs	n = 1 h⁻¹
Weekends	n = 1 h⁻¹
Lighting	None
Cooling	None
Climate	Würzburg

f = 71.9 %
g = 0.6
F_c = 0.4
T_{max} = 30.4 °C
$h_{T>26\,°C}$ = 199 h/a

f = 68.2 %
g = 0.33
T_{max} = 31.2 °C
$h_{T>26\,°C}$ = 170 h/a

f = 48.9 %
g = 0.6
T_{max} = 29.1 °C
$h_{T>26\,°C}$ = 220 h/a

f = 29.4 %
g = 0.6
T_{max} = 30.9 °C
$h_{T>26\,°C}$ = 204 h/a

f = 99.9 %
g = 0.6
F_c = 0.1
T_{max} = 30.0 °C
$h_{T>26\,°C}$ = 204 h/a

f = 74.1 %
g = 0.6
F_c = 0.15
T_{max} = 30.1 °C
$h_{T>26\,°C}$ = 205 h/a

f = 74.1 %
g = 0.33
F_c = 0.4
T_{max} = 30.7 °C
$h_{T>26\,°C}$ = 177 h/a

f = 58.5 %
g = 0.6
F_c = 0.2
T_{max} = 30.3 °C
$h_{T>26\,°C}$ = 207 h/a

f = 42.9 %
g = 0.2
F_c = 1.0
T_{max} = 30.8 °C
$h_{T>26\,°C}$ = 177 h/a

f = 31.1 %
g = 0.6
F_c = 0.4
T_{max} = 30.4 °C
$h_{T>26\,°C}$ = 199 h/a

f = 25.3 %
g = 0.6
F_c = 0.5
T_{max} = 30.5 °C
$h_{T>26\,°C}$ = 199 h/a

f = 25.3 %
g = 0.33
F_c = 1.0
T_{max} = 30.6 °C
$h_{T>26\,°C}$ = 185 h/a

f = 13.2 %
g = 0.6
F_c = 1.0
T_{max} = 30.7 °C
$h_{T>26\,°C}$ = 199 h/a

100 %
90 %
80 %
70 %
60 %
50 %
40 %
30 %
20 %
10 %
0 % Proportion of window area f

Fig. 2.32 Achievable proportions of window area shown in relation to the selected solar screening system on the south facade (T_{room} > 28 °C for less than 50 h/a during the period of building use)

The figure shows the achievable proportions of window area for various solar screening concepts if a limiting value for the room climate in summer is set so that there are no more than 50 h per year when the room operating temperature exceeds 28 °C. The maximum temperatures are all approximately 30 °C. The over-temperature hours > 26 °C generally total approximately 200 h/a, or 10 % less with lower g-values.

Fig. 2.33 **Over-temperature hours during the period of use and room operating temperatures on three very hot days shown for various types of solar screening**

Variation: Solar screening
External (F$_c$ = 0,1)
Canopy (depth = half window height) + internal (F$_c$ = 0,4)
Canopy (depth = window height)
Internal (F$_c$ = 0,4)

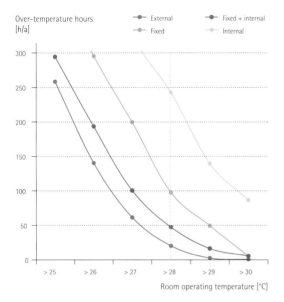

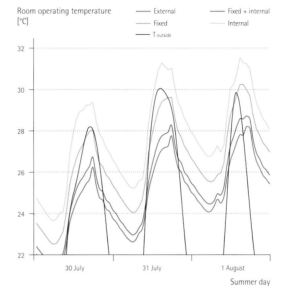

With an external system room temperatures remain within an acceptable range, even on hot days. The efficiency of fixed solar screening depends on the ratio of the window height to the depth of the projection. This solution alone may not suffice, even with a very long projection. A good arrangement for weather-independent solar screening is a combination of projecting and internal elements. Uncomfortable room temperatures often result from completely internal systems.

Boundary conditions to Figs. 2.33 and 2.34, unless varied as a parameter

Office floor area	22.5 m²
Orientation	South
Facade area	13.5 m²
Proportion of window area	70 %
U-value external wall	1.1 W/m²K
g-value	0.6
F$_c$-Value	Varies
Solar screening control	Closed from I$_{facade}$ > 180 W/m²
U-value external wall	0.30 W/m²K
Internal walls	Lightweight, adiabatic
Ceilings	Solid, adiabatic
Loads	Weekdays
8:00–18:00 hrs	2 pers. + 2 PCs
Ventilation	Weekdays
8:00–10:00 hrs	n = 5 h⁻¹
10:00–18:00 hrs	n = 2 h⁻¹
18:00–8:00 hrs	n = 1 h⁻¹
Weekends	n = 1 h⁻¹
Lighting	None
Cooling	None
Climate	Würzburg

Fig. 2.34 **Cooling energy demand and the required cooling system output with room operating temperatures on three very hot days shown for various types of solar screening with active cooling**

Variation: Solar screening
External (F$_c$ = 0,1)
Canopy (depth d = half window height) + internal (F$_c$ = 0.4)
Canopy (depth d = window height)
Internal (F$_c$ = 0.4)

Ideal cooling at T$_{room}$ > 26 °C during the period of use of the building

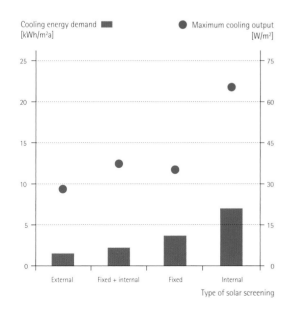

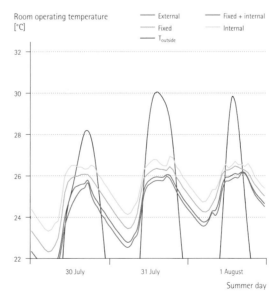

Internal solar screening leads to higher cooling energy demand and requires increased cooling system output. This cannot be provided with passive cooling strategies. The result is a considerably more complex technical system. The combination of a semi-overhang and an internal screening system is very advantageous in terms of the cooling energy demand, although the required cooling system output is slightly raised.

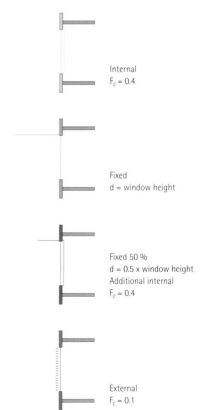

Internal
F$_c$ = 0.4

Fixed
d = window height

Fixed 50 %
d = 0.5 x window height
Additional internal
F$_c$ = 0.4

External
F$_c$ = 0.1

Hotel Tower
Hotel in Dubai, UAE

With its unique design, this landmark development reflects its function as one of the leading hotels in Dubai. Its dynamic shape and innovative shading system combine excellence in design with a future-oriented approach towards sustainability in hotel design.

Due to its unique external shading structure, the building has to be regarded as on of the first low-energy high-rise hotels in Dubai.

Facade and Shading Structure

The concept for the control of the indoor climate aims for the maximisation of comfort while keeping the energy consumption on the lowest level possible. The most effective way to keep the cooling loads down is to employ external shading through the use of external louvres, which are positioned according to the path of the sun.

Calculations by Bartenbach Lichtlabor have shown, that the total cooling loads are reduced to less than 60% if compared to a plain facade without external shading. The curtain wall facade is consisting of a aluminium-glass structure, which is prefabricated to be mounted easily to a large structure such as the DSC hotel. The glazing has a g-value of approx. 30 % and U-value of 1,5 $W/(m^2K)$.

The external shading structure consists of a light metal structure with a depth of 1,6 m, which is mounted at a distance to the facade of 90 cm, allowing the facade cleaning system to move in the gap between the glazing and the metal louvers. The vertical distance of the louvers is approx. 3,6 m. As the louvers follow the path of the sun on the west facade, they are positioned vertically at the entrance of the building.

Lighting Concept: Use of Daylight

The design of the facade and shading structure allows for an optimum use of daylight, giving the building a special atmosphere which is characterised by light, transparency and openness during the day as well as the night. Although the building is fully transparent throughout most of the facade, the special shading structure keeps the cooling loads low.

Highly effective low-energy glazing with g-values below 30 % maintain a high transparency and allow for undisturbed visual contact, which will affect the interaction of the guest with the surroundings as much as giving the building a unique appearance at night.

While regular glass buildings have a intense green, blue or grey colour and only little transparency due to regular glass coatings, the DSC Hotel will be an inviting and open element, which stands for light and airiness.

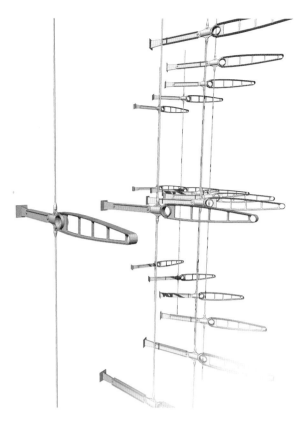

Fig. 2.35 **Exterior view**

Fig. 2.36 **Suspended steel brackets adjustable to any geometrical requirement**

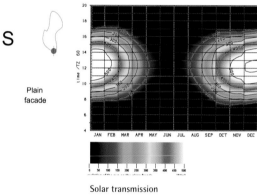

S

Plain facade

Solar transmission

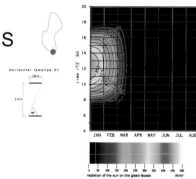

S

Horizontal lamellas H1

Fig. 2.37 **Reduction of solar transmission if compared to facade without external shading structure**

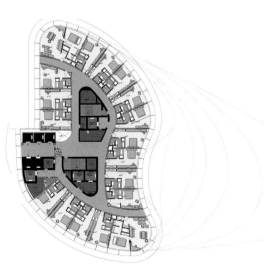

Fig. 2.38 **Detail view of external shading structure and floor plan**

Architects: Lang Hugger Rampp, Munich
Lead consultants: Shankland Cox Ltd., Al Ain, UAE
Civil Engineers: Sailer Stepan Partner, Munich
Daylighting/Shading: Bartenbach Lichtlabor, Aldrans, Austria
Building Climate and Simulations: IB Hausladen, Kircheim, IB Bauklimatik Hausladen + Meyer, Kassel
Facade Engineering: R + R Fuchs, Munich
Aerodynamic Studies: Ruscheweyh Consult, Aachen

The facade concept has to allow the option of natural ventilation. If facades are hermetically sealed, the objective comfort parameters can be fulfilled by mechanical ventilation but many subjective aspects of achieving an overall feeling of well-being are neglected. Our perception of the environment in the form of odours, sounds, air movements, fluctuations in moisture and temperature is limited. Our consciousness of the seasons and time of day is much reduced. The introduction of supply air through the facade allows the user to take quick and direct action to remedy a need for fresh air and appreciate that the air change is immediate. At locations with good quality outside air a facade which allows supply air to be introduced comfortably and limits the entry of noise can take the place of a ventilation system, whilst offering the additional advantages of reduced technical complexity, space requirement for installation and drive energy demand. If building use means that mechanical ventilation must be provided then it should be supplemented by natural ventilation. Natural ventilation can have good effects on room climate in summer. With the appropriate design it can provide considerable cooling.

Ventilation

The potential of free cooling

In our moderate climate we can use free ventilation at certain times of the year. Openings in the facade admit air, which flows though the interior, moved only by buoyancy or the wind. We know from experience that this method can work the whole year round in the domestic environment. It is often not the case in office buildings due to more intensive use and higher thermal loads.

If we take the simplest case of a room sealed off from the rest of the building by a thick door, the air in the room can only be exchanged with the outside air as a result of buoyancy forces created by the difference between inside and outside temperatures. Wind pressure has little influence if the room is sealed off from the rest of the building and the windows are on one side of the building only. The difference between inside and outside temperatures is large in winter, approximately 30 °C, but is very small in summer. Therefore the openings in the facade must be very small in winter and large in summer; at least 100 times larger and infinitely adjustable!

There is a lower limit to the outside temperature and an upper limit to the thermal loads inside the room which, if not complied with, will result in draughts in winter. Thermal loads of over 30 W/m^2 in rooms more than about 5 m deep produce air speeds greater than 15 cm/s, which would be felt as uncomfortable. Sensitive people feel draughts when outside temperatures fall below 10°C. If an air speed of 18 cm/s is permitted, then ventilation can be provided through narrow window openings at low outside temperatures as long as the gaps can be set small enough. Lower thermal loads also permit ventilation with fresh air at lower outside temperatures. The window openings in this case are very small, preferably thin continuous slots, which are positioned as high as possible and extend over the whole width of the room.

As soon as the outside temperatures drop below 8°C, it is not considered possible to provide adequate continuous ventilation through window gaps as the temperatures at floor level become too low. In these circumstances "purge ventilation" with its well-known inconvenient secondary effects usually results in the users preferring to have poor room air quality rather than ventilation. The better approach would be to use gap ventilation to its limits more extensively and augment this when required with purge ventilation.

In summer the limits of free ventilation are determined by the permissible room temperatures. As long as the temperatures outside are lower than those inside and are between 23 to 25 °C, the windows have to be opened as wide as possible. As soon as outside air temperatures exceed this value it becomes necessary to use the thermal storage effect of the building in combination with night cooling to keep temperatures comfortable. Then windows may only be opened a small amount during the day and placed at least into the tilt setting at night. The limit for thermal loads in the room by experience is somewhere around 30 W/m^2 during an approximately eight-hour office working day.

Prof. a.D. Dr.-Ing. Klaus Fitzner

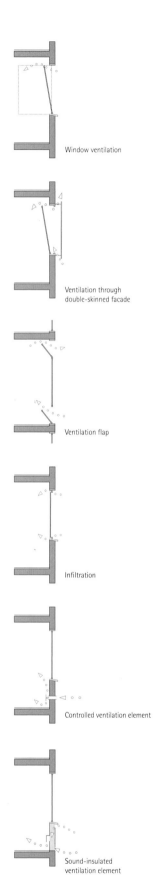

Window ventilation

Ventilation through
double-skinned facade

Ventilation flap

Infiltration

Controlled ventilation element

Sound-insulated
ventilation element

Fig. 2.39 **Overview of ventilation openings**

Ventilation elements

Most buildings are ventilated through their windows. In traditional perforated facades they were the only openings and combined the functions of ventilation, daylight entry and views out in one element. The linking of several functions makes it difficult to obtain the best performance in each respect.

For natural ventilation the opening light of a window must be finely adjustable in order to offer a certain degree of weather protection, ensure complete air exchange, contribute to limiting thermal discomfort and prevent the entry of noise. Conventional tilt-turn fittings alone are usually not enough to allow the option of natural ventilation over the whole year. Further ventilation elements are required depending on the building location and use with the objective of providing the perfect setting to permit air exchange in all outside conditions. The ventilation openings should allow continuous trickle ventilation as well as purge ventilation. In principle window ventilation can be provided in the facade with various kinds of fittings or by ventilation elements.

Window ventilation Window ventilation can be by horizontally or vertically sliding elements, tilt-turn elements, turning or hinged windows or by parallel action windows. These window elements are differentiated by their air change performance, ease of regulation and complexity of construction. Window ventilation is suitable for locations with little noise load and low wind speeds. They provide unobstructed views out and permit purge ventilation with their high rate of air change.

Ventilation through double-skinned facades Double-skinned facade elements may prove advantageous in noisy or windy locations. They may be incorporated as double-skinned facades, box windows or baffle panels. Ventilation solely through a double-skinned facade is somewhat less satisfactory in summer as temperatures in the facade cavity can be rather high and therefore it should be augmented by some means of direct ventilation. The second skin of glass prevents a direct view out. However, the second skin protects the users from noise and wind, and heats supply air during colder months. A further advantage is the option of the cavity providing weather protection to solar screening.

Ventilation flaps In the case of tall buildings in particular, wind pressures on the facades can be so high that the user cannot safely operate the windows. The designer still has to provide some basic weather protection so that rain or wind cannot cause damage if a window is inadvertently left open. Small flaps can allow facade ventilation even in high wind speeds. Their small area also makes them safe to use in strong winds. These flaps should have a wide range of set opening angles to allow the amount of ventilation to be finely adjusted. The ventilation flap, being on the outside skin, provides some protection in wet weather, making it safe to leave them open for night ventilation. This type of flap is a useful addition to box or conventional windows.

	Air changes	Controllability	Sound insulation	View out	Notes
Window ventilation	1–20 h⁻¹	Medium	Low	Very good	Low cost
Ventilation through double-skinned facade	0.5–5 h⁻¹	Low	Good	Low	Risk of overheating
Ventilation flap	1–3 h⁻¹	Good	Low	Good	Additive solution
Infiltration	0.5–2 h⁻¹	Good	Good	–	Low complexity
Controlled ventilation element	0.5–1 h⁻¹	Good	Very good	–	Medium complexity
Sound-insulated ventilation element	1–3 h⁻¹	Medium	Very good	–	High complexity

Tab. 2.4 **Characteristics of ventilation openings**

Infiltration ventilation Basic air exchange with little entry of noise can also take place from a controlled amount of leakage around window joints. High air flow speeds and thermal discomfort can be lessened in this way. As infiltration ventilation is not immediately apparent to the user, there is the risk of unnecessarily high rates of air changes taking place in winter through the permanent infiltration openings, which leads to increased heat losses.

Controlled ventilation elements The basic level of air changes can also be provided by means of a controlled ventilation element. This allows user controlled ventilation without additional fans. Criteria for control can include the air quality, the presence of people or air flow. It can be effective for the control of the ventilation openings to be dependent on outside conditions. In summer a temperature-controlled system will produce the best thermal conditions in the room.

Sound-insulated ventilation element At noisy locations a sound-insulated ventilation element can be a useful addition to a conventional window and an alternative to a double-skinned facade or a box window. In addition a conventional window with an opening light will provide a good view out.

Tab. 2.5 **Advantages and disadvantages of ventilation elements for various locations and building types**

Ventilation elements	Advantage	Disadvantage	Location and outside conditions
Double-skinned facade	Wind-protected solar screening Comfortable introduction of supply air in winter Night ventilation	High cost No view out Risk of summer overheating	
Window ventilation and ventilation flaps	Cost-effective Direct view out	Unprotected solar screening	
Window ventilation and box windows	Direct view out Very flexible solution Night ventilation	Only partially protected solar screening	
Window ventilation and controlled ventilation element	Direct view out Night ventilation User-dependent ventilation	Requires control system Higher cost Unprotected solar screening	High-rise, exposed to wind
Box window	Night ventilation Comfortable introduction of supply air in winter	No direct view out Risk of summer overheating	
Window ventilation and box windows	Direct view out Very flexible solution Night ventilation		
Window ventilation and infiltration	Sound-insulated basic ventilation Direct view out Cost-effective	Limited sound insulation	
Window ventilation and sound-insulated ventilation element	Sound-insulated ventilation Direct view out	High complexity	Noisy location
Window ventilation	Direct view out Cost-effective	No protected night ventilation	
Window ventilation and baffle panel	Night ventilation	Limited view out	
Window ventilation and infiltration	Direct view out Basic air changes Basic night ventilation	Unnoticed air changes	
Window ventilation and controlled ventilation element	Direct view out User-dependent basic ventilation	Higher cost Requires control system	Quiet location

Air change with natural ventilation

With ventilation through the facade it is difficult to determine the number of air changes exactly, as there are many influences to be taken into account. The main factors are the type and position of the facade openings and the driving forces of thermal buoyancy and wind. These driving forces can be active in a room or in certain circumstances combine to affect the whole of a building. They can act to reinforce or cancel one another. The strength and direction of thermal buoyancy and wind cannot be influenced and are subject to continuous fluctuations. The size of the facade openings influences air exchange and therefore particular attention should be paid to their design and position. The best approach is to design the ventilation openings very flexibly and with an appropriate reserve capacity as it is only possible to make rough predictions about natural air exchanges. Moreover the aspects of sound insulation, room climate in summer and comfortable introduction of supply air need to be considered as they often require special detailing of the ventilation openings.

Ventilation by thermal buoyancy Differences in air density resulting from differences in temperature between inside and outside air give rise to vertical air movements. This effect depends on the effective height and the temperature difference. The effective height is determined by the position and design of the facade openings in the room and by the height difference of the openings in the building, providing the air can circulate throughout the building. Large effective heights can result in considerable pressure differences. In the upper storeys this can produce a thermally induced pressure, which causes air to flow out of the building.

In winter, when large temperature differences between inside and outside normally prevail, air changes are generally assured. The task is more one of limiting air changes and avoiding discomfort problems caused by cold supply air and excessive air speeds. In summer, when temperature differences are less, the task is to ensure sufficient air changes. The facade openings and the effective height must be adequately large. Therefore windows with a vertical aspect ratio and openings in the balustrade and skylight area are more effective than a centrally placed window with little height.

Fig. 2.40 **Indicative supply air volume flows for an opening width of 6 cm shown in relation to the temperature difference between inside and outside. Range of values based on various theories and measurements [graphic after Hall]**

Boundary conditions
Window height: 1.23 m
Window width: 0.94 m

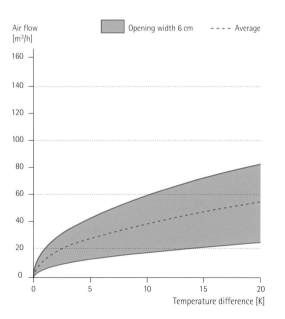

Fig. 2.41 **Indicative supply air volume flows for an opening width of 10 cm shown in relation to the temperature difference between inside and outside. Range of values based on various theories and measurements [graphic after Hall]**

Boundary conditions
Window height: 1.23 m
Window width: 0.94 m

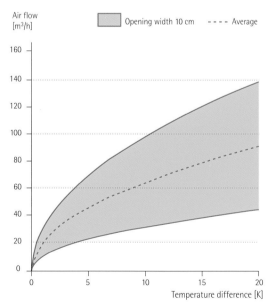

Ventilation by the wind Wind-conditioned air change can be brought about in two ways. If the openings in a room or a building are situated in different aerodynamic pressure zones then air flows from the positive pressure zone to the suction zone. Local pressure peaks may form along with considerable suction, depending on the shape of the building and its position. Air exchange depends greatly on wind speed. Another influence factor is turbulence in the air. No through-flow of air takes place in rooms with only one opening, However, intensive air change can take place as a result of fluctuations and changes in direction of wind pressure. Changes in wind pressure are generally caused by wind turbulence or gusts.

Extensive wind-conditioned air exchange takes place in the transition months, when higher wind speeds tend to occur. Openings must be designed so that they can limit the speed of the air entering the room. This applies in particular when air can flow through the building between different pressure zones. Furthermore the design of ventilation openings in the facade and overflow openings should ensure that no whistling noises are generated by narrow openings.

Assessment of natural ventilation In winter air change is easy to achieve. The main aim is thermal comfort. In the transition months wind generally causes adequate air changes but air flow speeds need to be limited. Even in still conditions, the temperature difference between inside and outside is normally enough to ensure adequate air exchange. Summer weather often has periods of high outside air temperatures and still wind conditions, which can limit air exchange. If a building has no mechanical ventilation, the openings in its facade must be large. In some cases air can flow through the building via an atrium to optimise air exchange. This can be useful in removing heat from a building by improved night ventilation.

Fig. 2.42 **Supply air volume flows with open windows shown in relation to temperature difference [graphic Pültz]**

Fig. 2.43 **Supply air volume flow shown in relation to wind speed and window position with respect to wind direction [graphic Blum]**

Boundary conditions
Window height: 1.20 m
Window width: 1.00 m

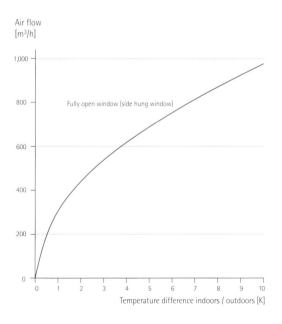

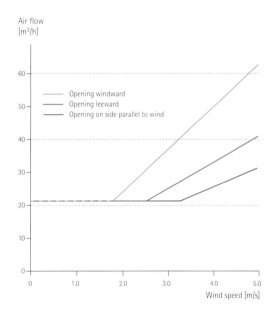

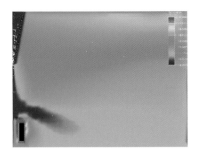

Fig. 2.44 **Supply air provided through an open window**
When outside temperatures are low, direct ventilation through opened windows leads to high air flow speeds and low air temperatures in the floor area. This effect cannot always be satisfactorily intercepted by heating radiators.

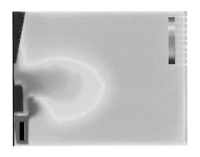

Fig. 2.45 **Supply air provided through an optimised facade**
Excessively low temperatures in the floor area can be avoided by the formation of a supply air mixing zone in which the cold outside air is mixed with the warm room air.

Tab. 2.6 **Comparative evaluation of supply air introduction**

Comfortable introduction of supply air in winter

For ventilation in very low temperatures ($T_a < 5\,°C$) constructional or technical precautions are necessary in the facade to avoid thermal discomfort (Figs. 2.44 and 2.45). The basic strategies for this include preheating the supply air, mixing the supply air with the room air or a combination of preheating and mixing (Fig. 2.46). Introducing air through the facade allows cost savings in building services, which can justify higher investment in the facade.

Preheating the supply air Preheating can be performed by the heating system, by waste heat from technical equipment and lighting or by the supply air collectors. Preheating by the heating system, e.g. by radiators or convectors, usually requires additional heating energy. In addition, higher flow temperatures can also bring with them higher energy generation costs. Preheating by collectors is only worthwhile at the south facade, it relies on the amount of solar energy entering the facade and the construction costs are relatively high. The ideal is to be able to use the waste heat from technical equipment or lighting for preheating the supply air. Construction costs are high. Air distribution and preheating can take place in the double floor cavity in systems where room conditioning is by thermally activated components and double floors. This solution is highly attractive in terms of energy but from a hygienic point of view it presents serious problems and also requires a drive.

Mixing of the supply air Preheating by mixing supply air can be done in suspended ceilings, a supply air duct or mixing zone near the facade. Large rooms are better ventilated even at depths when air is introduced through the ceiling or a duct. The heat energy demand may be less as supply air preheating can be reduced to compensate for internal heat loads. The disadvantage of mixing is lower air quality. Dust deposits can further reduce air quality when air is introduced through the ceiling or a duct. Delivering air through a duct requires a fan to drive it.

	Thermal comfort	Air exchange and air quality	Energy efficiency	Application and comments
Supply air preheating by heating radiators	Risk of cold air drop	Low air change rate, high air quality	Possible increased heating energy demand	For low air volumes, very simple solution
Supply air via mixing zone	Medium	Medium air change rate, high air quality	Increased heating energy demand	Simple solution for medium air change rates
Supply air via mixing zone with convector	High	Medium air change rate, displacement ventilation	Increased heating energy demand	Possible dirt deposits, high inlet temperatures
Supply air via technical equipment zones	Depends on waste heat	Medium air change rate, possible with waste heat	Use of waste heat	With high heat loads, complex detailing
Supply air via supply air collector	Depends on entry of solar radiation	Very high air change rate with entry of solar radiation	Use of solar radiation	Only for south facades, complex facade design
Supply air via ventilation duct	Very high	Very high air change rate, mixed ventilation	Drive energy, controlled ventilation	For large room depths, drive required
Supply air via double floor	Possible low floor temperature	Low air change rate, displacement ventilation	Drive energy, low inlet temperature	For activated ceilings, hygiene may be a problem
Supply air via suspended ceiling	Very high	High air change rate, mixed ventilation	Low energy requirement	For large room depths, no drive required

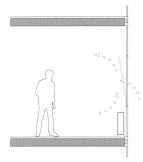

Supply air preheating by heating radiators

A radiator under the window heats the supply air flowing in through the opened window. For low rates of air change this can limit cold air drop.

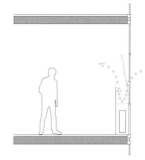

Supply air via a mixing zone

A supply air mixing zone is required with very cold outside temperatures and high air change rates. Cold supply air is mixed and heated with the room air with the result that discomfort is avoided.

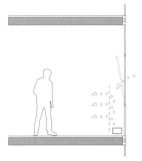

Supply air via a mixing zone with a convector

A supply air mixing zone can be designed so that cold air first travels downwards, where it is heated by a convector and then flows slowly into the room through a perforated element. Larger volumes of fresh air can be introduced into the room in this way.

Supply air from technical equipment zones

If technical equipment, for example computers or lighting elements, are integrated into a specific zone close to the facade and supply air is passed through it, the waste heat from the devices can be used to preheat the air. In summer the direction of air circulation can be reversed to carry the waste heat directly out of the building.

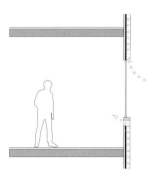

Supply air via a supply air collector

The supply air is heated by a supply air collector integrated into the facade. This system is independent of orientation of the building.

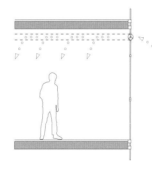

Supply air via ventilation ducts

A supply air duct carries out the mixing and distribution of air into the depth of the room. The fan allows precise adjustment of the pressures in the room. Filters and sound insulation can be incorporated. There is no need for long ducts associated with a central ventilation system.

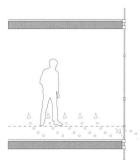

Supply air via double floors

Supply air can be heated by passing through a double floor and distributed into the depth of the room as displacement air. Hygiene is an aspect which should not be ignored. A drive is required to ensure a defined rate of air change.

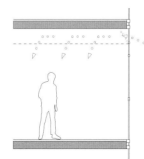

Supply air via a suspended ceiling

The void in a suspended ceiling can be used to conduct mixed supply air into the depth of the room and introduce it evenly. Low outside temperatures mean a drive is necessary.

Fig. 2.46 **Overview of concepts for comfortable introduction of supply air**

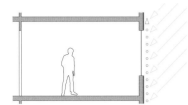

Fig. 2.47 **Boundary layer at the facade**
In summer, depending on reflection conditions and colours, the temperature of a facade surface can rise to 40°-80°C. This rise in temperature heats the air immediately in front of the facade.

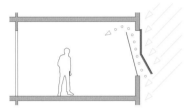

Fig. 2.48 **Excessive supply air temperature due to solar screening**
The radiation absorbed by the solar screening can lead to an increase in supply air temperature of between 2-5 K as it enters through the facade.

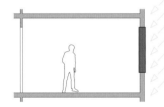

Fig. 2.49 **Facade-related excess temperature of the supply air**
With box windows or double-skinned facades the excess temperature may be up to 30 K, depending on the degree of opening.

Boundary conditions to Fig. 2.50

Office floor area	22.5 m²
Room height	3.0 m
Room volume	67.5 m³

Influence of ventilation on room climate in summer

In summer, ventilation has a considerable influence on comfort in buildings. High outside air temperatures, especially when combined with high rates of air change, can result in additional heat energy entering the building. This may be increased by further increases in temperature related to the facades. However, when outside temperatures are lower than room operating temperatures then heat loads can be removed from the building, especially when the temperature difference is large. Therefore night ventilation is particularly suitable for heat removal.

Entry of thermal energy by ventilation So that room climate in summer is not made worse by ventilation, the rate of air change must be limited when outside air temperatures are higher than room temperature, and in particular when the supply air temperature is higher than outside air temperature due to facade-related factors (Tab. 2.7). The facade surface can reach temperatures of up to 80 °C, depending on its colour. This causes an air boundary layer to form directly in front of the facade in which the air temperature can be up to 10 K higher than the ambient temperature (Fig. 2.47). Wind weakens this boundary layer effect, with the temperature increase then being only up to 5 K. In the cavity of box windows or double-skinned facades considerable temperature in-

creases of up to 30 K can result from the solar radiation absorbed by the solar screening (Fig. 2.49). Depending on how open the outside skin is and the rate of air change in the facade cavity, typical temperatures in the cavity can reach 30 to 40 °C. A further risk of heating the supply air arises behind the solar screening, especially if an awning type of system is used (Fig. 2.48). In general, it is beneficial to admit supply air into the building from the sides facing away from the sun.

Cooling potential of day ventilation The amount of heat removed by ventilation is determined by the rate of air change and the temperature difference between inside and outside. Therefore a particularly efficient way of heat load removal is to adopt purge ventilation in the mornings. In summer the rate of air change during the day should be set higher rather than lower, as in practice the user cannot be relied upon to optimise temperatures by using the windows. Even with outside temperatures which are only slightly above the average room operating temperatures it can still be possible to remove heat as the internal loads themselves are released at a higher temperature. The possibility of heat entry because of increased air change rates is really quite small as high outside temperatures generally coincide with high inside temperatures and therefore the temperature difference is only slight. In addition there is a comfort gain from increased air movement.

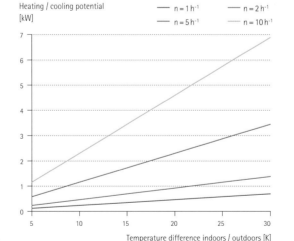

Fig. 2.50 **Theoretical cooling and heating potential from ventilation shown in relation to rate of air change and temperature difference**

	Typical	Maximum
Boundary layer, no wind	5 K	10 K
Boundary layer, with wind	2 K	5 K
Heat-absorbent facade surface	10 K	15 K
Box window	5–15 K	20 K
Box window, sound insulated	5–20 K	30 K
Unsegmented double-skinned facade	5–20 K	30 K
Controlled double-skinned facade	5–10 K	20 K
Solar screening louvres	2–5 K	10 K
Awning	5–10 K	15 K

Tab. 2.7 **Typical supply air temperatures for different facades shown in relation to outside air temperatures for high insolation in summer**

Fig. 2.51 Over-temperature hours during the period of building use and room operating temperatures on three hot days with increased supply air temperatures around midday (10:00 to 14:00 hrs)

Variation: Supply air temperature between 10:00–14:00 hrs
$T_{supply} = T_{outside\ air}$
$T_{supply} = 30\,°C$
$T_{supply} = 35\,°C$
$T_{supply} = 40\,°C$

Increased supply air temperatures caused by the boundary layer effect or heating up of the facade cavity have a detrimental effect on conditions in summer. Even an increase in the supply air temperature to 30 °C during the middle of the day means comfortable conditions cannot be achieved. An alternative source of supply air is required.

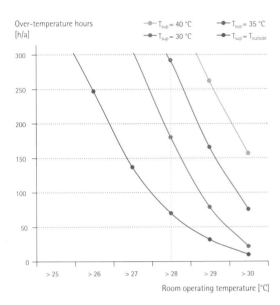

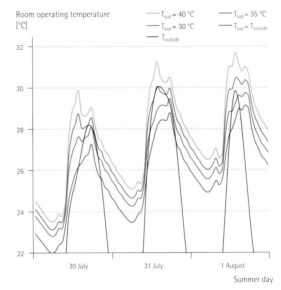

Fig. 2.52 Over-temperature hours during the period of use and operating room temperatures on three hot days shown in relation to the daytime ventilation strategy

Variation: Ventilation strategy
Continuous ventilation:
8:00–10:00 hrs n = 5 h⁻¹
8:00–10:00 hrs n = 2 h⁻¹

Morning purge ventilation:
8:00–10:00 hrs n = 5 h⁻¹
10:00–18:00 hrs n = 2 h⁻¹
8:00–10:00 hrs n = 10 h⁻¹
10:00–18:00 hrs n = 1 h⁻¹

With room operating temperatures up to 28 °C, a thermally optimised ventilation strategy can improve room climate in summer. In addition the influence of air change rate is less significant, as the temperature differences between outside air and the room operating temperatures are small.

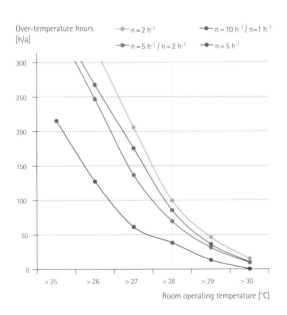

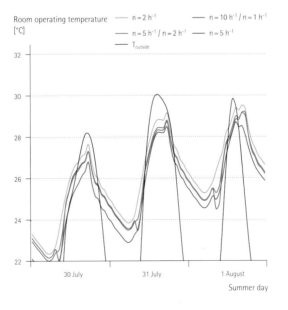

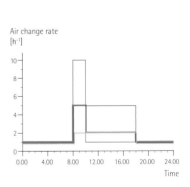

Night ventilation

With night cooling, the lower air temperatures during the night are used to remove heat from the exposed thermal storage masses by ventilation. The storage masses are then available as sources of cooling energy for the next day. Night cooling provides an effective method of cooling without additional operating costs.

Night cooling is particularly suitable for locations with large temperature movements between day and night. A favourable situation arises when outside air temperatures drop by about 15 °C during the night. As thermally usable storage masses increase the effectivenss of night cooling (Fig. 2.53), it is beneficial to construct ceilings from concrete and dispense with suspended ceilings and double floors. For ideal conditions the internal walls should also be of solid construction. If necessary PCMs (Phase Change Materials) can augment or take the place of thermal storage masses. Rates of air change of $n = 4\ h^{-1}$ or higher are desirable (Fig. 2.55). Adequately large ventilation openings are required, which must also be weather- and intruder-proof. Controlled ventilation openings allow the cooling performance to be optimised and can avoid the creation of excessively low room temperatures in the mornings during the transition months. On the other hand this incurs higher costs for fittings and controls. In practice this is only economic if controlled openings were necessary for other reasons, e.g. for controlled natural ventilation or smoke removal. A buoyancy or wind-induced through-flow of air in a building increases the cooling effect. Therefore it is necessary to have vertical air spaces or opposing facade openings.

Night ventilation allows heat loads of between 200 and 250 Wh/m^2d to be removed to achieve good climatic conditions in rooms with moderate thermal loads in summer. However, the dependence on outside climate means that no temperature limits can be guaranteed. Higher thermal loads can be accommodated given favourable outside climatic conditions and adequate thermal storage masses. However, this is also associated with excessively cool room temperatures in the mornings. Although optimum conditions cannot be created with low rates of air change, which can also be achieved with conventional windows using infiltration, these measures can produce considerable improvements in room climate (Fig. 2.54).

Boundary conditions for Fig. 2.53, unless varied as a parameter

Office floor area	22.5 m^2
Orientation	South
Facade area	13.5 m^2
Proportion of window area	70%
U-value window	1.1 W/m^2K
g-value	0.6
F_c-value	0.2
Solar screening control	Closed from I_{facade}> 180 W/m^2
U-value external wall	0.30 W/m^2K
Internal walls	Varies, adiabatic
Ceilings	Varies, adiabatic
Loads 8:00–18:00 hrs	Weekdays 2 pers. + 2 PCs
Ventilation 8:00–10:00 hrs	Weekdays $n = 5\ h^{-1}$
10:00–18:00 hrs	$n = 2\ h^{-1}$
18:00–8:00 hrs	$n = 4\ h^{-1}$
Weekends	$n = 1\ h^{-1}$
Lighting	None
Cooling	None
Climate	Würzburg

Fig. 2.53 **Influence of thermally effective storage mass on the number of over-temperature hours and the room operating temperature on three hot days**

Variation: Construction
Lightweight construction: Internal walls lightweight, double floors, suspended ceilings
Medium-heavy construction: Internal walls lightweight, exposed ceilings
Heavyweight construction: Internal walls solid, exposed ceilings
Night air change rate $n = 4\ h^{-1}$

Storage mass is essential for efficient night cooling.
Construction must be at least medium-weight. Extensive storage masses can efficiently limit the times of high room temperatures but users may feel temperatures in the mornings are too cool.

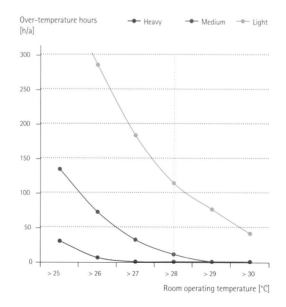

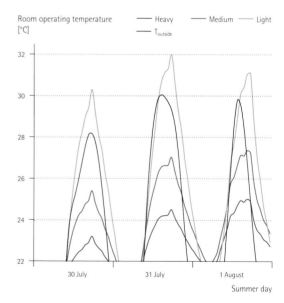

Fig. 2.54 Over-temperature hours during the period of use and operating room temperatures on three hot days shown in relation to night infiltration ventilation

Variation: Infiltration air change 18:00–8:00 hrs
n = 0 h⁻¹, n = 0.5 h⁻¹, n = 1.0 h⁻¹, n = 1.5 h⁻¹
Weekend 00:00–24:00 hrs: n = weekday 18:00–8:00 hrs
Medium-heavy construction

Even a low rate of air change through gaps and small openings can considerably improve room climate in summer. Therefore in summer a user-independent minimum number of air changes takes place during the night. This is also possible without any special night ventilation openings.

Boundary conditions to Figs. 2.54 and 2.55, unless varied as a parameter

Office floor area	22.5 m²
Orientation	South
Facade area	13.5 m²
Proportion of window area	70 %
U-value window	1.1 W/m²K
g-value	0.6
F_c-value	0.2
Solar screening control	Closed from I_{facade} > 180 W/m²
U-value external wall	0.30 W/m²K
Internal walls	Lightweight, adiabatic
Ceilings	Solid, adiabatic
Loads Weekdays 8:00–18:00 hrs	2 pers. + 2 PCs
Ventilation Weekdays	
8:00–10:00 hrs	n = 5 h⁻¹
10:00–18:00 hrs	n = 2 h⁻¹
18:00–8:00 hrs	Varies
Weekends	n = 1 h⁻¹
Lighting	None
Cooling	None
Climate	Würzburg

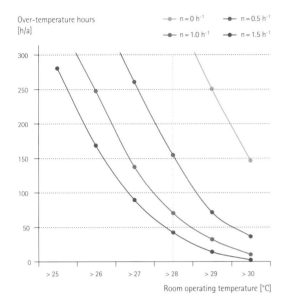

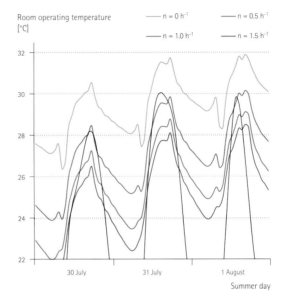

Fig. 2.55 Over-temperature hours during the period of use and room operating temperatures on three hot days shown in relation to night air exchange

Variation: Rates of air change 18:00–8:00 hrs
n = 2 h⁻¹, n = 4 h⁻¹, n = 6 h⁻¹, n = 8 h⁻¹
Medium-heavy construction

Even a low rate of air change can considerably improve room climate. A rate of air change of at least n = 4 h⁻¹ is desirable to achieve good conditions.

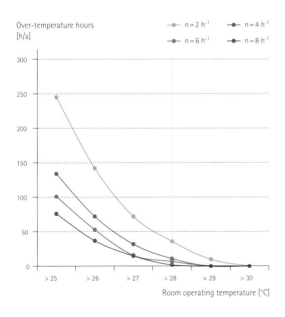

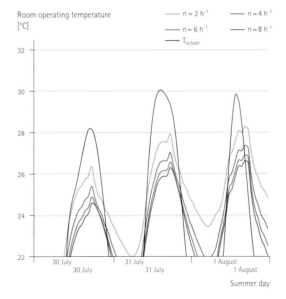

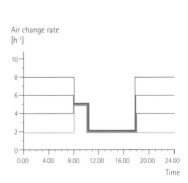

Air and water
Competition entry, Botanical Garden, Shanghai

The 200 ha Botanical Garden site lies some 30 km southwest of the centre of Shanghai in an area of intensive agricultural use. Nine hills provide spatial orientation points and are popular local recreation areas. The new Botanical Garden will be used by the university as a research facility whilst fulfilling the role of a popular leisure park. It is expected to attract around 30,000 visitors per day. The Botanical Garden is planned to open at the same time as Expo 2010.

The Botanical Garden Shanghai aspires to put extensive sustainability and recycling to the test on all levels. This extends from resource saving and energy efficiency to ecological systems for water purification and the conversion of wastes and biomass into energy. The garden is intended to be recognised as an exemplary demonstration project beyond its immediate location.

Energy concept The client wishes the building to have an energy consumption of 50% of the general average for China whilst minimising the energy required for heating in winter and cooling in summer. The climatic conditions present a serious challenge: Winter temperatures in Shanghai can fall below –5 °C. In summer the outside temperature climbs to 35 °C with relative air humidities of around 75%. The building incorporates measures such as good thermal insulation of the facade, efficient solar screening, excellent provision of daylight and the use of rainwater for irrigation.

Ventilation concept A ventilation system with heat recovery, supply air conditioning through an earth pipe and heating and cooling registers (dehumidification) ensures the air changes necessary for hygienic purposes.

Plants need to have moisture added to the room air. In summer this humidification produces an additional cooling effect in the interior. The greenhouses can also be naturally ventilated with outside air through opening flaps.

Layout

Fig. 2.56 **Layout**
Like a shell, a large sculptural ring encloses the inner garden and one of the hills. All the important buildings such as the reception, restaurant and exhibition halls, greenhouses and the botanical research centre are integrated into the large ring sculpture and together form a single morphological unit.

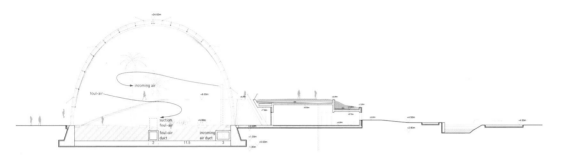

Winter ventilation concept

Fig. 2.57 **Winter ventilation concept**
Winter ventilation concept: The ventilation system is powered in circulatory mode in conjunction with a combined heat and power plant. If necessary, outside air can be mixed into the system. Supply air is introduced laterally through chimneys and extracted centrally close to ground level.

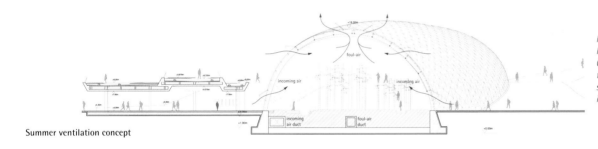

Summer ventilation concept

Fig. 2.58 **Summer ventilation concept**
Plants are shaded by internal solar screening. Outside air flows past the solar screening from flaps in the lower parts of the building skin and some of the heat absorbed by the solar screening is carried away.

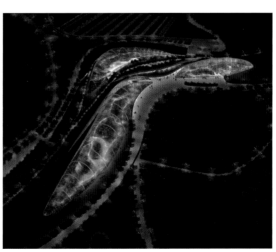

Fig. 2.59 **Perspective of the research centre**

Fig. 2.60 **Perspective of the greenhouse**

Completion: Competition, planned 2010
Use: Botanical garden
Client: Chenshan Botanical Garden Shanghai Project Team, China
Architect: Auer+Weber+Assoziierte, Munich
Landscape architects: Valentien + Valentien Landschaftsarchitekten und Stadtplaner SRL Straub + Thurmayr Landschaftsarchitekten
Energy concept: IB Hausladen, Kirchheim b. Munich, Cornelia Jacobsen

The use of daylight in buildings is essential for the feeling of well-being of their occupants. This is particularly true because the dynamic changes of daylight allow us to appreciate the passage of the day and seasons. Furthermore it reduces lighting energy demand and cooling loads. However, it can be accompanied by the risk of increased entry of solar thermal energy and glare, especially where there are computer monitors. A considerable influence on the use of daylight is the facade. Window size and position as well as the natural light transmittance of the transparent surfaces have a considerable influence on the entry of daylight. Further aspects include the form of solar screening and the use of light-redirecting systems. The reflection properties of the internal surfaces determine the illuminance at the working plane and the distribution of illuminance in the room.

Daylight

Influence of daylight on the comfort and performance of the user

Natural or artificial light? The subjective and spontaneous answer to this question is almost always "natural light". However, there are also many "technocrats" who do not readily agree. In their opinion, using today's technology we can manufacture all the components of "primary light", that is to say all the qualities of natural light; the distribution, radiation types, inherent luminous density of the light sources, colour temperatures and spectrums. In principle this is correct, however in practice the theories of reproducing the important characteristics, such as the changes in intensity, the direction of the radiation and the spectrum are impractical or can only be realised under laboratory conditions.

During the process of evolution, humans have become biologically attuned to natural light. The mechanisms and functions of optical perception are based on the properties of natural light and have developed from them. The processing powers of our brains developed in parallel to this. The continuous change of natural light and the diversity of the images this produces provide people with information and we have learned to interpret it. When intensively viewing exhibits in a museum that is naturally lit but otherwise visually cut off from the outside world, it is still possible to discern the weather and even the time of day from changes in secondary textures of light.

Artificial light always has a static effect. As the primary light emitted is determined by the type of emitter and undergoes no changes, the information it gives out is limited and influenced by the light source. Artificial light cannot therefore be said to produce the same effects in all respects as natural light – it is at best a plagiarism of natural light at a single moment in time. The nature of artificial light makes it most suitable for use as a supplement to natural light or exclusively at night.

Measurements based on optical perception for computer monitor work carried out on 30 subjects at the Bartenbach Light Laboratory, Austria showed that, for eight different brain functions, better mental performances and fewer signs of fatigue occur when natural light is used.

The window is thought of as a means of relating to the outside world and thus provides the important factor of a room visually open to the outside. It is certainly not possible to dispense with the view out. Extensive research on opening sizes of windows shows that a room should have a window area some 20–30 % of its floor area, thus satisfying the human attachment to visual contact and primordial need for an escape route. Windows connect an observer with the "external" world. However, the luminance of the sky immediately presents itself as a source of glare luminance. The luminance of the sky is in the range 8,000 cd/m^2 and above, depending on the outdoor brightness. As these luminances extend over large areas and come into the field of view through the active spatial perception and the type of room geometry, they induce a disturbance in the stable optical perception state of the observer. When these areas of luminance occur, the associated direct and reflective glare can jeopardise the use of electronic information screens. Measures are necessary to counter glare, on the one hand to reduce window luminance and, on the other, to allow the entry of natural light. These high window luminances can be reduced to the required value of 100–400 cd/m^2 with the help of suitable light-redirection systems. Offices must have an average daylight factor of 3 %. The evenness of distribution within the room is important. Light-redirecting louvres, which provide solar screening through their reduced luminance and counteract glare, combined with a light-redirecting ceiling can best fulfil the 3 % requirement. Fatigue measurements show a clear preference for light-redirecting louvres. Whilst clear windows and conventional blinds place excessive loads on the eye due to their too high or too low brightness (adaptation glare), light-redirection systems (perforated or solid) produce fatigue values which are compatible with continuous and relaxed levels of activity.

The following requirements for natural light must be fulfilled by light-redirection systems, the appropriate match of materials and luminances and an adequate view out: sufficient amounts of natural light, light distribution appropriate to the room and its use, solar screening and passive use of solar energy, perception psychology characteristics such as stress prevention, low fatigue and maximum mental performance and the feeling of well-being of the users. Too little natural light can result in serotonin deficiency in humans, which in turn is a significant cause of depressive illnesses (e.g. SAD), and this is precisely what these systems can prevent.

Prof. Dipl.-Ing. Christian Bartenbach

Natural light outside buildings

Natural light is subject to continuous variation. The intensity, colour, angle of incidence and direction of light change with the time of day, the seasons and the weather. The aim of a holistic daylighting design is to set the limits on this dynamic wide enough to fulfil the criteria for visual comfort whilst retaining views out and the perception of changes in light. At the same time the user should be aware of the passage of time and able to appreciate the outdoor climate. It is important to provide natural light, even in the depth of the room.

The use of natural light has a considerable influence on the energy demand of a building. The direct saving comes from the reduction in electricity used for lighting. In summer a good daylighting design can save cooling energy and improve thermal comfort. In winter the heating energy demand can be reduced if solar radiation can penetrate into the room without causing glare.

The appearance of natural light Natural light (daylight) can occur in the forms of directional or diffused nondirectional light. Direct light occurs with a clear sky and sun. It can be directed over long distances on to the desired area. Direct light generally leads to large differences in luminance and direct glare. With diffused solar radiation the light is scattered. Scatter can be due to moisture or particles in the atmosphere, to the light passing through translucent materials or being reflected from rough surfaces. Diffused light at about 120 lm/W is considerably lower in energy than direct light with

a luminous efficacy of 60 to 90 lm/W and is therefore preferable in summer in terms of comfort. Diffused light can be directed over short distances only and cannot be aimed. Direct light can be deflected and aimed deep into the depth of the room.

Influence of the seasons The intensity of daylight changes with the solar altitude, the turbidity of the atmosphere and the amount of cloud cover. These climatic factors influence the illuminance, colour, luminance and therefore the atmosphere of the room. Day length and luminance change with the seasons. The luminance at midday under a diffuse sky in summer is approximately 18,000 lx, in winter approximately 7,000 lx. As the seasons change so does the path of the sun, which determines the angle of incidence of direct sunlight.

The direct radiation of the low sun improves the lighting conditions in the depth of the room, although there is a severe risk of glare. Light-redirection systems can be helpful in delivering the light via the ceiling into the depth of the room.

Influence of building orientation Facade orientation plays a subordinate role in the use of diffused natural light as the brightness of the sky depends mainly on the elevation angle and is a factor of three higher at the zenith.

Local influence factors on lighting conditions indoors are shading and reflectance outdoors. Depending on the reflection properties of the surrounding buildings light may be reflected as diffused or direct light. Direct reflection can give rise to glare.

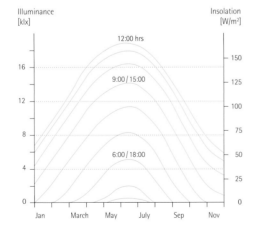

Fig. 2.61 **Horizontal illuminance shown in relation to the time of day and season**
Illuminance is directly proportional to solar radiation.

Tab. 2.8 **Horizontal illuminance shown in relation to sky state**
Illuminance is considerably influenced by cloud cover and solar altitude.

Sky state	Illuminance
Overcast sky winter noon	7,000 lx
Overcast sky summer noon	18,000 lx
Overcast sky summer morning	10,000 lx
Clear sky no sun	50,000 lx
Clear sky with sun	100,000 lx

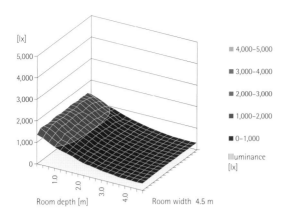

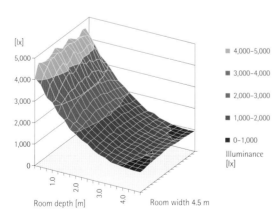

Spring, 21 March

Summer, 21 June

Illuminance
with diffuse sky, 12:00 hrs

Mood
with sun, 11:00 hrs

Boundary conditions to Fig. 2.64

Office floor area	22.5 m²
Orientation	South
Facade area	13.5 m²
Proportion of window area	70%
Natural light transmittance	80%
Frame width	0.08 m
Reflectance	
Ceiling	80%
Internal walls	80%
Floor	20%
Location	Würzburg

Visual comfort

Natural light is more dynamic than artificial light and therefore it increases our feeling of well-being. A further criterion for good visual comfort is the view out. Good distribution of light is important, as is high illuminance. This must avoid leading to glare, in any case a minimum of contrast and shadow is required for good spatial and material perception.

View out The openings for the view out must be positioned at the user's eyelevel. As high a window position as possible is advantageous to daylighting. Therefore with a very small proportion of window area, it can be worthwhile to have a window for the view out and a fanlight for providing daylight in the depth of the room.

Visual perception The human eye cannot perceive illuminance, only luminance. Luminance is determined by the illuminance and reflectivity of the materials. The perceivable luminance range is between 10^{-6} and 10^5 cd/m². The human field of vision, the area within which visual impressions can be detected, is 180° horizontal and 140° vertical. The eye requires a certain time to adjust to changing light conditions. Too high a difference in luminance in the field of vision leads to contrast glare.

Illuminance The visual task determines the required illuminance The more detailed the visual task, the higher the illuminance should be. The range of required illuminance extends from 200 lx for filing to over 750 lx for drawing production. Very detailed activities may require considerably higher illuminance. Very high illuminance brings the risk of glare. Glare can be limited by a suitable choice of materials and colours.

Glare Glare arises from high luminance or luminance contrast. It can be in the form of direct glare, contrast glare or reflection glare and is limited by glare protection and the choice of compatible surfaces.

Direct glare is a result of excessively high luminance. It occurs with direct sunlight, looking into an artificial light source or from the reflection of strong light sources at reflective surfaces. Absolute glare occurs when luminance exceeds 10,000 cd/m². The pupil can no longer limit the light entering the eye and vision is reduced.

To avoid contrast glare the difference in luminance between the central field of vision, the working area, and the surrounding field of vision, the direct surroundings should be kept in an optimum relationship to one another.

The introduction of computers into the workplace has intensified the problem of reflection glare. Reflection glare on monitor screens occurs when a light source reflects from it, thus creating high luminance on the screen. Glare protection at the facade can ensure that surfaces in the area of the work station are no longer subject to direct sunlight and therefore reflect less light. To avoid reflections, monitor screens should be arranged to be at right angles to the widow. One of the main causes of reflection glare is smooth surfaces, for example desk tops.

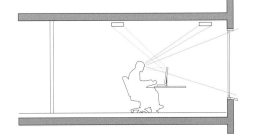

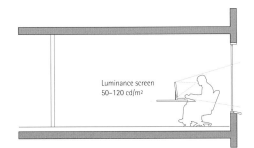

Luminance screen
50–120 cd/m²

Fig. 2.63 **Glare in offices**
Direct glare can occur in an office from windows or lamps with an unfavourable arrangement of desk and monitor (red). Light sources behind the user can be reflected in the monitor and cause reflection glare (orange)..

Without measures

cd/m²
4,750
4,250
3,750
3,250
2,750
2,250
1,750
1,250
750
250

Antiglare film with
internal light shelf

cd/m²
4,750
4,250
3,750
3,250
2,750
2,250
1,750
1,250
750
250

cd/m²
4,750
4,250
3,750
3,250
2,750
2,250
1,750
1,250
750
250

Solar shading
louvres with light
direction setting

Luminance distribution
with sun, 21 March, 11:00 hrs

Mood
with sun, 21 March, 11:00 hrs

Natural light and entry of solar radiation

Direct sunlight usually results in uneven room lighting, which produces direct and contrast glare. Therefore solar screening, glare protection and light-redirection systems are required. The system chosen should allow a good view out.

Solar screening louvres Solar screening louvres are an efficient and finely adjustable option for regulating the entry of solar radiation. Some view out is usually still possible, depending on the louvre setting. The louvres can be set so that diffused light and a proportion of direct light can still penetrate the room. The louvres in the top part of the facade can be set at a flatter angle to provide better lighting in the depth of the room. Depending on the shape of the louvre surfaces this can produce an improvement of visual comfort or direct light into the depth of the room.

Glare protection Glare protection is essential for computer workstations near windows. Glare protection should be fully adjustable over its full depth so that the working area can be effectively protected from direct solar radiation. To ensure that the room does not become too dark,

light should be able to enter the room through the top area. Light-scattering or light-redirecting elements in the fanlight area can be used to adjust the lighting for different requirements. Large differences in luminance on the side walls caused by light striking them at a flat angle should be avoided.

Light redirection Light-redirection systems produce even room lighting. With large room depths in particular light redirection can improve the entry of natural light . The bright ceiling creates the impression that the room is flooded with light. Light direction systems can be internal, in the plane of the glazing, or external. Then light can be directed by reflectors, curved louvres, prismatic panels, or mirror louvres. A suitably designed system is able to direct a certain angular proportion of direct light and in this way can become most effective at certain times of the year. A ceiling with a high reflectance is required for effective light redirection. In some cases highly reflective metallic ceiling elements may be considered. The curvature of the elements can be selected to optimise light redirection. Internal light-redirection systems are not exposed to the weather and therefore provide better performance.

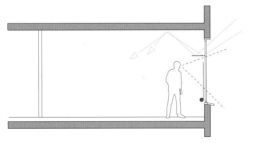

Fig. 2.65 **Antiglare film with internal light shelf**

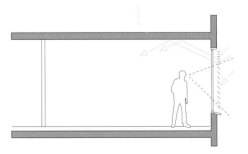

Fig. 2.66 **Antiglare louvres with light-direction setting in the top zone**

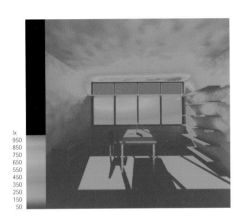

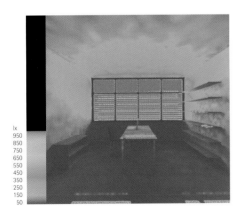

Illuminance distribution
with sun, 21 March, 11:00 hrs

Without light-
control measures

Antiglare film
with internal
light shelf

Solar shading louvres
with light-direction
setting

Luminance distribution
with sun, 21 March, 11:00 hrs

Proportion of window area

Fig. 2.68 **Influence of proportion of window area on room lighting conditions**

In rooms with a proportion of window area of 30 %, only the workstations close to the windows will receive adequate natural light on days with diffused daylight. The luminance distribution over the whole room is even because of low amount of admitted light falling upon the side walls. The room feels cut off from the outside world. The room lighting improves with proportions of window area greater than about 50 %, especially in the corners close to the facade. The irradiation of the room side-walls produces excessive differences in luminance in the field of view. The presence of a lintel means that the areas in the depth of the room remain relatively dark. Lintel-free facade construction can be adopted even with ribbon facades with a proportion of window area of 70 %. This improves lighting conditions in the depth of the room. The bright ceiling and the large transparent areas create an impression of openness in the room. With proportions of window area greater than 70 % the spandrel wall zone requires transparency. There is only a minimal improvement in the lighting conditions in the depth of the room. The view of the horizon creates an impression of openness in the room.

Boundary conditions to Fig. 2.68

Office floor area	22.5 m²
Orientation	South
Facade area	13.5 m²
Proportion of window area	30/50/70/90 %
Natural light transmittance	80 %
Frame width	0.08 m
Reflectance	
Ceiling	80 %
Internal walls	80 %
Floor	20 %
Location	Würzburg

Proportion of window area 30 %

Proportion of window area 50 %

Proportion of window area 70 %

Proportion of window area 90 %

Mood
with a diffuse sky, 21 March 12:00 hrs

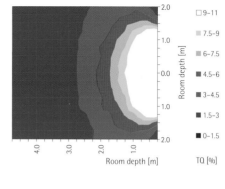

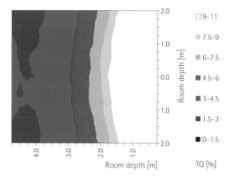

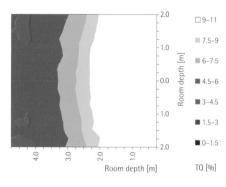

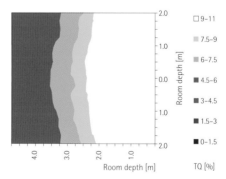

Distribution of daylight factor

Proportion of
window area
30 %

Proportion of
window area
50 %

cd/m²
9,500
8,500
7,500
6,500
5,500
4,500
3,500
2,500
1,500
500

lx
950
850
750
650
550
450
350
250
150
50

Proportion of
window area
70 %

Proportion of
window area
90 %

cd/m²
9,500
8,500
7,500
6,500
5,500
4,500
3,500
2,500
1,500
500

lx
950
850
750
650
550
450
350
250
150
50

cd/m²
9,500
8,500
7,500
6,500
5,500
4,500
3,500
2,500
1,500
500

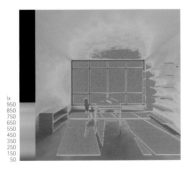

lx
950
850
750
650
550
450
350
250
150
50

cd/m²
9,500
8,500
7,500
6,500
5,500
4,500
3,500
2,500
1,500
500

lx
950
850
750
650
550
450
350
250
150
50

Mood
with sun, 21 March, 11:00 hrs

Luminance distribution
with sun, 21 March, 11:00 hrs

Illuminance distribution
with sun, 21 March, 11:00 hrs

Light transmittance through glazing

Fig. 2.69 Influence of light transmittance of the glazing on the natural lighting conditions in the room interior

Solar control coatings to limit the entry of solar radiation also have effects on natural light transmittance. Solar control glass with low g-values reduces light transmittance to about 40%. With standard glazing with a light transmittance of 80% there is only a slight reduction in natural light admitted. Good daylighting is possible under a diffuse sky even in the depth of the room. The entry of direct sunlight creates high luminance at the window. With light transmittances of the order of 60% good light conditions are possible up to the centre of the room. If light transmittance is reduced further, then only workstations close to the windows will have adequate daylighting. The area in the depth of the room is relatively dark, so that artificial lighting is necessary as a rule. Direct glare when looking though the window is reduced by the lower light transmittance. The capacity of the eye to adapt can even out the influence of differing transmittances to a certain degree.

Transmittance
40%

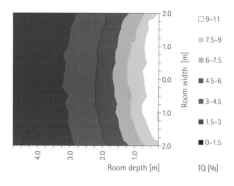

Transmittance
60%

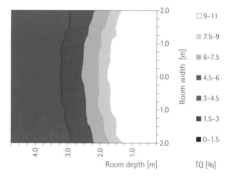

Boundary conditions to Fig. 2.69

Office floor area	22.5 m²
Orientation	South
Facade area	13.5 m²
Proportion of window area	70%
Natural light transmittance	40/60/80%
Frame width	0.08 m
Reflectance	
Ceiling	80%
Internal walls	80%
Floor	20%
Location	Würzburg

Transmittance
80%

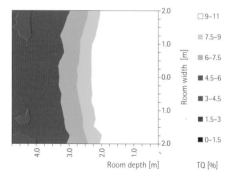

Mood
with a diffuse sky, 21 March 12:00 hrs

Distribution of daylight factor

Transmittance
40 %

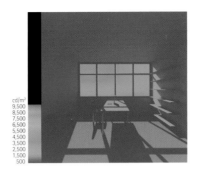

Transmittance
60 %

Transmittance
80 %

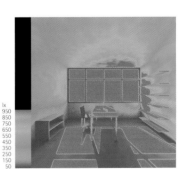

Mood
with sun, 21 March, 11:00 hrs

Luminance distribution
with sun, 21 March, 11:00 hrs

Illuminance distribution
with sun, 21 March, 11:00 hrs

Reflectance of internal walls

Fig. 2.70 Influence of the reflectance of the internal surfaces on the use of daylight inside rooms
The reflectance of walls and ceilings influence the lighting conditions in the depth of the room. With low reflectance walls there is still insufficient daylight beyond the middle of the room. With medium or high reflectance walls the whole of the room is well lit. Lower reflectance reduces the risk of contrast glare at the room-enclosing surfaces.

Room dark

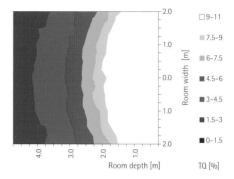

Room medium

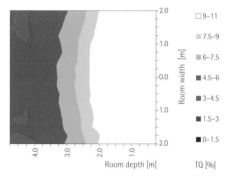

Boundary conditions to Fig. 2.70

Office floor area	22.5 m²
Orientation	South
Facade area	13.5 m²
Proportion of window area	70%
Natural light transmittance	80%
Frame width	0.08 m
Reflectance	
Room dark	
Ceiling	40%
Internal walls	40%
Floor	10%
Room medium	
Ceiling	80%
Internal walls	80%
Floor	20%
Room light	
Ceiling	95%
Internal walls	90%
Floor	50%
Location	Würzburg

Room light

Mood
with a diffuse sky, 21 March 12:00 hrs

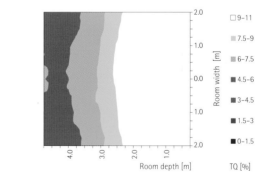

Distribution of daylight factor

Room dark

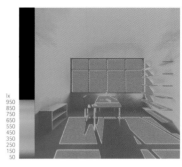

Room medium

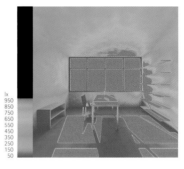

Room light

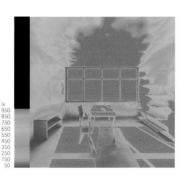

Mood
with sun, 21 March, 11:00 hrs

Luminance distribution
with sun, 21 March, 11:00 hrs

Illuminance distribution
with sun, 21 March, 11:00 hrs

Illuminance and daylight factor

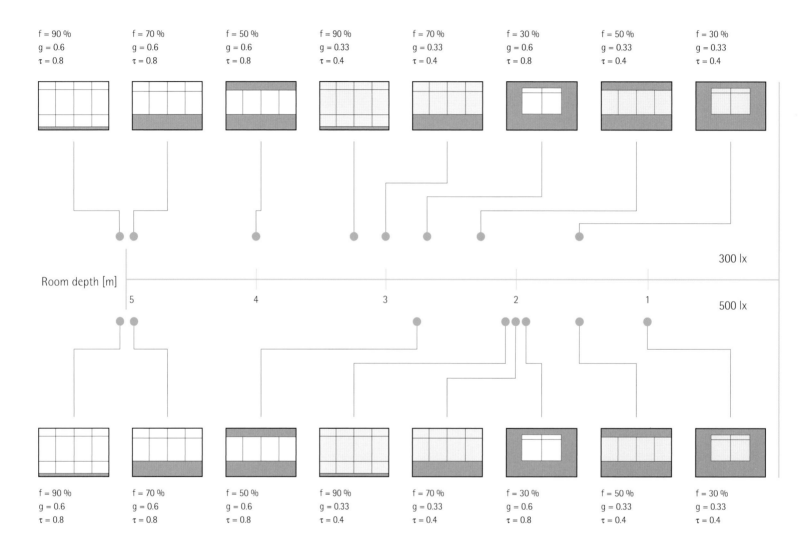

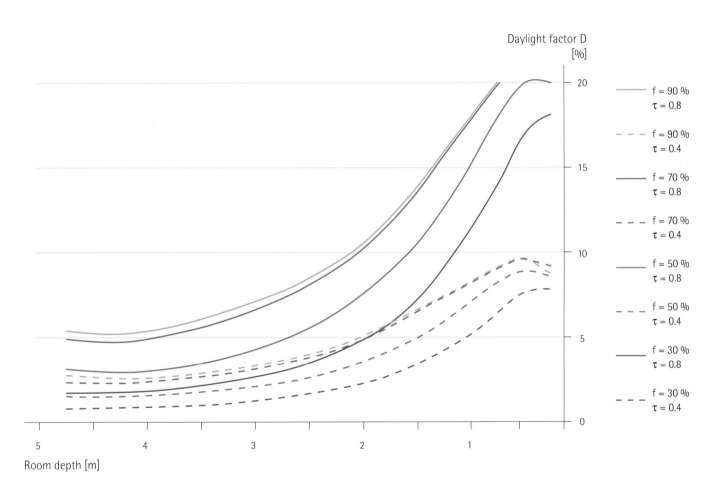

Daylight factor D [%]

f = 90 %
τ = 0.8

f = 90 %
τ = 0.4

f = 70 %
τ = 0.8

f = 70 %
τ = 0.4

f = 50 %
τ = 0.8

f = 50 %
τ = 0.4

f = 30 %
τ = 0.8

f = 30 %
τ = 0.4

Room depth [m]

Boundary conditions to Figs. 2.71 and 2.72

Office floor area	22.5 m²
Orientation	South
Facade area	13.5 m²
Proportion of window area	30/50/70/90 %
Natural light transmittance	40/80 %
Frame width	0.08 m
Reflectance	
Ceiling	80 %
Internal walls	80 %
Floor	20 %
Location	Würzburg
Outdoor lighting conditions	10,000 lx

Genzyme Center, Cambridge, USA
Artificially natural

The basic concept of the Genzyme Center was a green building with the aim of achieving the highest rating, "Platinum". This means using natural resources to provide people with the best possible environment whilst using a minimum amount of energy. As a natural energy source, daylight plays the crucial role.

The central atrium is surrounded on all sides by office areas. Tracking the sun automatically, seven heliostats on the roof guide sunlight via mirrors into the atrium, where it is distributed by a chandelier consisting of freely moving prismatic panels resembling a nursery mobile. Total reflection of the sunlight takes place at ceiling level and the sunlight, decomposed into its spectral components, enlivens the atrium. The dynamic of sunlight is perceived not only as a far-off source of light – the motion of the chandelier elements and the sun can be actually experienced.

A so-called "lightwall" of highly polished reflective vertical louvres also distributes the daylight dynamically in the atrium under computer control. The coordinated surfaces reflect the outdoor light in specific directions to create brilliant light, even when the sky is overcast. On the ground floor these effects combine to produce a real experience, flooding the space with daylight, giving it brilliance and a feeling of transparency in its relationship with the outside world. This is intensified by shallow trough water features with minimum water depths and highly polished stainless steel bottoms, which emphasise the natural quality of the building by means of light, water and plants. Light striking these features is reflected on to the ceiling, carrying the inimitable motion of water to all the areas above them.

Augmenting these measures, all the balustrade areas in the atrium are clad in various aluminium finishes so that light can be redirected deep into each floor, even on overcast days.

The external facade with its storey-height glazing has special, partially perforated, anti-glare louvres which track the sun fully automatically and distribute daylight by reflective ceilings into the interior and contribute to providing daylight even in the deepest room zones. The furnishing concept has also been carefully designed to ensure every work space remains in contact with daylight.

Artificial light is there purely in the form of supplementary lighting; it was designed around and intended to complement the daylighting provisions.

These installations have improved the working environment for the employees to such an extent that absences due to illness have been reduced by up to a massive 70%.

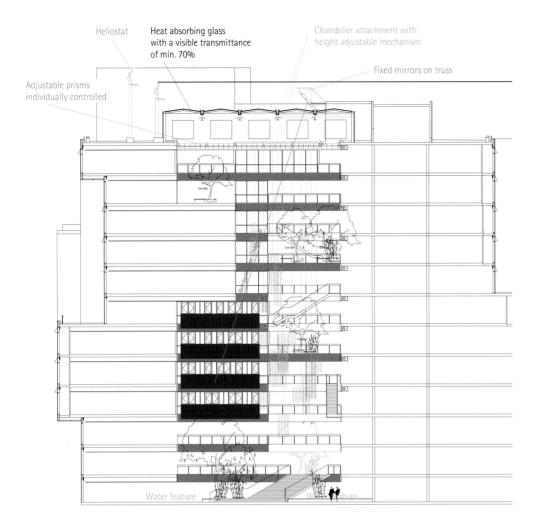

Heliostat

Heat absorbing glass with a visible transmittance of min. 70%

Chandelier attachment with height adjustable mechanism

Fixed mirrors on truss

Adjustable prisms individually controlled

Water feature

Water feature

Section

Heliostat

Adjustable prisms individually controlled

Detail chandelier

Fig. 2.73 **Cross-section**
Seven heliostats and fixed mirrors redirect the sunlight. Automatically controlled prisms block the unwanted entry of solar radiation but allow zenith light into the interior. Reflective louvres distribute daylight in the atrium. Like a nursery mobile, the chandelier decomposes and distributes the redirected sunlight into all interior spaces. The light distribution and transparence of the ground floor are created by sunlight. The reflective insides of the water troughs throw up brilliant dynamic light effects, which reach up to all the floors above them.

Fig. 2.74 **Light figurations**
Sunlight creates dynamism, transparence and a highly acceptable, pleasant room atmosphere.

Fig. 2.75 **Artificial light**
Although supplementary artificial lighting is used sparingly, these artificial sun and wall lighting effects complete the lighting mood.

Planning and Construction: 2000–2003
Clients: Lyme Properties LLC, Cambridge, MA, USA
Genzyme Corporation, Cambridge, MA, USA
Architect and General Planner, Building and Interior:
Behnisch, Behnisch & Partner, Inc., Venice, CA, USA
Green Building / Lead Consultant: Natural Logic,
Arlington, MA, USA
Environmental Consultancy, Structural and MEP
Engineers: Büro Happold, Bath, GB and New York,
NY, USA
Natural and Artificial Lighting Consultancy: Barten-
bach LichtLabor GmbH, Aldrans, Austria

Facade concepts

"The art gallery stands in the light of Lake Constance. Its body is built from glass panels, steel and a mineral mass of formed concrete, which defines the texture and space in the interior of the building. Observed from the outside the building resembles a luminous block of light. It absorbs the changing light from the sky, the haze of the lake, it reflects light and colour and gives some intimation of its inner life, depending on the angle of view, time of day and weather conditions.

"The skin of the building consists of finely etched glass. It creates an effect like slightly ruffled plumage or a jointed shingle cladding composed of large glass panels. The glass panels, which are all the same size, are neither drilled nor cut. They are supported on metal brackets. Large clamps keep them in place. The edges of the glass are left intact and exposed. Wind wafts through the open joints of the shingles. Lake air penetrates the fine mesh of the space frame, flows into the steel structure of the self-supporting facade, which rises out of the basement pit and encloses the monolithic sculpture inside with a sophisticated system of facade glazing, thermal insulation and solar screening, without being solidly connected to it.

"The multilayered facade construction is a structurally independent cladding structure in complete accord with the interior, which acts as a weather skin and daylight moderator, solar protection and thermal insulation layer."

Peter Zumthor

Source: Peter Zumthor, Kunsthaus Bregenz, 1999, p. 7

Facade principles

Facade typology

Every facade fulfils a wide range of functions. These functions are defined by the location of the building and the conditions required by the users inside it. Among the functions are the provision of natural light, views out and in, solar screening, ventilation and energy generation. The conceptual design of the skin must consider the basic arrangement of the various functions within the skin – adjacent, behind one another or combined. Depending on the requirements, positive synergic effects may arise from the chosen arrangement.

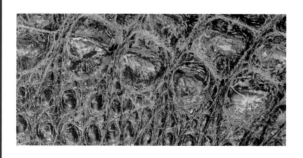

Facade principles

The role of the facade in historical change

In his publication "Learning from Las Vegas" Robert Venturi only differentiated between two forms of buildings or facades: the symbol and the decorated shed. With architectural symbolism, the function of a building determines the complete appearance, a restaurant serving poultry dishes therefore looks like a duck; with a decorated shed, the function or role of the building can be read from the facade, which is placed in front of the building like an advertising sign. However, Venturi presents the subject of facades in a rather too simplistic or exaggerated manner, as from his perspective of Las Vegas architecture even Amiens Cathedral is just a decorated shed.

The need to protect buildings against changing climatic conditions, in particular against moisture, and to temper the interior for the user has always determined the design of facades. This occurred either directly in the materials used for the enclosure, for example solid masonry and timber construction, or in the structure, such as traditional timber- and brick-framed buildings, or in the surface, which was often covered with natural stone slabs, plastered or clad with brick or timber boards, depending on the region and the available materials. A prestigious ornamental form can be developed from any material; this includes sawn or painted weather boarding, specially shaped masonry and plasterwork decorations, show-facade frontages or the expensive marble incrustations overlaid on Roman temples, Christian churches or royal palaces. Representative and specific expressions of facades vary enormously depending on the epoch, building use, urban planning context and the financial strength of the client. However, if the principle constructional forms of facades are extracted from the never-ending abundance and all the stylistic variations, then it could be rather crudely concluded that the surfaces of buildings result either from enclosing a solid or skeletal structure or by simply being placed in front of one.

A crucial change in respect of this fundamental structure of facades arose with the emerging distinction between solid and skeletal construction and between load-bearing and non-load-bearing components. Although there are examples of skeletal construction from all ages, it was not until the development of steel and reinforced concrete construction during the 19th century that a new form of facade became possible, because a large part of the building surface could be almost completely detached from the structural frame. Or expressed the other way around: The building skin was suspended in front of the structure as a "curtain wall". This separation of facade and load-bearing structure, of appearance and content, led to serious changes; the building skin no longer needed to follow the traditional constructional make-up from base to roof but could in large part be freely formed, and the building envelope as a glazed skin could leave the underlying structure to a large extent exposed, whilst still protecting it against climatic effects. These possibilities of treatment of the building skin determine the appearance of modern architecture: On the one hand the design of the skin was much more an expression of the artistic imagination of architects, viz., buildings became sculptures, facades works of art, the architect a facade decorator. On the other hand the building became a closed climatised box, the ideal of international style, which could be "parked" anywhere in the world.

Following the development of a new sensitivity towards problems of ecology and energy use coupled with a fresh view of history, regional differences and the environment, designers produced buildings that related to place and context in the 1970s instead of universal sealed enclosures. These new buildings have skins which react flexibly and manage energy expenditures appropriately to suit changing climatic conditions, in the same way an open system can. The structural frame is no longer the most important element in a building. This title has been claimed by the building skin, which now exchanges energy and reacts to the actual local conditions.

Whilst climate design is based primarily on architectural requirements, the continuously increasing importance of communication media in our globalised world over recent years has led to the development of media facades: The surface of the building becomes a computer screen; the building skin is transformed into an information carrier or an element of public events and entertainment. Whilst the climate facade offers many promising new avenues in a future increasingly dominated by considerations of energy, neither the show facade *pièces de résistance* of artist-architects nor the domination of public open space by commercially or politically controlled media facades are worthwhile or acceptable developments.

Prof. Dr.-Ing. Winfried Nerdinger

Arrangement of facade elements

Single-skinned facades – parallel arrangement of facade elements Single-skinned building envelopes are generally made up of transparent and opaque areas all in the same plane. Perforated facades are one example. In the simplest form they consist of solid wall surfaces with windows, but they can also be equipped with a multitude of functional elements. Single-skinned facades can also be constructed as transom-mullion frames. The functional elements for ventilation, solar control, energy gain or light redirection are generally arranged adjacent to one another. Each of these elements can be designed and positioned optimally for its functions independently of the others. The normal rule is that a lower proportion of window area has a positive effect on room climate. Large proportions of glazing are only feasible with external solar screening. As single-skinned facades offer no weather protection for solar screening, the latter must be made robust, for example by the elements being fixed in position. A combination of fixed cantilever projections and internal solar screening can provide a weather-independent system for a south facade. Wind can pose problems to window ventilation, hence additional, specially designed ventilation elements are necessary for high-rise buildings. These units are a common means of providing sound-insulated ventilation in noisy locations.

Double-skinned facades – series arrangement of facade elements With double-skinned facades the primary facade has a second glass plane in front. The facade cavity can be unsegmented, vertically divided (shaft facade), horizontally divided (corridor facade) or vertically and horizontally divided (box window). The functional elements are placed one behind the other, with the result that they may adversely influence one another. An unrestricted relationship with the outside world in respect of ventilation and outside view is not possible. The entry of daylight is reduced as the solar radiation has to pass through several layers. Solar screening can be installed in the facade cavity to be protected against the effects of wind and weather. The radiation they absorb heats the facade cavity, which can lead to the undesirable entry of solar thermal energy. Normally facades like this require mechanical ventilation. In winter and in the transition months, the facade cavity temperature allows extensive natural ventilation to take place without adversely affecting comfort. The outer skin protects the opening in the facade for problem-free night ventilation. Double-skinned facades reduce wind pressures on high-rise buildings, allowing the users to open windows. Natural ventilation is possible even in locations exposed to noise. Adjustable flaps in the outer skin can control pressures in the facade cavity, allowing air flows to be created and directed.

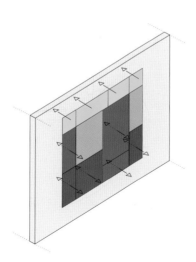

Fig. 3.1 **Single-skinned facade**
Parallel arrangement of facade elements

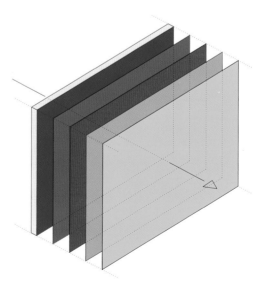

Fig. 3.2 **Double-skinned facade**
Series arrangement of facade elements

Alternating facades – a combined concept The alternating facade is combination of single- and double-skinned facades. The principles of both facade types are united in one overall system. The disadvantages of the interaction of the various layers of a multilayered system are avoided by the presence of single-skinned facade elements. On the other hand the system can make use of the advantages of the double-skinned facade such as sound insulation and wind protection, sheltered solar screening and comfortable introduction of supply air. In the area of the single-skinned facade the low glazing fraction means that solar screening can also be positioned inside the building. The result is a weather-independent overall system. The opening light in the single-skinned facade gives the users a direct visual relationship with the outside world. The different facade openings and solar screening settings allow the users extensive opportunities to adjust the building skin to suit their personal visual and ventilation requirements. The ratio of single- and double-skinned facade areas has a definitive effect on the appearance and functionality of the overall facade. However, the homogenous and multilayer overall effect of a double-skin facade is normally lost.

Double-skinned facade with direct ventilation – a combined concept Summer problems can be considerably reduced if a double-skinned facade is augmented by some means of providing natural ventilation, through which fresh air can be introduced directly into the room. Direct ventilation openings allow supply air to be introduced on hot days without increasing the temperature in the facade cavity. The ventilation openings can be of different designs: They can be small penetrations of the facade cavity or room-high box-shaped connection which allow extensive air exchange and improves the outside view. The amount of radiation admitted shows no or only a slight increase. If required the areas incorporating direct ventilation openings can be made opaque. Appropriate detailing can improve the sound insulation performance of direct ventilation openings. The user can choose whether to ventilate through the direct ventilation openings or through the double-skinned facade. If direct ventilation is provided then it is feasible to dispense with mechanical ventilation for buildings with double-skinned facades. The small area of the direct ventilation openings and the homogenous character of the outer facade ensures that the appearance of a double-skinned facade is retained.

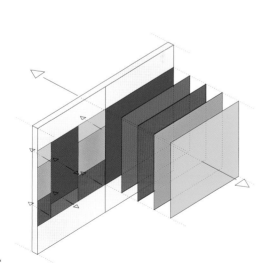

Fig. 3.3 **Alternating facade**
Combined concept

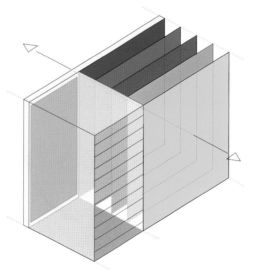

Fig. 3.4 **Double-skinned facade with direct ventilation**
Combined concept

Light redirection

Solar screening

Energy generation

Ventilation

Views out and in

Facade function zones

Facades can be typically divided into three zones arranged vertically one above another. These zones can be allocated various principle functions and the various functional elements are integrated into the appropriate zones.

Daylight zone The daylight zone is located in the upper parts of walls. Natural light from this zone also penetrates into the depth of the room. It is advantageous if this fanlight area extends over the full width of the room. For the depth of the room to be well lit, the fanlight should extend to the ceiling. Ideally this daylighting should be optimised with a light-redirection system. This is particularly important for rooms more than 6 m deep

and for workstations that are remote from the facade. In order for there to be no restriction on the entry of natural light, the fanlight area should not be shaded or the solar screening in this area should have louvres capable of being set at different angles. If a higher rate of air change is required for thermal reasons, e.g. for night cooling, then it may be advantageous for the fanlight to be an opening light so that the effective height is increased for the thermal buoyancy effect.

Outside-view zone The middle facade zone provides the view out and natural lighting. This area is shaded by solar screening to reduce the energy entering the room and the exposure of the users to direct sunlight in summer. In winter internal glare protection can improve visual com-

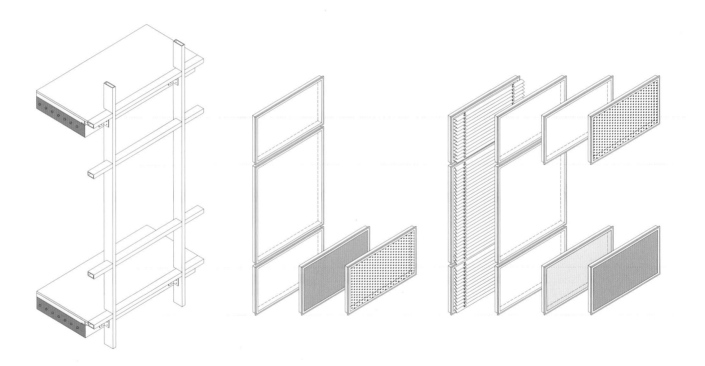

	Views out and in			Solar screening			
Top area	Window			Lamellae	Solar-control glass	Switchable glass	Screen-printed glass
Middle area	Window			Lamellae	Solar-control glass		
Lower area	Window	Opaque material	Screen-printed glass	Lamellae	Solar-control glass	Translucent glass	Opaque material

Tab. 3.1 **Arrangement of functional elements in different facade areas**

fort, especially for people working at computer monitors, whilst allowing the sun's heat into the room. Blinds can be individually operated by the users to allow them to sit in the sun if they wish. The window is also integrated into the middle zone of the facade. This allows the user to have direct visual contact with the outside world and provides purge ventilation. It is not necessary for the middle zone to be transparent over the full width of the facade. Opaque areas around the edges are convenient for room furnishings and reduce the entry of solar radiation in summer.

Spandrel-wall zone The spandrel-wall zone plays a very minor role in daylighting. The room climate can be improved in summer by reducing the amount of solar radiation admitted through this area. This can be achieved whilst retaining the required transparent appearance, e.g. by detailing solar-control glazing with a very low total solar-energy transmittance, screen-printed glass or grids in front of the glass. These measures retain some of the view out. Observers outside cannot see into the room, which gives the user a feeling of security. However, it is best for this zone to be opaque, because of the advantages in terms of summer room climate and winter heating energy demand. The spandrel-wall zone can accommodate ventilation elements or decentralised ventilation equipment. This allows supply air to be introduced through the facade with no detrimental effects on comfort. The spandrel-wall area is also suitable for the integration of energy generating systems.

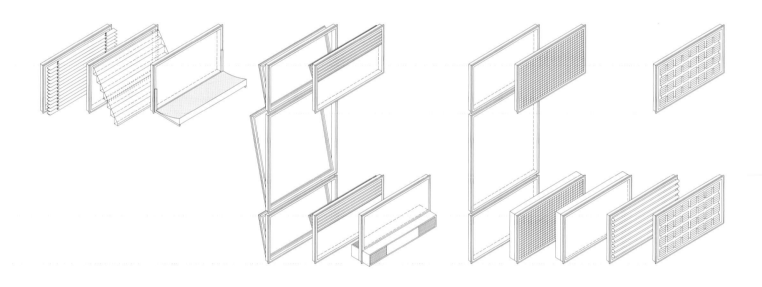

Light redirection systems			Ventilation			Energy generation				
Lamellae	Prismatic panel	Light shelf	Window	Ventilation flap		Passive	TI			Photovoltaics
			Window			Passive				
			Window	Ventilation flap	Decentralised ventilation equipment	Passive	TI / storage	Air collector	Water collector	Photovoltaics

Sports Hall, Tübingen
Sporting efficiency

This national-standard, multisports centre opened in 2004 and is situated in the bottom of the Neckar valley to the southwest of Tübingen, Germany. The sports hall is used as an area for competitions watched by up to 3,000 spectators, school sporting activities, athletics and as a venue for the latest popular leisure sports. The design of the centre's external walls was derived from the large range of different uses made of the building. The northwest facade is configured as an outdoor climbing wall, with the roof overhang providing a more difficult climbing feature and protection against rain. The southwest facade is designed as a photovoltaic solar facade. The electricity not used by the hall is fed into the national grid. The roof is designed largely as a green roof and incorporates skylights.

Photovoltaic facade The green colour of the 20,000 solar cells was selected to complement the sports and landscaped areas and to emphasise the transition from the city to the open countryside of the river valley. This colour sets this facade apart from the usual blue appearance of most solar facades. With a top output of 43.7 kWp, the wall generates about 24,000 kWh of electrical energy per annum, despite its vertical orientation. A total of four different large module types were used. The glass-foil laminate solar modules comprise a front glass panel of 8 mm toughened glass and a white plastic foil at the back. The solar cells are embedded between them. The modules act as a suspended facade and form a continuous flush-jointed surface. The delicate point fixings in the form of clips create open joints between the modules, which gives the facade its smooth overall appearance.

   The shimmering green effect of the surface is produced by an anti-reflective coating applied to the modules. The solar cells are arranged in a rectangular pattern and the peripheral edge welds, which otherwise would normally be visible, are concealed in order that the outer edges of the laminated modules should all appear white.

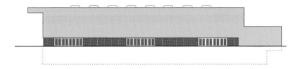

View from southwest

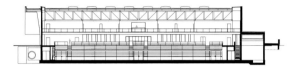

Section

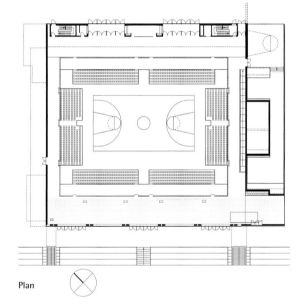

Plan

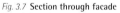

Section through facade

inside   outside

Fig. 3.5 **Elevation and section**
*The facade design suits the specific use of each
external wall. A number of different facade designs are used. Each one is constructed with the
orientation and intended function in mind: The
northwest facade is designed as a climbing wall,
the roof overhang provides a more difficult climbing feature and protection against rain. An open
area for the latest popular leisure sports such as
streetball, in-line skating and skateboarding extends in front of the southeast facade. The green-
glass northeast facade is the entrance, the southwest facade is designed as a solar facade.
The visible roof of the large hall is designed largely
as a green roof and incorporates skylights.*

Fig. 3.6 **Plan**
*The large sports hall, which offers a competition
venue with seats for 3,000 spectators, is also used
for school, athletics and leisure sports.*

Fig. 3.7 **Section through facade**
*The reinforced concrete wall is backed (from inside
to outside) by insulation and a ventilation cavity,
which also accommodates the point fixings for the
solar modules. This arrangement of point fixings
ensures that the facade has a smooth and solid
appearance.*
Wall construction:
30 cm   reinforced concrete wall
10 cm   mineral wool
3 cm   photovoltaic facade

Fig. 3.8 **Hall interior**

Fig. 3.9 **Photovoltaic facade**

Completion: 12 / 2004
Use: Sports hall
Client: Universitätsstadt Tübingen
Architect: Allmann Sattler Wappner
Architekten, Munich
Solar modules: Sunways Solartechnik

The facade of a building forms the interface between the environment outside and the user inside. It must ensure a comfortable interior climate in winter and prevent the entry of too much solar radiation in summer. It has to provide daylight deep to the interior during the period of building use and extensive natural ventilation. These requirements lead to conflicts of objectives. The solar screening required in summer normally results in a reduction in the amount of daylight entering the interior. The optimum use of natural light and the admission of the desired amount of solar radiation in winter are often accompanied by glare. Predominantly natural ventilation of buildings in heavily trafficked areas is linked with the entry of unwanted noise. The objective in the design of facades is to find the most favourable compromise between the specific location and the various requirements of the planned use.

Facade typology

The interaction between facade concept, building use and location

Which facade concepts can offer advantages and disadvantages relevant to investment costs and which have the most influence on operating costs? How high are the energy costs (for lighting, heating, cooling, ventilation), the costs for operating and cleaning the building, as well as its upkeep (inspection, servicing and maintenance)? And the uses offered by each concept? Every building design project (building function and design, construction and schedule of accommodation) and every location (macro- and microclimate) should be individually analysed with respect to the above questions. There are, however, some generally applicable statements relating to the requirements of facades from the point of view of the building and its location.

The design and the method of construction and the question of whether it is a new-build, conversion or a renovation have a crucial influence on the requirements and options for the manufacture and installation of the facade. The facade concept is considered from the aspects of manufacture and installation. Punched windows are generally used in solid construction, whilst skeleton construction features ribbon windows or curtain-wall facades. Mullion-and-transom facades are common on smaller low-rise skeletal frame buildings, whilst prefabricated curtain-wall facades have become the established solution for high-rise buildings.

Outside air temperature and wind speed can influence working conditions on site. A suitably higher degree of prefabrication should be adopted for facades on sites where the weather is poor. It is not just in this respect that elemental facades prove to be the best option. As they can be supplied on a just-in-time basis to the construction site outside peak traffic hours and fitted into the structural frame, they are particularly suitable for city centre sites, where storage space is usually limited.

When considering the future use of the building, the design of the facade must take particular account of the building function and form, the method of construction, the floor and accommodation schedules and the question of whether it is for use by the client himself, or for sale or lease by an investor. For example, office buildings differ from hotels in terms of their operating hours, in-ternal heat loads and their spatial and comfort requirements. Operating costs and flexibility for change of use, comfort and safety emerge as more important to clients who adopt longer-term views. In this respect as well, different building projects have different expectations of the performance of the facade in relation to room comfort, especially thermal, hygienic, visual and acoustic comfort, operational comfort and energy use (heating and lighting, ventilation and cooling). This in turn results in different requirements for protection against heat and moisture, solar radiation and glare and noise, for the use of solar energy, daylight and natural window ventilation. The floor and accommodation schedules have an influence on the possible options for daylighting and natural ventilation.

Flexibility is essential in facades today; the ways we interact, house ourselves and work are changing ever more rapidly, along with advances in technology. Normally the costs of manufacture and installation of a facade increase with the degree of flexibility. This initial additional expenditure can be offset against the lower costs of conversion if the costs associated with the building that is no longer to be used for its original purpose are taken into account.

The location's typical macroclimate, which could be temperate, cold, dry-hot or humid-hot, also has an influence on the facade requirements. Urban surroundings create a microclimate featuring local air movements with noise, dust and pollutants. The resulting noise and exhaust gases pose particular problems for facades and may limit the scope for window ventilation. Unless there are compelling grounds to preclude the use of window ventilation during most of the year, its provision should always be considered. Building skins that have been properly designed to meet their climatic and usage requirements react to changing outside conditions as a semipermeable membrane with dynamic properties instead of presenting a rigid, impenetrable barrier between the room and the outside environment. Facades with movable components have proven advantages in this respect, particularly if combined with a control system and sensors for optimum positioning. Automatic controls that allow the user some influence over the system reduce the accuracy of its predictive ability but enjoy better user acceptance.

Dr.-Ing. Winfried Heusler

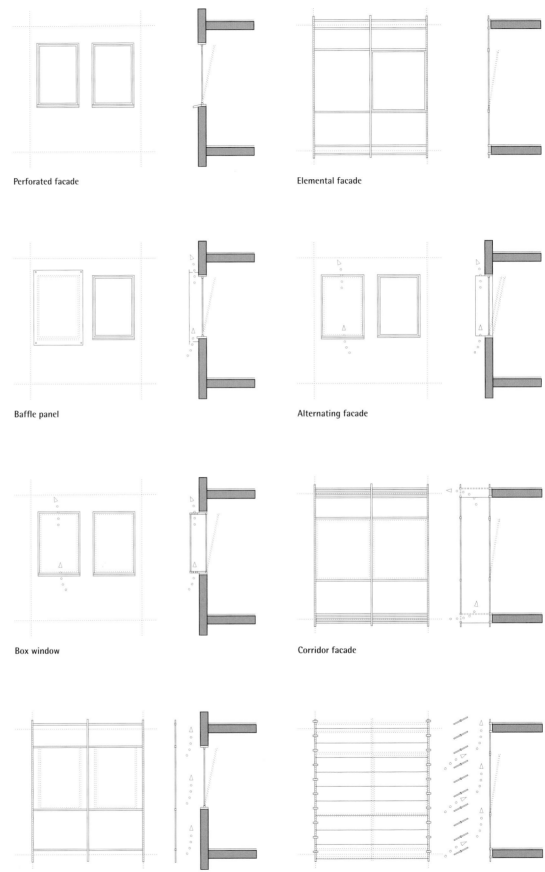

Perforated facade

Elemental facade

Baffle panel

Alternating facade

Box window

Corridor facade

Unsegmented double-skinned facade

Controlled double-skinned facade

Fig. 3.10 **Facade concepts**
*A principal differentiating feature between fa-
cade concepts is whether a facade is single- or
double-skinned or single-skinned with some areas
of double-skinned surfaces. The direct view out,
sound insulation and ventilation characteristics
are determined by these factors.*

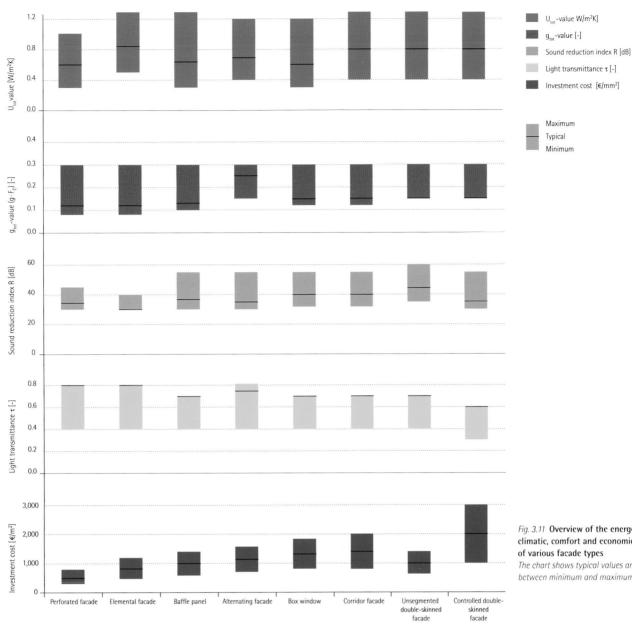

Fig. 3.11 Overview of the energetic, room climatic, comfort and economic performance of various facade types
The chart shows typical values and the range between minimum and maximum.

	Sound insulation during window ventilation	Transmission of sound / odour	Overheating in the facade	Space requirement	Cleaning costs
Perforated facade	Low	–	–	Low	Low
Elemental facade	Low	–	–	Very low	Medium
Baffle panel	Medium	–	Low	Low	Medium
Alternating facade	High	–	– / high	Medium	Medium
Box window	High	–	High	Medium	High
Corridor facade	High	Medium	High	High	High
Unsegmented double-skinned facade	Very high	High	Very high	High	Very high
Controlled double-skinned facade	Very high	Very high	Low	High	Very high

Tab. 3.2 Overview of the energetic, room climatic, comfort and economic performance of various facade types

Perforated facade

The perforated facade is the original form of building skin. It consists of a solid load-bearing wall with openings to provide light and ventilation. There may be additional functional elements which direct light or generate energy, admit fresh air or mechanically ventilate the interior. Opaque surfaces have low U-values and create very few heat bridges. The thermal storage mass of solid construction can be used. This type of facade is economical to construct and has low maintenance and cleaning costs.

	Typical	Min.–max.
Glazing fraction	40%	25–60%
U-value total	0.6 W/m²K	0.3–1.0 W/m²K
U-value (glazing)	1.1 W/m²K	0.7–1.4 W/m²K
U-value (opaque)	0.3 W/m²K	0.2–0.5 W/m²K
g_{tot}-value	0.12	0.08–0.30
g-value (glazing)	0.60	0.30–0.65
Sound reduction index R	34 dB	30–45 dB
Light transmittance τ	0.80	0.40–0.80
Investment cost euro/m²	500	300–800

Tab. 3.3 **Typical values and indicative ranges for perforated facades**

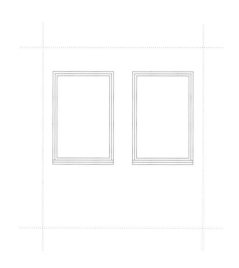

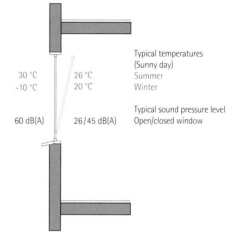

Typical temperatures
(Sunny day)
Summer
Winter

30 °C   26 °C
-10 °C   20 °C

Typical sound pressure level
Open/closed window

60 dB(A)   26/45 dB(A)

Fig. 3.12 **Temperature conditions and sound pressure levels for perforated facades**

Boundary conditions to Fig. 3.13

Insulation	WLG 035
Insulation thickness	10/30 cm

| 2-pane insulating glazing | U = 1.1 W/m²K |
| Frame fraction 10% | U = 1.4 W/m²K |

| 3-pane insulating | U = 0.7 W/m²K |
| Frame fraction 10% | U = 0.8 W/m²K |

Boundary conditions to Fig. 3.14

Room dims. L/W/H	5.0/4.5/3.0 m
Facade area	13.5 m²
Opaque wall	R_w = 50 dB
Insulation glazing	R_w = 30 dB
Sound reduction glass	R_w = 40 dB

Fig. 3.13 **Influence of insulation thickness and glazing quality on the U-value of the whole building skin**
From a minimum insulation thickness of the order of 10 cm it is more effective in achieving lower transmission heat losses to opt for 3-pane glazing instead of having very thick insulation.

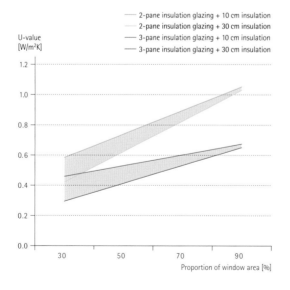

— 2-pane insulation glazing + 10 cm insulation
— 2-pane insulation glazing + 30 cm insulation
— 3-pane insulation glazing + 10 cm insulation
— 3-pane insulation glazing + 30 cm insulation

Fig. 3.14 **Influence of proportion of window area and sound reduction index R of glazing on the sound insulation performance of the facade**
The influence of the proportion of window area on sound reduction is approximately 5 dB; the influence of glass quality approximately 10 dB.

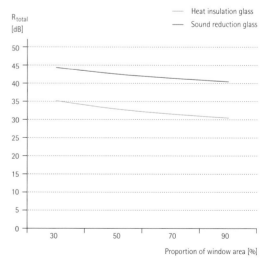

— Heat insulation glass
— Sound reduction glass

Construction
- structural facade
- predominantly solid construction
- reinforced concrete
- masonry
- timber-stud construction

Typical applications
- residential buildings
- administration buildings
- low wind-speed locations
- low noise-load locations

Heating energy demand
- low U-values
- high surface temperatures at
  facade inner side
- few problems from heat bridges
- low solar gain

Ventilation
- thermal discomfort in winter ($T_a < 5 \,°C$)
- heat entry in summer ($T_a > 24 \,°C$)
- wind forces on window
- no transmission of odour from room to room

Room climate in summer
- smaller proportion of window area
- external solar screening exposed to wind
- thermal storage mass available with
  solid construction

Daylight
- external glare protection required
- possible dark room corners
- usually window lintels
- deeper window reveals
- high light transmission through glass

Room climate in summer
- smaller proportion of window area
- external solar screening exposed to wind
- thermal storage mass available with solid construction

Functional aspects
- direct view out
- low cleaning costs
- low maintenance costs
- difficult to modify or retrofit

Sound insulation
- poor sound insulation with window ventilation
- good sound insulation with closed windows
- little sound transmission from room to room by the facade

Disadvantages
- natural ventilation may be uncomfortable
- external solar screening exposed to wind

Elemental facade

Elemental facades are made up of prefabricated facade elements. They have transparent and opaque surfaces. They may also have integrated functional elements for ventilation, daylighting or energy generation. Opaque components generally lead to greater wall thicknesses, which may create recesses or projections on the room side of the wall. Vacuum insulation panels may offer a solution here. They may also improve the insulation at the wall/floor connections. Glazing quality has a crucial influence on thermal performance. With large proportions of window area, the designer should opt for 3-pane insulation glazing as a means of improving comfort.

	Typical	Min.–max.
Glazing fraction	70%	50–90%
U-value total	0.85 W/m²K	0.5–1.3 W/m²K
U-value (glazing)	1.1 W/m²K	0.7–1.4 W/m²K
U-value (opaque)	0.3 W/m²K	0.2–0.5 W/m²K
g_{tot}-value	0.12	0.08–0.30
g-value (glazing)	0.60	0.30–0.60
Sound reduction index R	30 dB	30–40 dB
Light transmittance τ	0.80	0.40–0.80
Investment cost euro/m²	800	500–1200

Tab. 3.4 **Typical values and indicative ranges for elemental facades**

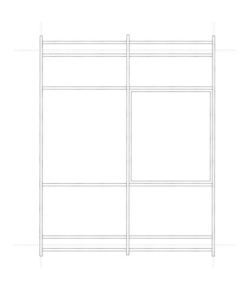

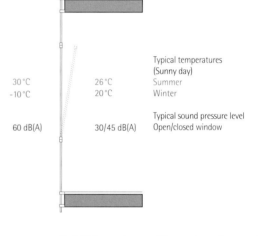

30 °C	26 °C	Typical temperatures (Sunny day)
-10 °C	20 °C	Summer / Winter
60 dB(A)	30/45 dB(A)	Typical sound pressure level Open/closed window

Fig. 3.15 **Temperature conditions and sound pressure levels with elemental facades**

Fig. 3.16 **Influence of spandrel-wall construction and glazing quality on the U-value of the facade**
The high proportion of window area means that the glazing quality is more critical than the insulation quality of the spandrel wall.

Boundary conditions to Fig. 3.16

Facade area	13.5 m²
Window area	70%
Spandrel wall	30%
Insulation	WLG 035
Insulation thickness	10 cm
2-pane insulation glazing	U = 1.1 W/m²K
3-pane insulation glazing	U = 0.7 W/m²K
Vacuum insulation	U = 0.16 W/m²K

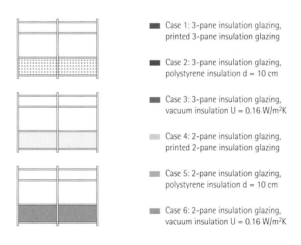

- ■ Case 1: 3-pane insulation glazing, printed 3-pane insulation glazing
- ■ Case 2: 3-pane insulation glazing, polystyrene insulation d = 10 cm
- ■ Case 3: 3-pane insulation glazing, vacuum insulation U = 0.16 W/m²K
- ■ Case 4: 2-pane insulation glazing, printed 2-pane insulation glazing
- ■ Case 5: 2-pane insulation glazing, polystyrene insulation d = 10 cm
- ■ Case 6: 2-pane insulation glazing, vacuum insulation U = 0.16 W/m²K

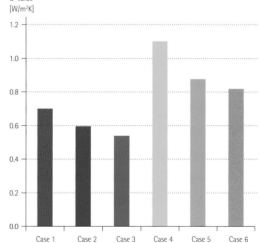

Construction
- non-load bearing, additional supports
  needed inside room
- elemental, prefabricated construction
- mullion-and-transom construction

Typical applications
- administration buildings
- high-rise buildings with mechanical ventilation
- low wind-speed locations
- low noise-load locations

Heating energy demand
- U-value depends on glazing fraction,
  generally unfavourable
- lower surface temperatures at facade inner side
- heat bridges especially at frames,
  opaque elements and between storeys

Ventilation
- thermal discomfort in winter ($T_a < 5\ °C$)
- heat entry in summer ($T_a > 24\ °C$)
- wind forces on window
- no transmission of odour from room to room

Room climate in summer
- usually high proportion of window area
- external solar screening exposed to wind
- no thermal storage mass

Daylight
- high proportions of window area possible
- high light transmission through glass
- small window reveals

Sound insulation
- little sound transmission from room to room
- poor sound insulation with open windows

Functional aspects
- poor thermal insulation
- lower surface temperatures at facade inner side
- no noise reduction for ventilation
- solar screening difficult to incorporate

Advantages
- can be prefabricated
- short construction time
- little space requirement

Disadvantages
- poor thermal insulation
- lower surface temperatures
  at facade inner side
- no noise reduction for ventilation
- solar screening difficult to incorporate

Baffle panel

A baffle panel is an additional panel that is fixed a short distance in front of a window in a perforated or an elemental facade. It is a means of minimising the disadvantages of single-skinned facades with respect to sound insulation and ventilation. Baffle panels also provide protection to solar screening, allowing it to be operated in almost any wind conditions. They are simple to incorporate and offer reliable protection against weather and intruders during night cooling. Baffle panels restrict the user's view out only to a limited extent. The effective cross-section for ventilation may be considerably reduced if the gap between the baffle panel and the facade is too small. Solar gain and daylight entry are reduced to a certain extent by the second plane of glass.

	Typical	Min.–max.
Glazing fraction	50%	30–90%
U-value total	0.65 W/m²K	0.3–1.3 W/m²K
U-value (glazing)	1.0 W/m²K	0.6–1.4 W/m²K
U-value (opaque)	0.3 W/m²K	0.2–0.5 W/m²K
g_{tot}-value	0.13	0.10–0.30
g-value (glazing)	0.40	0.25–0.50
Sound reduction index R	38 dB	30–55 dB
Light transmittance τ	0.70	0.40–0.70
Investment cost euro/m²	1000	600–1400

Tab. 3.5 **Typical values and indicative ranges for baffle plates**

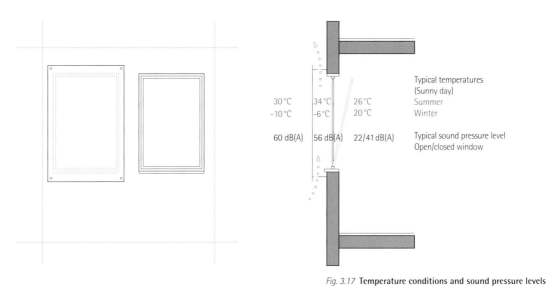

Typical temperatures
(Sunny day)
Summer
Winter

Typical sound pressure level
Open/closed window

Fig. 3.17 **Temperature conditions and sound pressure levels for baffle panels**

Fig. 3.18 **Influence of baffle panel size and facade gap on the ratio of available ventilation cross-section to the open window area**
The available ventilation may be considerably reduced by a small gap and a poor choice of baffle panel size. The windows may not be able to provide adequate ventilation in these circumstances..

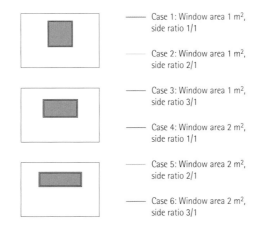

—— Case 1: Window area 1 m², side ratio 1/1

—— Case 2: Window area 1 m², side ratio 2/1

—— Case 3: Window area 1 m², side ratio 3/1

—— Case 4: Window area 2 m², side ratio 1/1

—— Case 5: Window area 2 m², side ratio 2/1

—— Case 6: Window area 2 m², side ratio 3/1

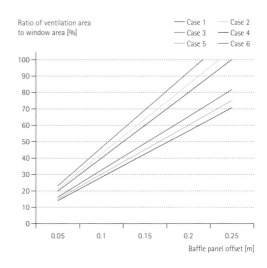

Construction
- in front of perforated facades
- in front of elemental facades
- size and distance of the baffle panel
  depends on the desired function
- panel offset 5-25 cm

Typical applications
- administration buildings, residential buildings
- high-rise buildings with natural ventilation
- medium wind-speed locations
- higher noise-load locations
- night cooling

Heating energy demand
- transmission heat loss dynamic,
  dependent on panel offset and
  insolation
- little improvement on single-skinned facades
- little reduction of solar gain

Ventilation
- comfortable introduction of supply air in winter
- increased entry of heat in summer
- no transmission of odour from room to room
- attenuation of wind effects
- possible impairment of air exchange

Room climate in summer
- very little sound transmission from room to room
- improved noise reduction with natural ventilation

Daylight
- Reduction of natural light transmittance
  by second pane
- possible integration of light-related functions
  into the baffle panel

Sound insulation
- cost-effective way of optimising a facade
- can be retrofitted
- simple night cooling
- little overheating in summer

Functional aspects
- possible limited purge ventilation
- weather protection
- intruder protection
- view out restricted
- difficult to clean outer face of facade

Advantages
- cost-effective way of optimising a facade
- can be retrofitted
- simple night cooling
- little overheating in summer

Disadvantages
- view out restricted
- purge ventilation limited

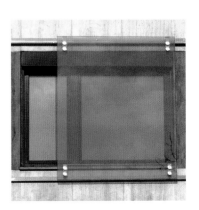

Alternating facade

The alternating facade is a combination of single- and double-skinned facades with the advantages of both. In each room there is at least one element of each type. Depending on the outside and inside climatic conditions, ventilation can be provided through the single- or double-skinned facade to ensure comfortable conditions in the room at almost any time of the year. If the surface area of the single-skinned facade is small it can also be fitted with internal solar screening. The ratio of the areas of single- and double-skinned elements determines the properties of the combined facade with respect to ventilation, noise reduction and the entry of solar radiation.

	Typical	Min.–max.
Glazing fraction	50 %	40–90 %
U-value total	0.7 W/m²K	0.4–1.2 W/m²K
U-value (glazing)	1.0 W/m²K	0.6–1.3 W/m²K
U-value (opaque)	0.3 W/m²K	0.2–0.5 W/m²K
g_{tot}-value	0.25	0.15–0.30
g-value (glazing)	0.55	0.25–0.60
Sound reduction index R	35 dB	30–55 dB
Light transmittance τ	0.75	0.40–0.80
Investment cost euro/m²	1100	700–1600

Tab. 3.6 Typical values and indicative ranges for alternating facades

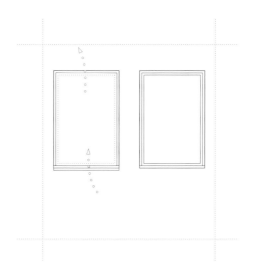

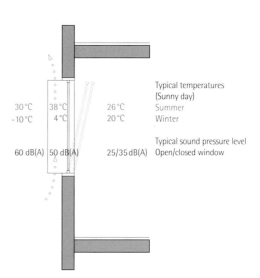

30 °C	38 °C	26 °C	Typical temperatures (Sunny day) Summer
-10 °C	4 °C	20 °C	Winter
			Typical sound pressure level
60 dB(A)	50 dB(A)	25/35 dB(A)	Open/closed window

Fig. 3.19 Temperature conditions and sound pressure levels for alternating facades

Fig. 3.20 Energy transfer for alternating facades shown in relation to the ratio of areas of single- and double-skinned elements to the total facade area

Boundary conditions to Fig. 3.20

Room dims. L/W/H	5.0/4.5/3.0 m
Facade area	13.5 m²
Double-skinned facade g_{tot}-value	0.15
Single-skinned facade g-value	0.6
F_c-value	0.5

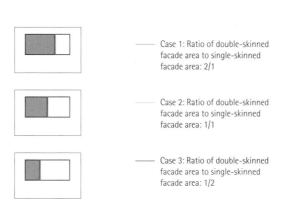

Case 1: Ratio of double-skinned facade area to single-skinned facade area: 2/1

Case 2: Ratio of double-skinned facade area to single-skinned facade area: 1/1

Case 3: Ratio of double-skinned facade area to single-skinned facade area: 1/2

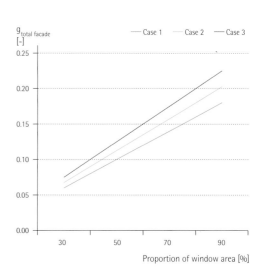

Construction
- in perforated facades
- elemental facades
- area proportions and panel offsets
  varied to suit the required function
- panel offset 10-30 cm

Typical applications
- administration buildings, residential buildings
- high-rise buildings with natural ventilation
- high wind speeds high noise-load areas
- night cooling

Heating energy demand
- U-value dynamic, depends on proportion of
  double-skinned facade and entry of solar radiation
- only a slight improvement compared
  with a single-skinned facade

Ventilation
- comfortable introduction of supply air in winter
- direct ventilation in summer
- no transmission of odour from room to room
- attenuation of wind effects

Room climate in summer
- wind-protected solar screening
- possible unwanted entry of heat from
  overheating in the facade cavity
- purge ventilation at high temperatures

Daylight
- reduction of daylight by depth of facade
- reduction of natural light transmittance
  by second pane
- uneven room lighting
- light redirection systems may be installed in
  facade cavity

Sound insulation
- additional sound level reduction with
  natural ventilation
- very little sound transmission from room
  to room

Functional aspects
- flexible user intervention possible
- uneven effects in room
- possible increased space requirement
- difficult to clean outer face of facade

Advantages
- very high user-acceptance
- very good level of comfort
- many ventilation options
- can be prefabricated

Disadvantages
- high construction costs

Box window

The box window as a second glass plane in front of the opening window, which allows a ventilated cavity to be formed. The cavity can be ventilated vertically or through the continuous peripheral joint. Box windows can be integrated into perforated and elemental facades. The system provides weather-protected solar screening, good noise reduction and comfortable introduction of supply air in winter and the transition months. Smaller ventilation openings perform better in terms of noise reduction but present a greater risk of overheating in summer. If necessary the openings in the external skin should be variable to allow the box window to be adjusted to suit different requirements.

	Typical	Min.–max.
Glazing fraction	50%	30–90%
U-value total	0.6 W/m²K	0.3–1.2 W/m²K
U-value (glazing)	0.9 W/m²K	0.5–1.3 W/m²K
U-value (opaque)	0.3 W/m²K	0.2–0.5 W/m²K
g_{tot}-value	0.15	0.12–0.30
g-value (glazing)	0.50	0.25–0.50
Sound reduction index R	40 dB	32–55 dB
Light transmittance τ	0.70	0.40–0.70
Investment cost euro/m²	1300	800–1800

Tab. 3.7 **Typical values and indicative ranges for box windows**

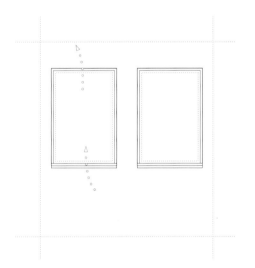

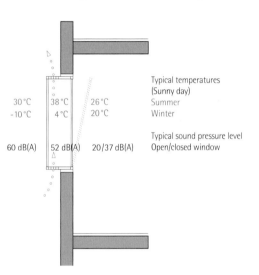

Typical temperatures
(Sunny day)
Summer
Winter

Typical sound pressure level
Open/closed window

30 °C	38 °C	26 °C
-10 °C	4 °C	20 °C
60 dB(A)	52 dB(A)	20/37 dB(A)

Fig. 3.21 **Temperature conditions and sound pressure levels for box windows**

Fig. 3.22 **Sound reduction index range for a box window**
The noise reduction performance of a box window depends on the proportion of openings in the external facade skin and the sound absorption properties of the facade cavity. A small proportion of openings may lead to overheating in summer but provides better noise reduction. [Graphic after Oesterle]

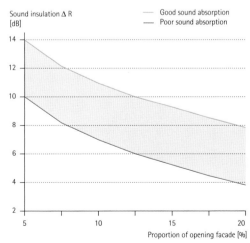

Construction
- in perforated facades
- in elemental facades
- inner skin 2-pane insulation glazing
- outer skin single-pane glazing
- distance between panes varies to suit the required function
- pane offset 10–50 cm

Typical applications
- administration buildings, residential buildings
- high-rise buildings with natural ventilation
- for high wind speeds for high noise-load areas
- night cooling

Heating energy demand
- transmission heat loss dynamic, dependent on the openings in the cavity and insolation
- improvement compared to a single-skinned facade
- use of solar gain

Ventilation
- comfortable introduction of supply air in winter
- heated supply air in summer
- no transmission of odour from room to room
- attenuation of wind effects
- impairment of air exchange

Room climate in summer
- wind-protected solar screening
- overheating in the facade cavity
- night cooling

Daylight
- reduction of daylight by depth of facade
- reduction of natural light transmittance by second pane
- light direction systems may be installed in facade cavity

Sound insulation
- comfortable ventilation in winter and in the transition months
- can be prefabricated
- suitable for renovation

Functional aspects
- weather protection
- intruder protection
- limited view out
- difficult to clean outer face of facade
- possible condensation formation on outside glass pane

Advantages
- comfortable ventilation in winter and in the transition months
- can be prefabricated
- suitable for renovation

Disadvantages
- direct view out limited
- purge ventilation limited
- overheating in the facade cavity
- high construction costs

Corridor facade

The corridor facade is a double-skinned facade in which the facade cavity is separated storey by storey with bulkheads. Air exchange in the facade cavity is either vertically at a floor level, horizontally at the corners of the building, or both vertically and horizontally. If the double-skinned facade is ventilated horizontally it is often designed so as to be able to control the pressures in the facade cavity. In this way the facade flaps can be opened or closed depending on the desired pressure conditions (over- or underpressure), wind direction and speed. This allows specific pressure conditions to be set up in the building and the ventilation drive energy demand to be minimised. Facade corridors can transmit unwanted odours and sounds between rooms.

	Typical	Min.–max.
Glazing fraction	90%	70–100%
U-value total	0.8 W/m²K	0.4–1.3 W/m²K
U-value (glazing)	0.9 W/m²K	0.5–1.3 W/m²K
U-value (opaque)	0.3 W/m²K	0.2–0.5 W/m²K
g_{tot}-value	0.15	0.12–0.30
g-value (glazing)	0.50	0.25–0.50
Sound reduction index R	40 dB	32–55 dB
Light transmittance τ	0.70	0.40–0.70
Investment cost euro/m²	1400	800–2000

Tab. 3.8 **Typical values and indicative ranges for corridor facades**

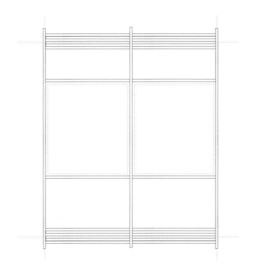

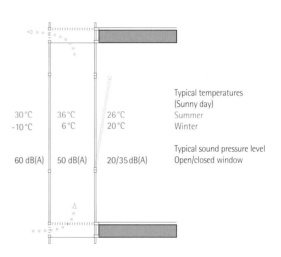

Typical temperatures
(Sunny day)
Summer
Winter

Typical sound pressure level
Open/closed window

Fig. 3.23 **Temperature conditions and sound pressure levels for corridor facades**

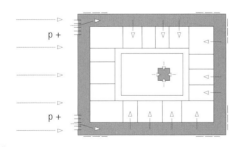

Fig. 3.24 **The facade as a positive pressure zone**
By opening the flaps on the side facing the wind the whole of the building is placed under positive pressure. This configuration of the facade is most suitable for introducing supply air into the building.

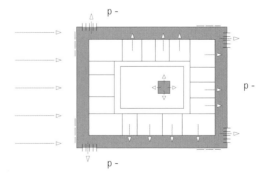

Fig. 3.25 **The facade as a negative pressure zone**
By opening the flaps in the wind-suction regions the whole of the building becomes a negative pressure zone. This configuration of the facade is most suitable for removing exhaust air from the building.

Construction
- elemental facade
- distance between panes varies to suit the required function
- inner facades are often made of wood
- panel offset 20–120 cm

Typical applications
- administration buildings
- high-rise buildings with natural ventilation
- for high wind speeds for high noise-load areas
- with aerodynamic ventilation concepts

Heating energy demand
- U-value dynamic, depends on air
  exchange and insolation
- improvement compared to a single-skinned facade
- possible use of solar gain
- possible movement of energy around the building

Ventilation
- comfortable introduction of supply air in winter
- risk of summer overheating
- transmission of odour from room to room
- pressure conditions can be defined with
  suitable controls

Room climate in summer
- wind-protected solar screening
- overheating in the facade cavity
- night cooling

Daylight
- reduction of daylight by depth of facade
- reduction of natural light transmittance
  by second pane
- integration of light redirection systems possible

Sound insulation
- good noise reduction with natural ventilation
- transmission of sound from room to room

Functional aspects
- facade cavity can carry pedestrian traffic
- increased space requirement
- intruder protection
- possible condensation formation on outside
  glass pane

Advantages
- pressure conditions can be controlled
- natural ventilation is possible even under difficult
  outside conditions
- homogenous appearance to the facade

Disadvantages
- overheating in summer
- high construction costs
- limited view out
- transmission of sound and odour
- high fire-safety requirements

Unsegmented double-skinned facade

Unsegmented double-skinned facades have no horizontal or vertical divisions in the facade cavity. They may be constructed as a double-skinned facade with a cavity less than one metre wide or as a glass front wall at an offset of several metres. The two skins are often structurally independent of one another. The ventilation openings are typically placed at the bottom and top only. This considerably increases the problem of overheating in the facade cavity, particularly if the distance between the glass skins is small. This effect can be moderated by additional ventilation openings or mechanical ventilation. There is the possibility of sound and odour transmission from room to room. If the distance between the skins is small the view out for users is very much limited. The building interior normally requires mechanical ventilation.

	Typical	Min.–max.
Glazing fraction	90%	50–100%
U-value total	0.8 W/m²K	0.4–1.3 W/m²K
U-value (glazing)	0.9 W/m²K	0.5–1.3 W/m²K
U-value (opaque)	0.3 W/m²K	0.2–0.5 W/m²K
g_{tot}-value	0.15	0.15–0.30
g-value (glazing)	0.50	0.25–0.50
Sound reduction index R	45 dB	35–60 dB
Light transmittance τ	0.70	0.40–0.70
Investition euro/m²	1000	600–1400

Tab. 3.9 **Typical values and indicative ranges for unsegmented double-skinned facades**

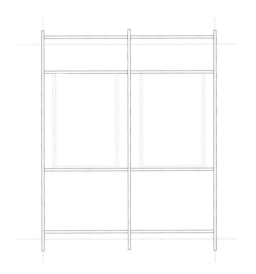

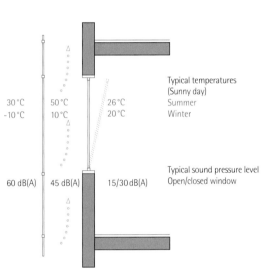

Fig. 3.26 **Temperature conditions and sound pressure levels for unsegmented double-skinned facades**

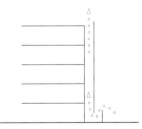

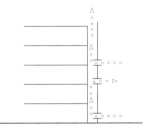

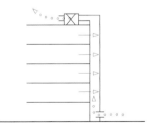

Fig. 3.27 **Ventilation of the facade with optimised sound insulation**
Adopting a small open cross-section and noise-reduction linings results in very little entry of noise.

Fig. 3.28 **Thermally optimised ventilation of the facade**
Ventilation flaps spaced over the height of the facade reduce overheating in the cavity.

Fig. 3.29 **Mechanical ventilation of the facade for exhaust air concepts**
Mechanical air extraction can set up specific pressure conditions.

Construction
- in front of perforated facades
- in front of elemental facades
- distance between skins varies to suit the required function
- outer skin can be self-supporting
- panel offset 1–5 m

Typical applications
- administration buildings, residential buildings in high noise-load areas
- buildings with mainly mechanical ventilation
- in building renovation, heritage buildings

Heating energy demand
- U-value dynamic, depends on air exchange and insolation
- formation of a climatic buffer zone
- possible use of solar gain

Ventilation
- comfortable introduction of supply air in winter
- considerable risk of summer overheating
- transmission of odour from room to room
- can be incorporated into the ventilation concept
- mechanical ventilation is normally required

Room climate in summer
- wind-protected solar screening
- unwanted heat entry from severe overheating in the facade cavity
- can provide night cooling

Daylight
- reduction of natural light transmittance by the second glass skin and construction of the outer skin
- diffuse light admitted by the arrangement of the solar screening on the outer skin

Sound insulation
- very good noise reduction with natural ventilation
- transmission of sound from room to room

Functional aspects
- view out limited depending on offset
- increased space requirement
- intruder protection
- cavity useable if offset large
- possible condensation formation on outside glass pane

Advantages
- very good noise reduction
- natural ventilation is possible even under difficult outside conditions
- homogenous appearance to the facade
- can be simply retrofitted

Disadvantages
- considerable summer overheating
- high construction costs
- severely limited view out
- transmission of sound and odour
- high fire-safety requirements

Controllable double-skinned facade

The controllable facade is the most complex type of facade to design and construct. It could extend over the whole of the outer facade skin or be restricted to individual opening flaps in the floor and ceiling area of each storey. The control system adjusts the facade to different outside climatic conditions. The user can still retain a good view out and a high degree of natural ventilation is possible. A conflict arises in summer between noise reduction and overheating in the facade cavity. The large number of moving parts and control system devices leads to very high maintenance costs.

	Typical	Min.-max.
Glazing fraction	90%	70–100%
U-value total	0.8 W/m²K	0.4–1.3 W/m²K
U-value (glazing)	0.9 W/m²K	0.5–1.3 W/m²K
U-value (opaque)	0.3 W/m²K	0.2–0.5 W/m²K
g_{tot}-value	0.15	0.15–0.30
g-value (glazing)	0.50	0.25–0.50
Sound reduction index R	35 dB	30–55 dB
Light transmittance τ	0.60	0.30–0.60
Investition euro/m²	2000	1000–3000

Tab. 3.10 **Typical values and indicative ranges for controllable double-skinned facades**

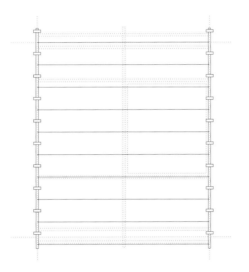

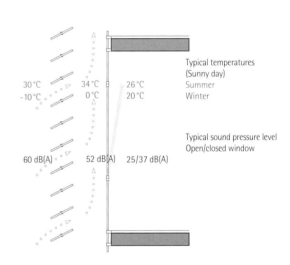

Typical temperatures
(Sunny day)
Summer
Winter

Typical sound pressure level
Open/closed window

30 °C   34 °C   26 °C
-10 °C   0 °C   20 °C

60 dB(A)   52 dB(A)   25/37 dB(A)

Fig. 3.30 **Temperature conditions and sound pressure levels for controllable facades**

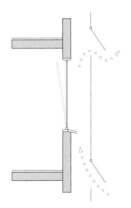

Fig. 3.31 **Storey by storey ventilation of the facade**

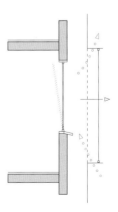

Fig. 3.32 **Ventilation by ventilation elements**

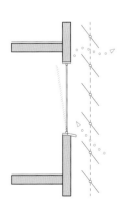

Fig. 3.33 **Completely opening facade**

Construction

- elemental facade
- variable opening of angle outer skin
- many moveable parts required
- panel offset 30–120 cm

Typical applications

- administration buildings
- high-rise buildings with natural ventilation
- higher noise-load locations
- front curtain wall in building refurbishment

Heating energy demand

- U-value dynamic, depends on settings
  of the ventilation flaps and insolation
- formation of a climatic buffer zone
- possible use of solar gain

Ventilation

- comfortable introduction of supply air in winter
- little risk of overheating in summer
- possible transmission of odour from room to
  room
- less noise reduction when ventilation flaps
  opened

Room climate in summer

- wind-protected solar screening
- overheating of the cavity avoided
  by opening the outer skin
- can provide night cooling

Daylight

- reduction of natural light transmittance
  in the depth of the room
- reduction of natural light transmittance
  by the second glass skin and construction
  of the outer skin

Sound insulation

- very good noise reduction depending on
  the setting of the ventilation flaps
- little noise reduction with open facade
- possible transmission of sound from room to room

Functional aspects

- direct view out depending on
  ventilation flap setting
- increased space requirement
- very high maintenance costs
- high cleaning costs

Advantages

- variable facade settings
- no overheating in summer
- improvement of view out possible
- can be controlled to adjust to outside climate

Disadvantages

- very high construction costs
- very high maintenance costs
- high technical costs

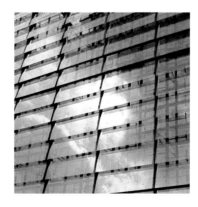

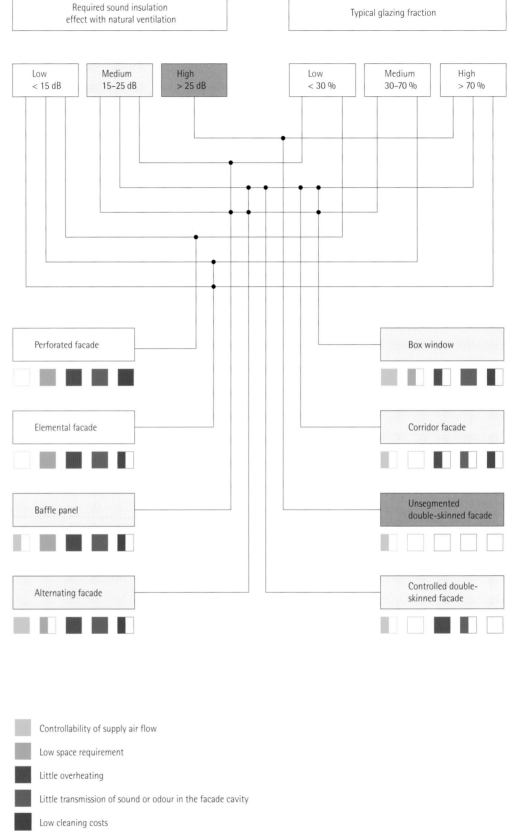

Fig. 3.34 **Decision chart for facade concepts**
The important criteria in the selection of facade systems are the noise reduction effect of the facade when the windows are open and the transparency of the building, which depends on the glazing fraction. The chart can be used to select the most suitable system by linking the desired output criteria. The characteristics of each system are made clear in the colour-coded squares. Each square indicates a characteristic as good (fully filled), average (half-filled) or poor (empty). As an example, a controllable double-skinned facade arises from the combination of average noise reduction requirement with a very high glazing fraction. This solution provides good ventilation in windy conditions (yellow) and has a high space requirement because of the second facade skin (orange). Its controllability avoids overheating in the facade cavity (red). This system transmits sound and odour from room to room via the facade even with the ventilation flaps closed (green). Cleaning costs are high because of the large areas of glass and the technical installations (blue).

Required sound insulation effect with natural ventilation

Typical glazing fraction

| Low < 15 dB | Medium 15–25 dB | High > 25 dB |
| Low < 30 % | Medium 30–70 % | High > 70 % |

Perforated facade

Box window

Elemental facade

Corridor facade

Baffle panel

Unsegmented double-skinned facade

Alternating facade

Controlled double-skinned facade

Controllability of supply air flow

Low space requirement

Little overheating

Little transmission of sound or odour in the facade cavity

Low cleaning costs

The choice of facade concept is focussed on user requirements and the conditions around and construction of the building. The user-specific requirements mainly influence the degree of transparency of the building and ventilation type. These aspects are often flexible and should be reanalysed during the design stage. The building-specific aspects influence wind exposure, noise load and insolation and are only variable to a very limited extent. These parameters have a decisive influence on the facade concept.

Tab. 3.11 **Suitability of facade concepts for various outdoor conditions and locations shown in relation to ventilation concept**

+ suitable
o neutral
- less suitable

Facade concept	Adequacy of natural ventilation for building use		Mechanical ventilation required for building use		Location and outdoor conditions
Perforated facade	–	Special fittings necessary, solar screening wind-exposed	+	Cost-effective, solar screening wind-exposed	
Elemental facades	–	Special fittings necessary, solar screening wind-exposed	o	Cost-effective, increased entry of solar radiation	
Baffle panel	o	Solar screening wind-protected	+	Night cooling, solar screening wind-protected	
Alternating facade	+	Very comfortable, flexible	o	Higher cost, solar screening wind-protected	
Box window	+	External openings adequately dimensioned	o	Higher cost, solar screening wind-protected	
Corridor facade	+	External openings adequately dimensioned	o	Higher cost, solar screening wind-protected	
Unsegmented double-skinned facade	–	Severe overheating	–	Risk of overheating	
Controllable double-skinned facade	+	Very flexible, cost intensive	–	Uneconomic	High-rise, exposed to wind
Perforated facade	–	High noise load	+	Cost-effective, good thermal insulation	
Elemental facade	–	High noise load	o	Possible limited noise reduction	
Baffle panel	o	Small offset necessary	+	Night cooling	
Alternating facade	+	Very comfortable	o	High cost, night cooling	
Box window	+	Possible overheating in summer	o	High cost, night cooling	
Corridor facade	o	Possible overheating in summer	o	High cost, night cooling	
Unsegmented double-skinned facade	–	No view out, risk of overheating	+	Very high noise load	
Controllable double-skinned facade	+	Little overheating of the facade, flexible	–	Uneconomic	Noisy location
Perforated facade	+	Cost-effective, possible thermal discomfort	+	Cost-effective, good thermal insulation	
Elemental facade	+	Possible limited thermal insulation	+	Be aware of thermal insulation	
Baffle panel	+	Night cooling	+	Night cooling	
Alternating facade	o	Cost intensive, comfortable	–	Uneconomic	
Box window	–	Uneconomic	–	Uneconomic	
Corridor facade	–	Uneconomic	–	Uneconomic	
Unsegmented double-skinned facade	–	Uneconomic	–	Uneconomic	
Controllable double-skinned facade	–	Uneconomic	–	Uneconomic	Quiet location

Buddha Memorial Hall

The construction of a new Buddhist memorial hall is planned for a location near the Taiwanese capital Taipei. The funding for the new building is provided on behalf of a local monastery by a Buddhist industrialist. In spite of this generosity, the aim will be to create a building which requires the minimum of room conditioning technology, in order to reduce the amount of initial investment and ensure the building can be operated cost-effectively and in a manner which conserves natural resources.

The building

The most conspicuous feature of the building is the 50 m diameter globe, which houses the actual memorial hall. The globe rests on a multistorey plinth which is flanked by towers. Religious motifs are projected from the tops of the towers onto the surface of the globe during periods of darkness.

Inside the globe a walkway winds up and along the wall up to about half its height. On reaching this point, the visitor finds himself at the same level as a relic standing at the centre of the globe on a slender stele.

Taiwan is in a typhoon region and therefore the whole structure must be able to resist high wind forces. The globe is formed from a robust mesh of steel profiles and has large water tanks in the basements of the plinth to give the building extra weight.

Facade concept

The facade of the globe is constructed using two skins. It is planned to use a lightweight, almost opaque plastic material for the inner skin, which is fitted into the spaces between the structural members. Light can only enter the building through small transparent spots in the walls, which creates the illusion of a star-covered sky on the inside surface of the globe.

The outer facade skin consists of translucent panels, which permit enough air to pass through them to ventilate the facade cavity. Their solar screening effect reduces the heating up of the inner facade skin by solar radiation.

Climatisation concept

The interior of the globe is completely naturally ventilated through the openings near the crown. The air temperature in the area open to visitors, extending up to half the height of the globe, should not become much hotter than the outside air. Using air flow modelling, it was calculated that an area of about 20 m² would be necessary for ventilation, which is the equivalent of a circle with a 5 m diameter.

The perceived temperature inside the sphere is higher than the air temperature, especially on the side exposed to the sun, because the facade heats up. The possibility of using the water in the basement tanks required for structural stability to compensate for this effect by cooling the supply air or the facade is being investigated.

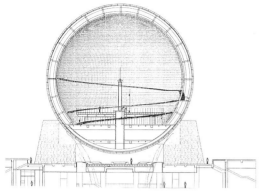

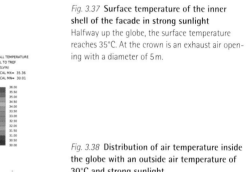

Section

Fig. 3.35 **Section through the Buddha Memorial Hall**
A walkway winds its way up the wall to the equator of the globe. The top of the stele, where the relic is positioned, is at the centre of the globe.

Fig. 3.36 **Structural system based on steel triangles**

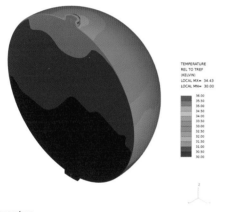

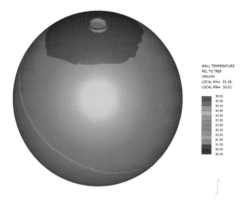

Surface temperature

Air temperature

Fig. 3.37 **Surface temperature of the inner shell of the facade in strong sunlight**
Halfway up the globe, the surface temperature reaches 35°C. At the crown is an exhaust air opening with a diameter of 5m.

Fig. 3.38 **Distribution of air temperature inside the globe with an outside air temperature of 30°C and strong sunlight**

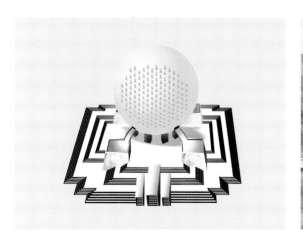

Figs. 3.39 and 3.40 **Digital 3D models in elevation and plan view (simplified model)**

Completion: Planned 2009
Use: Buddhist memorial hall
Client: Buddhist monastery in Kaohsiung
Architect: Artech Inc. Taiwan
Architectonics: Prof. Wienands, Munich
Structural engineering: Dr. Kurt Stepan, Munich
Climatisation concept: Ingenieurbüro für Bauklimatik Hausladen & Meyer, Kassel

adidas Factory Outlet Center
Dynamic ventilation

A natural ventilation concept was developed for the adidas Factory Outlet Center in Herzogenaurach, Germany. Through ventilation openings in the roof, the wind suction forces on the roof surface thoroughly ventilate the sales hall – a symbol for themes of sport, dynamism and freshness. The aerodynamic behaviour of the building is further improved by the canopy, which resembles a landing flap of an aircraft. The deep overhang also ensures optimum shading of the facade. In winter and summer supply air is brought to the building through an earth pipe and is preheated or precooled respectively as required. Direct exhaust air discharge through the roof is an efficient way of removing the waste heat given off by the luminaires. In addition the tempering effect of the ceilings ensures a comfortable room climate throughout the year.

Ventilation and room-climate concept for the summer The supply air is introduced into the room through an earth pipe and is precooled. Wind forces acting on the roof removes air from the building naturally through the ventilation openings in the roof. The surface heating systems are cooled with groundwater in the summer to create a comfortable room climate. The canopy produces extensive shading and a suction zone on the roof of the building. This suction zone can help through-ventilate the building.

Ventilation and room-climate concept for the winter The building is designed to make as much use of regenerative energy as possible in order to minimise the heating energy demand. Supply air is preheated in an earth pipe, which allows extensive air exchange to take place with low ventilation heat losses. Room conditioning is performed by a surface heating system, which works very efficiently with a heat pump fed with groundwater. The waste energy contained in the exhaust air is recovered using an exhaust heat pump and stored in the surface heating system.

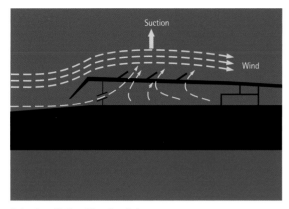

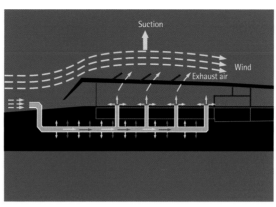

Fig. 3.41 **Ventilation and room–climate concepts for winter and summer**
Through the use of wind forces and the creation of regenerative heat and cold, the building achieves a good room climate and good ventilation with the use of very little energy.

Natural ventilation driven by wind

Ventilation concept for summer

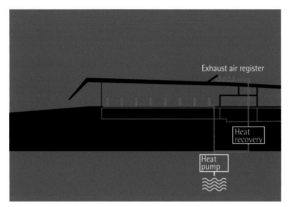

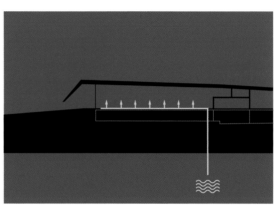

Room climate concept for winter with floor heating

Room-climate concept for summer with groundwater cooling

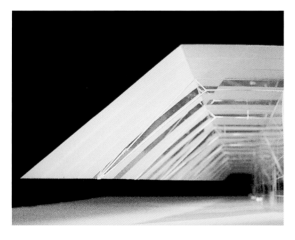

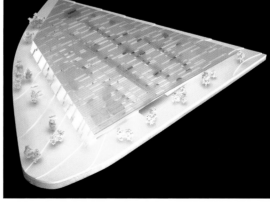

Fig. 3.42 **Canopy resembling an aircraft landing flap**

Fig. 3.43 **Model photo, view from above**

Completion: Competition entry, 2002
Use: Retail
Client: adidas AG
Architects: Auer+Weber+Assoziierte, Munich
Building services: IB Hausladen, Kirchheim

Facade technologies

"... our stadiums are perceptual mechanisms between the spectators and the playing field.

"... I love football. I grew up next to the earlier football ground here, in the back yard of FC Basel so to speak. I also played for a long time myself, and today I am a passionate spectator at games in the stadium. Therefore I am well qualified to understand the subject from the point of view of the spectator.

"... It is like a child's drawing, just dot, dot, comma, line and the elevation is done. There are three or four key aspects at the heart of the concept. First of all the esplanade; it forms an almost ceremonial route along which streams of visitors meander their way from the underground station towards the stadium, which hides behind a gentle hill and reveals itself only gradually as they walk down the other side. The spectators move in an embracing gesture around the stadium. The ritual of approach is continued by the cascade of stairs. A further aspect is the stadium as an icon, a body of light that can change its colour from white to red and blue, like a membrane transmitting the energy contained inside to the outside. Thirdly the radicalisation of the space inside which, as an interactive mechanism for perception, is almost like a classical arena.

"... A building is either better or worse, correct or less correct, appropriate or less appropriate — those are our criteria. Whether the expression of form is minimum or maximum, affected or less affected, is less important to us. As we have no preferences, it all depends on the particular project."

Jacques Herzog & Pierre de Meuron

Source: DETAIL, Munich, Vol. 9/2005, pp. 900–901

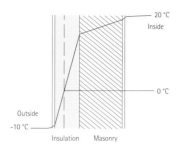

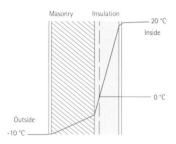

Fig. 4.1 **Temperature profile in a single-leaf wall with external and internal insulation**
Internal insulation produces low temperatures within the wall construction where water vapour may condense and lead to building damage.

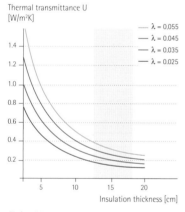

Fig. 4.2 **U-values shown in relation to insulation thickness and thermal conductivity group**
The graph is nonlinear with respect to insulation thickness. From a thickness of about 15 cm any further increase in insulation leads to only a slight increase in thermal insulating effect. It is more efficient to choose insulation with a lower thermal conductivity.

Insulation

Insulating materials improve the thermal and sound insulation of buildings. They reduce transmission heat losses and produce higher surface temperatures, which minimises ventilation heat losses in winter. They protect the building fabric from condensation and frost whilst contributing to a comfortable and hygienic indoor climate. The insulating effect of a material is based on the low thermal conductivity of enclosed air. This effect is greater with smaller and more numerous pores of air and more so if they are evenly distributed. To be described as insulation, a building material should have a thermal conductivity of less than 0.1 W/mK.

Insulating materials are classified into inorganic/mineral or organic types according to their constituent raw materials. Both may be made from natural or synthetic raw materials. Depending on their make-up they are subdivided into fibre, foamed and granulate or loose fill insulation. Air movement is prevented either by fibrous materials or by the entrained air enclosed within a solid cell structure. In terms of fire protection most inorganic insulation belongs to building material class A (non-combustible), organic insulation to class B (combustible). Mineral fibre insulation and rigid foam has over 90% of the market share. In recent years insulation made from renewable raw materials has been rediscovered and its use widened.

Constructional aspects Thermal insulation layers can be attached to the inside or the outside of a facade. Starting from the room side, the successive layers of materials making up a wall should be increasingly more open to diffusion, so that the movement of moisture is not obstructed. Thermal bridges are to be avoided particularly at wall and floor connections.

The insulating effect is not influenced by the position of thermal insulation in the structure; however external insulation generally creates fewer thermal bridges and better protects the load-bearing structure from temperature fluctuations. Thermal storage masses are effective inside the building and can improve indoor climate in summer. With internal insulation, the absence of thermal storage mass allows little-used rooms to be heated up quickly in winter.

Mineral insulation made from natural raw materials

One of these materials is expanded clay. Its thermal insulating effect is rather small. It is very resistant to compression and decomposition, which makes it popular as a levelling fill under screeds, a lightweight aggregate in concrete and mortar and as loose fill insulation above ceilings.

Finely ground raw perlite, a glassy stone material of volcanic origin with a relatively high water content, is heated to manufacture expanded perlite. After the expansion process it can be made hydrophobic or bituminised for special purposes. Expanded perlite can be used as aggregate, core insulation, thermal and impact sound insulation or as loose-fill insulation in roofs. It can be further processed to form perlite insulation boards.

Mineral insulation made from synthetic raw materials

Materials such as recycled glass, limestone or sand are melted, formed by various means into fibres and further processed with a binder for the manufacture of mineral fibres like glass or mineral wool. In addition to very good thermal and sound insulation properties, mineral fibres are open to diffusion and resistant to weather, which makes them suitable for thermal and sound insulation and fire protection.

Foamglass results from foaming a liquid glass melt with the addition of carbon as the foaming agent. The closed, gas-impervious cell structure makes foamglass an absolutely moisture- and waterproof material which is dimensionally stable and very resistant to compression. Foamglass boards are therefore primarily used as perimeter insulation, floor insulation, as floorboards and in flat roofs as well as for insulating components under high compressive stresses.

Thermal insulation boards of calcium silicate, also called mineral foam, consist of lime, silica sand and water, with the addition of cellulose when intended for use inside buildings. They are also capable of regulating indoor air humidity because their open pores and capillaries allow them to take up a large amount of water. For outside use they must be made hydrophobic by impregnation to protect them against water.

Organic insulation made from natural raw materials

Cellulose fibre insulation materials are made from waste paper and mixed with borax to improve their resistance to

Expanded clay

Mineral wool

Foamglass

fire and infestation. In addition to good thermal insulation properties, cellulose fibres are hygroscopic and open to diffusion. They are used in lightweight construction for thermal insulation in walls, ceilings, roofs and voids.

Wood off-cuts from sawmills are chipped and pulped in the manufacture of wood fibre insulation boards. Water is then added and the fibre pulp is pressed and dried to form boards. The resins in the wood provide the bond. Wood fibre insulation boards are hygroscopic, open to diffusion and wind-proof. They are used for external and internal walls, roofs and ceilings. Multilayer composite wood-wool boards are used in combination with boards made from polystyrene, polyurethane (PUR) or mineral fibres. They are used as permanent formwork, as insulation at heat bridges and as thermal insulation on the underside of basement ceilings.

Other insulation materials made from renewable plant or animal fibres include cork, coir, flax, reeds, cotton or wool. They are usually further processed into boards or insulation mats. These products are expensive because of the limited supply of raw materials and hence are used only to a small extent.

Organic insulation made from synthetic raw materials

Expanded polystyrene (EPS), marketed in some countries

under the name of Styropor, is produced by the polymerisation of styrene with the addition of a light, volatile blowing agent. Rigid polystyrene foam boards have good thermal insulation properties. They do not decompose but they become brittle under direct sunlight. They are temperature-sensitive and dissolve in many solvents. They are suitable as insulation on external walls and roofs. The high resistance to moisture diffusion should not be overlooked.

If molten polystyrene is expanded with a foaming agent (carbon dioxide) and then extruded this creates extruded polystyrene (XPS). With its uniform closed-cell structure, the material has a high compressive strength, very low water absorption capacity and high diffusion resistance. XPS is not UV-resistant and is dissolved by solvents. It is used to provide thermal insulation to surfaces under compressive loads, as perimeter insulation and for insulating inverted roofs and thermal bridges.

Polyurethane (PUR) rigid foam or foamed-in-place PUR are manufactured from crude oil or volatile components of renewable raw materials. Foamed-in-place PUR is used to fill voids on site. Closed-cell foam is resistant to chemicals and solvents and does not decompose. Thermal conductivity values are high. PUR rigid foam is used on walls, in roofs as insulation above rafters, in flat roofs and on surfaces under high compressive loads.

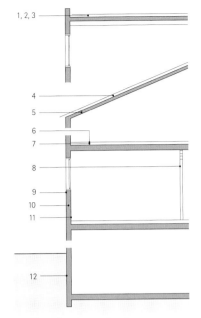

Fig. 4.3 **Uses of insulation in a building**

Roof
1 Inverted roof: XPS, foamglass
2 Cold roof: EPS, mineral wool, PUR
3 Warm roof: XPS, EPS, PUR
4 On rafters: EPS, XPS, PUR
5 Between rafters: Mineral wool, perlite, cellulose flakes, wool, wood-fibre insulation boards

Ceiling
6 Impact sound insulation: EPS, oak boards, perlite, wood-fibre insulation boards, mineral wool
7 Thermal insulation: Mineral wool, perlite, expanded clay, EPS, XPS, PUR, cork boards

Wall
8 Partition walls: Mineral wool, cork boards, wool, cellulose flakes, wood-fibre insulation boards
9 External insulation: Mineral wool, XPS, EPS, PUR, wood-fibre insulation boards
10 Core insulation: Foamglass, EPS, XPS, PUR,
11 Internal insulation: Mineral wool, foam glass, EPS
12 Perimeter insulation: Foam glass, XPS, PUR

	Expanded clay	Perlite	Mineral wool	Foam-glass	Cel-lulose	Wood fibre	Wool	Cork	Poly-styrene (EPS)	Poly-styrene (XPS)	Poly-urethane (PUR)
Bulk density ρ [kg/m³]	200–400	140–240	10–200	100–150	20–60	150–250	30–140	90–140	10–50	20–65	28–55
Thermal conductivity λ [W/mK]	0.100–0.160	0.045–0.065	0.030–0.050	0.038–0.055	0.035–0.045	0.035–0.060	0.035–0.045	0.040–0.055	0.030–0.050	0.026–0.040	0.020–0.040
Primary energy content [kWh/m³]	300–450	90–240	150–500	750–1600	50	600–1500	40–80	65–450	200–760	450–1000	800–1500
Water vapour diffusion resistance μ [-]	2	5	1	∞	2	5–10	1–2	5–10	60	150	60
Fire protection class	A1	A1–B2	A1–A2	A1	B1–B2	B2	B2	B2	B1	B1	B1–B2
Material form	Loose fill, aggregate	Board, loose fill	Board, mat, wool	Board, loose fill	Blown-in flakes	Insulation boards	Mat	Board, loose fill	Board, aggregate	Board	Board

Tab. 4.1 **Properties of common insulation materials**

Wood-fibre board

Cork

Polystyrene (EPS)

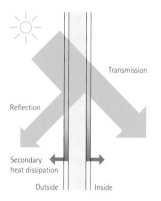

Fig. 4.4 **Solar radiation passing through glazing**
Transmission, reflection and absorption are the determining parameters when considering the amount of solar radiation passing through glazing. Absorption changes radiation energy into thermal energy, which increases the temperature of the absorbing pane. Longwave radiation and convection are responsible for the secondary heat dissipation into the room.

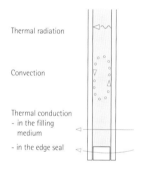

Fig. 4.5 **Heat transport in glazing**
Heat is transported in glazing by radiation, convection and conduction. With uncoated insulation glazing two-thirds of the total heat transport is by radiation and only one-third by convection. Coatings can almost completely prevent radiation exchange. An inert gas in the glazing cavity reduces heat transfer arising from conduction and convection.

Glass

Glass with as low a U-value as possible should be used in order to minimise transmission heat losses and achieve a good level of thermal comfort. A high natural light transmittance τ is necessary for good daylight provision. If solar heat gain in winter is important, then the total solar energy transmittance g should be as high as possible. On the other hand, a lower g-value is preferable for good indoor climatic conditions in summer. At noisy locations it is important to have glass with good sound reduction properties. Glazing should cause as little colour shift as possible and not reflect light when viewed from outside. Lower g-values normally lead to a reduction in natural light transmittance τ. The development of glass with very low U-values now means that more attention must be paid to frame design.

Manufacturing Most glass used today is float glass. The main ingredients of glass – quartz sand, soda and lime – are first melted. Then the homogenous glass melt flows out onto a bath of molten tin (float). After it has cooled slowly, the glass is cut into a maximum sheet size of 6.00 x 3.20 m.

Coatings can be applied to modify the properties of the glass. The position of the coating in a glazing unit is critical, as is the material and the type of coating. With so-called hard coatings, the coating material is applied during manufacture to the surface of the still-molten float glass. This firmly and solidly bonds the coating to the glass, which is therefore suitable for single glazing. Glass can also be coated after cutting. These coatings are not as resistant and therefore are only used for insulation glazing units and laminated safety glass. In the Sol-Gel process, a chemical synthesis method, the sheet is immersed in a liquid, so that both glass surfaces have the same properties. The magnetron sputtering process, in which different metal oxide coatings are applied one after the other, provides more scope for differentiation.

Physical aspects Glazing can have a wide range of different properties with respect to light, radiation and heat. Its performance is determined by the transmission, reflection and absorption properties of the glass. Parameters relating to light refer to visible light in the wavelength range 380 to 780 nm, whilst radiation parameters relate to the whole solar spectrum 300 to 2500 nm.

The transmission of heat in a glazing unit is determined by the thermal radiation between the panes resulting from the emissivity of the pane surfaces and the convection within the gas inside the glazing cavity. Low-E coatings can considerably reduce radiation exchange. Inert gases such as argon can considerably reduce the combined heat transport effects of conduction and convection in the glazing cavity compared with dry air. Combined heat transmission is the lowest with a 15 mm wide glazing cavity. The edge seal of insulation glazing units reduces the thermal insulation effect; this reduction is less significant with larger panes.

The radiation-related parameters of glazing can be modified by selecting specific coatings, for example for making it better at transmitting certain wavelengths than others. Selectivity is the ratio of light transmittance τ to total solar energy transmittance g. Higher ratios produce better daylight provision whilst admitting low amounts of radiation. The laws of physics limit the selectivity of colour-neutral glazing to a maximum of 1.8.

Colour affects the view out and the outside appearance of glazing. The colour-rendering index R_a is used to express the colour-rendering properties of glass. A high value signifies a more neutral colour rendering; a low value is associated with higher colour shifts. Glazing should have an R_a-value of at least 90. Colour in the external appearance of the glass is determined by its reflection spectrum. The transmission spectrum is responsible for the colour of the view out, which also determines the colour rendering inside the building.

Types of glass fixings

Thermal insulation glazing Thermal insulation glazing reduces heat transmission in two ways. A wafer-thin transparent coating on the outside of the internal pane reduces heat emissions so that almost no radiation interchange takes place between the panes. In addition an inert glass filling reduces heat exchange resulting from conduction. The gas is often argon or krypton. Two-pane glazing can achieve U-values as low as 1.0 W/m²K; with three-pane glazing this goes down to 0.5 W/m²K. These very low U-values minimise transmission heat loss and improve thermal comfort because of the higher surface temperature. The problem of cold-air drop, which usually occurs with high glazing, is also alleviated.

Solar-control glazing Special coatings on the inside of the external pane of solar-control glazing allow a lot of visible light but only a very small proportion of the energy of the rest of the solar spectrum into the room. The spectral composition of the proportion of light admitted is altered and the result is a colour shift. The coating's effect is the same throughout the year and therefore it also reduces solar gain in winter. In summer additional measures are generally necessary to ensure shading and glare protection. The reflection properties in the visible light spectrum determine the colour appearance and the strength of the reflection of the glass. Various colour

hues can result, the most common being blue, green and silver.

Solar-control glazing can achieve g-values as low as 0.15. However, these very low total solar energy transmittances reduce the amount of natural light admitted and the outside surfaces have a mirrorlike appearance, which may restrict their use to special applications or to parts of buildings only. In practice, offices can be completely glazed with glass with g-values as low as 0.30.

Printed glass Printing on glass is one way of reducing its g-value whilst preserving a transparent appearance. The view out is retained to a certain extent, depending on the coverage and pattern of printing. From outside, printed glass has an opaque appearance, which obstructs the view in.

In the screen-printing process a ceramic coating is baked on to the glass surface. The printing may be opaque or translucent. The dyes in translucent printing are specially modified so that they can be applied in different degrees of intensity and transparency.

Surface-treated glass The most popular forms of surface treatment for insulation glazing are etching and sandblasting. These techniques prevent people from looking in and admit only diffused light into the room.

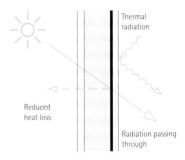

Fig. 4.6 **Low-e glass**
A special coating on the outside of the internal pane reduces heat loss from the room.

Fig. 4.7 **Solar-control glass**
A special coating or film on the inside of the external pane reduces the amount of solar energy admitted.

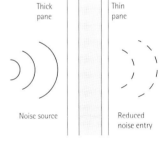

Fig. 4.8 **Sound reduction glass**
The sound reduction performance of insulation glazing can be improved by using two panes of different thicknesses and filling the glazing cavity with a special gas.

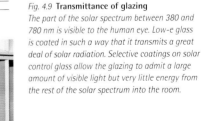

Fig. 4.9 **Transmittance of glazing**
The part of the solar spectrum between 380 and 780 nm is visible to the human eye. Low-e glass is coated in such a way that it transmits a great deal of solar radiation. Selective coatings on solar control glass allow the glazing to admit a large amount of visible light but very little energy from the rest of the solar spectrum into the room.

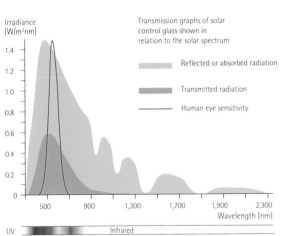

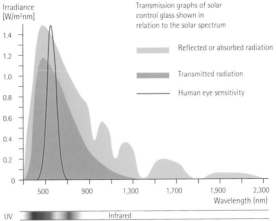

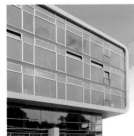

External appearance of solar control glazing

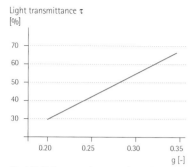

Light transmittance τ
[%]

Fig. 4.10 **Light transmittance τ shown in relation to total solar energy transmittance g**

Glazing with etched-glass surfaces appears smooth and silky. The period of exposure to the effects of the acid and its concentration determines the degree of etching. The treatment reduces light transmittance compared with untreated glass by only about 1 to 2%. In addition to treating the whole surface of a pane, it is also possible to create patterns by etching only parts of the glass surface. Surfaces treated in this way are less susceptible to mechanically caused defects such as scratches.

Sandblasting is another method of giving glass lighting properties. The glass is blasted with sand in a chamber to roughen its surface.

Sound reduction glass The effectiveness of sound reduction glazing increases with weight, elasticity and the distance between the panes. Other factors include the type of gas filling and the build-up of the panes. Sound reduction can be improved by having panes of different thicknesses. Sound reduction glazing can achieve a sound reduction index R_w of up to 50 dB. In the choice of glass it should be borne in mind that glass which improves sound reduction usually has reduced thermal insulation properties.

Safety glazing Safety glazing must be installed where there are increased requirements for intruder protection or resistance to bullets, in high facades and overhead glazing. Types include toughened glass and laminated safety glass. The pane is thermally prestressed (heat-treated) in toughened (fully-tempered) glass. It has a higher bending strength and when fractured it breaks into many grains of glass with no sharp edges. When this happens the glass loses its room-enclosing effect. Laminated safety glass is composed of two or more sheets bonded together by elastic interlayers. The strong bond between panes and interlayers ensures that in the event of breakage the glass has some residual strength. The room-enclosing effect is maintained and no dangerously large splinters are detached. Elasticity provides the protective effect of glass against throw-through or penetration and is created by the combination of glass with several interlayers or layers of cast-in-place resin.

Systems in the glazing cavity Elements in the cavity of insulation glazing reduce the amount of radiation admitted and influence daylighting conditions in the room. They are also able to take on the roles of solar control, anti-glare protection and light redirection to produce improved lighting conditions in the room. They can also cut out direct sunlight and only admit diffused light. The view in and out is normally limited. There are moveable and rigid systems. Rigid systems are cost-effective and have a long service life. If manually or motor-driven systems breakdown they may have to be completely replaced. Systems in the glazing cavity are highly efficient and can operate whatever the weather.

	Heat insulation glass	2-pane insulation glazing	3-pane insulation glazing	56/47 solar control glazing	40/24 solar control glazing	Sound reduction glazing
Build-up	6/12/6	4/12/4	4/12/4/12/4	6/16/6	6/16/6	13/16/9
U-value [W/m²K]	2.8	1.0	0.5	1.2	1.2	1.1
g-value [-]	0.74	0.53	0.50	0.47	0.24	0.53
τ-value [%]	0.81	0.71	0.70	0.56	0.40	0.75
Selectivity [-]	1.09	1.34	1.4	1.19	1.67	1.41
Weight [kg/m²]	30	20	30	30	30	52
R_w [dB]	31	31	32	34	34	48

Tab. 4.2 **Building-physical properties of glazing**

Appearance of surface-treated glass

Variochromic glass Controllable glazing allows the user to vary the amount of light and radiation transmitted through it and therefore offers a solution to one of architecture's most basic problems, namely, how to provide controlled shading that is both highly efficient and protected from the weather. Active systems change their optical and thermal characteristics at the press of a button, whilst passive systems work automatically. In combination with TI elements (see page 128), variochromic glass provides an additional option which allows the heat entering the room to be specifically controlled. Variochromic glass systems are at the testing stage and almost ready to be introduced to the market.

Electrochromic glass is an active system. It requires controls and switches. An active coating in the form of a film is embedded in laminated glass between two sheets. Its colour changes after switching, subject to a time delay. Visibility is retained, even in the switched state. Additional glare protection is required. Once installed, the glass has a bluish tint in the switched condition.

Gaschromic glass is also an active system. The glazing cavity is connected to control devices outside the glazing unit. The colour change is brought about by contact with a gas. Visibility through the glass is retained in operation but there is a blue colour shift. Glare protection must still be considered.

Thermotropic glazing is a passive system. The glazing becomes cloudy automatically once a certain threshold temperature is exceeded, which is determined during manufacture by the mixture of materials. The user cannot intervene in or control this process, the threshold temperature is fixed. As the temperature rises, the clear glass changes to diffuse the light. In this state the glass no longer allows clear visibility and therefore is mainly suitable for use in skylights or in combination with transparent panels.

PDLC glass (PDLC = Polymer-Dispersed Liquid Crystal) works in a similar way to thermotropic glass. As long as the correct voltage is applied, the liquid crystals are uniformly aligned and the visibility is clear. The system is used where visibility needs to be controlled or as an indoor switchable projection surface.

Photochromic coatings combine the functional aspects of electrochromic coatings and electrochemical solar cells. An external voltage is required only for the decolourising process. When not under voltage the coating appears blue in sunlight. Colouration in winter can be prevented by applying voltage.

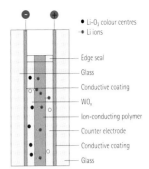

Electrochromic glass
The system normally consists of five layers: two conductive transparent electrodes, an ion storage layer and an active layer, usually of tungsten oxide. An electrical voltage is applied to this galvanic element. The ion exchange causes the colouration to take place..

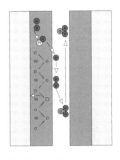

Gaschromic glass
A thin catalysing layer is placed on a layer of tungsten oxide. Atomic hydrogen, in a mixture at low concentration with a carrier gas, e.g., nitrogen, is introduced into the glazing cavity and diffuses into the tungsten oxide layer to bring about the colour change. Raising the oxygen concentration reverses the process.

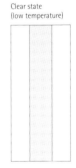

	Total solar energy transmittance g [-]		Light transmittance τ [-]		Switched visibility	Optical appearance	Controllability	Voltage required	Disadvantages
	Not switched	Switched	Not switched	Switched					
Thermotropic	0.5	0.15	0.74	0.16	No	Transparent–clear	No	No	No visibility, not controllable
Gaschromic	0.5	0.15	0.6	0.16	Yes	Neutral–blue	Yes	Yes	Glare risk
Electrochromic	0.36	0.12	0.5	0.15	Yes	Neutral–blue	Different switched states	Yes	Glare risk

Tab. 4.3 **Comparison of variochromic glass types**

Thermotropic glass
Two layers with different refractive indices are mixed. The plastics in the polymer blend mix well or less well according to the temperature and separate as the temperature rises. Light striking the layer is refracted, diffused or reflected to different degrees. With hydrogels, the polymer dissolves in the gel at low temperatures; at higher temperatures they separate and become cloudy.

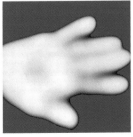

Appearance of variochromic glass

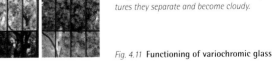

Fig. 4.11 **Functioning of variochromic glass**

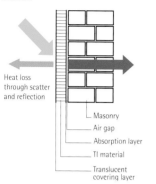

Insolation

Heat loss through scatter and reflection

— Masonry
— Air gap
— Absorption layer
— TI material
— Translucent covering layer

Fig. 4.12 **How TI works in a solid wall system**
Solar radiation striking the absorber wall is released over time into the room.

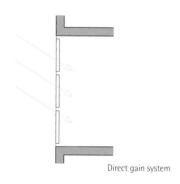

Direct gain system

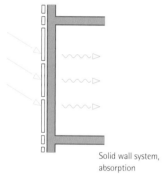

Solid wall system, absorption

Fig. 4.13 **Principles of operation**
Translucent insulation systems can use solar radiation directly, or transfer it into the room indirectly by absorption.

Translucent thermal insulation (TI)

Translucent thermal insulation is insulation that allows solar radiation to pass through it. This results in higher solar gain in the room and can reduce heat losses. TI can be used as a direct heat gain system without storage for heating and providing diffuse light or for time-shifted release of heat into the room. TI materials consist of hollow chamber structures (capillaries and honeycombs) of plastic or glass. These materials have optimum light transmittance and heat insulation properties. Small parallel tubes perpendicular to the absorber suppress convection movements. The thermal insulation effect arises from the low conductivity of the stationary air in these small tubes. The diameter of the small tubes is approximately 5 mm.

Heat gain Solar radiation penetrates the translucent insulation attached to the outside of the facade and the dark paint of the wall behind acts as an absorber to convert the radiation energy into heat. As the TI material has a very high resistance to the conduction of heat compared with the wall, the heat penetrates the wall where it is stored and released into the interior, subject to a time shift. The net heat gains depend on the type and quality of the TI system; they may be between 50 and 150 kWh/m²a.

Translucent thermal insulation can also be inserted between two glass panes. Solar screening is required to prevent the TI from overheating and the occurrence of unacceptably high room temperatures in summer or during the transition months. Variable solar screening can be regulated to suit the actual heat requirement. Optical systems that block the high summer sun by means of prismatic panels are being used in trial applications. Thermotropic glazing has passive self-regulating and reversible shading, which can be activated at a specific temperature.

Daylight optimisation If daylight use is paramount, translucent thermal insulation can be used to diffuse direct light and provide light in the depth of the room whilst improving thermal conditions. The scattering effect of the TI inserted between two glass panes produces an even and shadow-free distribution of light. A direct view out is not possible and therefore this system is suitable for skylights and roofs in offices, factories, sports halls and museums. The required shading and the high cost mean that where translucent insulation is used it is usually optimised to suit the building use.

Possible applications Translucent insulation can be used in new construction and in building refurbishment. The external walls of old buildings are generally very dense and can therefore form an energy-efficient combination with TI elements. It is particularly suitable for buildings that have a high heating energy requirement or with uses that need high room temperatures, such as indoor swimming pools.

Tab. 4.4 **Comparison of TI materials**

	Material					TI system	
	Honeycombs	Capillaries	Glass tubes	Makrolon	Aerogel	Solid wall	Direct gain
Thickness [mm]	100	80	80	70	20	131	49
U-value [W/m²K]	0.9	1.1	1.1	0.9	0.7	0.8	0.8
g-value [–]	0.82	0.78	0.68	0.40	0.70	0.59	0.63

Appearance of TI

Plastic ribs

Capillaries with glass render

Honeycombs

Vacuum insulation panels

The evacuation of air increases the insulating effect of the material because heat transport by convection and conduction is almost completely suppressed. Vacuum insulation consists of a core of microporous material, such as glass fibres or open-pored foam, which is capable of withstanding compression loads and of being evacuated of air. It is encapsulated in a gas- and water vapour-tight welded film. Fine-pored materials, such as aerogels or fumed silica, have very good insulating properties even without a vacuum. If they are also encapsulated in a gas-tight enclosure under reduced air pressure, their insulating effect is five to ten times greater than the same thickness of conventional insulation. Thermal conductivities of 0.004 to 0.008 W/mK can be achieved. Microporous silica fume is favoured for use in high-rise buildings because it does not substantially age and is heat resistant. Its good insulating properties make it ideal for thin construction components or for incorporation into narrow spaces.

Construction aspects Thermal problems may occur with vacuum insulation panels; if they lose vacuum their U-values increase by a factor of three. Larger panels perform better because the detrimental effect of thermal conductivity at their edge seals is less significant. Great care is required on site during and after installation to avoid loss of function.

The units have to be factory-made to accomplish the evacuation process. In principle they can be made in any shape and size. However, for reasons of cost, they are used in uniform standard sizes of 0.5 x 0.5 m to 0.5 x 1.0 m and in thicknesses of 10 to 40 mm. VIP cannot be cut to shape, hence connections and joints are made with conventional EPS boards. This may mean that heat bridges have to be tolerated as a result. The panels are attached to the walls with adhesive mortar or a system of rails when used as external or internal insulation.

Installation options Vacuum insulation panels are very thin and hence are very good for insulating areas below window sills and for preventing heat bridges, e.g., at floor connections. VIPs are particularly advantageous in refurbishment projects because of their minimal space requirement compared with conventional insulation materials.

VIPs are used for thermal insulation inside buildings, external wall insulation and for insulating flat roofs and floors where the available room height is restricted. The use of VIPs in the spandrel wall zones of facades avoids uneven projections into rooms.

Two aspects are important to the performance of vacuum insulation panels. VIP are expensive but they combine very good insulation properties with modest layer thickness. From an economic point of view the extra investment costs need to be balanced against a considerable gain in space. The units cannot be made to nonstandard sizes, which increases design costs.

VIP (λ = 0.004)
20 mm

Fumed silica (λ = 0.020)
100 mm

Polystyrene foam (λ = 0.035)
170 mm

Mineral wool (λ = 0.045)
200 mm

Fig. 4.14 **Comparison of insulation materials**
The evacuation of air gives vacuum insulation panels a significantly higher insulation value. Shown above are the thicknesses of various materials required to achieve a U-value of 0.2 W/m²K.

Fig. 4.15 **Comparison of U-values of vacuum insulation panels and EPS shown in relation to layer thickness**

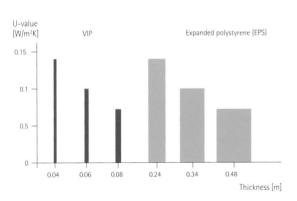

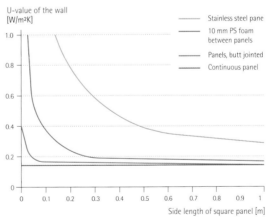

Fig. 4.16 **Panel sizes**
The graph shows the effective thermal transmittance of a VIP-insulated wall and relates it to the side length of square panels. 17.5 cm calcium silicate masonry, insulated with 3 cm VIP and 3 cm polystyrene. (After BINE)

Outside   Inside

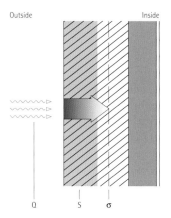

Fig. 4.17 **Penetration depth of heat and effective storage m**
The actual effective storage capacity S of a wall depends on the heat penetration depth σ for a period of 24 h. From S it is possible to calculate the surface area and mass that are necessary to be able to store a defined quantity of heat Q over a day-night cycle.

Latent heat storage – PCM

Phase change materials (PCM) are able to absorb heat and store it in the form of latent heat energy without an increase in surface temperature. This is in contrast to conventional heat storage materials. When the temperature rises a PCM changes from one physical state into another. In doing so it stores energy but its own temperature does not noticeably rise until after the phase change is complete. The temperature at which latent heat storage takes place is called the melting point. If the temperature falls below the melting point the PCM releases the stored thermal energy. This reversible process can be repeated any number of times. Salt hydrates or paraffins are normally used for PCMs, which are integrated into the materials used to construct internal features or facade components. The melting temperature creates a form of passive self-regulation, which smoothes out temperature fluctuations and peak loads. The advantages of PCM lie in their low space requirement and self-weight.

Materials PCMs with a melting temperature close to the comfort range of room air, between approximately 20 and 26 °C, can be used to increase the thermal storage mass in areas where people tend to spend time. Salt hydrates generally have a somewhat higher thermal storage ca-

pacity than paraffins, which are easier to work with but require special fire protection measures.

Using PCMs The phase change from solid to liquid prevents PCMs from playing a structural role in a building. Phase change is also accompanied by a change in volume, which presents a problem for processing the material into the finished construction product. The carrier material must have a high thermal conductivity and a large surface area so that direct exchange of heat can take place. The material may be processed in three different ways to ensure that it does not evaporate or flow out: macro-encapsulation, micro-encapsulation and immersion.

Area of application The potential of all modern commercially available PCM products is in smoothing out changes in temperature within a defined climate concept. They cannot replace a ventilation system or conventional passive measures to counteract overheating in summer. If PCMs are used in an appropriate way they can contribute to increased comfort and reduced building services plant. New lightweight construction and buildings with a high glazing fraction or facades exposed to direct sunlight are particularly suitable for PCM use, as are existing buildings with problems of high solar gain.

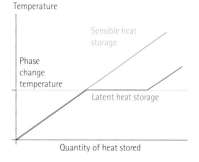

Fig. 4.18 **Heat storage of sensible and latent heat storage media**
When the phase change temperature is reached, the temperature stops increasing in the latent storage until the phase change is complete, at which time the temperature continues to increase again. The best known PCM material is water. The energy required to liquefy (melt) 1 kg of frozen (crystallised) water at 0 °C is approximately –333 kJ. As the temperature of the water hardly increases during this change of phase, the effect is described as latent (hidden) heat storage. The same amount of energy could heat cold water at 1 °C to about 80 °C, which would be sensible (perceptible) heat storage.

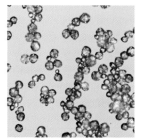

PCM internal structure

The capacity of PCM components depends largely on their quantity, the particular product, temperature range and the interchange of heat between the PCM and room air.

In a passive system PCM can be micro-encapsulated into internal walls (in the plaster or plasterboard) or macro-encapsulated above a suspended ceiling or used for buffering the solar energy entering a room behind a glass facade in order to smooth out daily temperature changes. For this to work the material must be able to release the stored energy again. Night ventilation can bring the air temperature back down below the melting temperature. The melting temperature of the PCM should be close to the maximum comfort temperature in order not to be constantly overloaded.

If it is not possible to completely discharge the PCM by night cooling then active systems can use cold energy specifically to accelerate and control the cooling process. Small fans, for example, can provide a constant flow of air over the thermal storage mass or cooling water can be pumped through integrated capillary mats. The economic feasibility of these systems is founded on the use of cheaper night tariff electricity or the generation of cold energy from a regenerative source, e.g., earth cooling. The optimum melting temperature for active systems is between 21 and 23 °C.

Other special forms include PCM heat storage as a latent heat store with water flowing through it or an intermediate PCM accumulator as a means of warming fresh air.

Material	Product	Description	PCM	Application	Melting energy, melting temperature	Dimensions, weight
Interior plaster	Maxit Clima	Machine-applied gypsum plaster single coat on internal walls	Micro-encapsulated paraffin, capsule size 5–20 µm	Passive: large surface area, thin wall or ceiling coating Active: large surface area cooling system on capillary tube mats	100 kJ/kg, 24–26 °C	–
Gypsum boards	BASF Smartboard	Gypsum board wrapped with glass-fibre non-woven fabric	Micro-encapsulated paraffin, capsule size 2–20 µm	Passive: in combination with a noncombustible gypsum board on internal walls and ceilings	330 kJ/m², 23–26 °C	15 x 2000 x 1250 mm, 11.5 kg
Granulate	Rubitherm GR	Heat storage granulate in the form of bulk fill	Paraffin bound in a silicate mineral	Passive: in voids or air-conditioned storage Active: dry subscreed as part of underfloor heating systems	72 kJ/kg approx. 28 °C	0.75 kg/l, 1–3 mm grain size
Aluminium bag	DÖRKEN Delta-Cool 24	Heat storage in bags, dimpled membrane or twin-wall sheet	Macro-encapsulated salt hydrate based on calcium hexahydrate	Passive: on metal boxes in suspended ceilings	158 kJ/kg, 22–28 °C	Bag 300 x 600 mm, 8–10 kg/m²

Tab. 4.5 **Properties and applications of various PCMs**

PCM
Gypsum plasterboards
d = 1.5 cm

A = 10.22 m²

m = 50 kg

Reinforced concrete
(2 %) steel
d = 16.9 cm

A = 3.13 m²

m = 900 kg

Brickwork
d = 8.8 cm

A = 10.74 m²

m = 1,070 kg

Solid wood
d = 5.8 cm

A = 19.3 m²

m = 330 kg

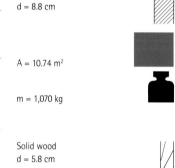

Fig. 4.19 **Comparison of the storage capacities of various construction materials**
Materials in the wall surface facing into the room can store a cooling load of 1 kWh with a temperature increase of 4 K as thermal energy. Taking the heat penetration depth σ into account a material requires a certain surface area A and mass m. The period of time considered is a 24-hour day-night cycle. The values shown for each PCM apply for a temperature increase of between 21 and 25 °C.

PCM raw material

Room operating temperature
[°C]

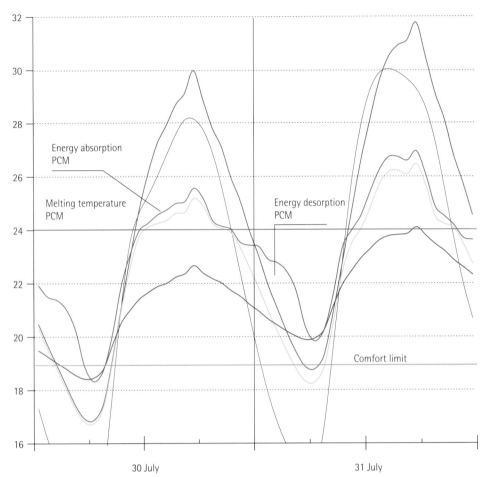

Fig. 4.20 **Dynamic graph of room temperature fluctuations for different forms of construction, based on typical values**
PCM use can considerably improve room climate in lightweight construction buildings. As the PCMs only have any effect above the melting temperature (24 °C), temperature levels are higher than for a comparable example of conventional weight construction.

—— T$_{outside}$

—— Lightweight construction

—— With PCM

—— With PCM, activated

—— Heavyweight construction

Boundary conditions to Fig. 4.20

Standard office	22.5 m²
facade	south, 70%
Solar screening	external
Ventilation day	n = 2.0–5.0 h⁻¹
Ventilation night	n = 4.0 h⁻¹
Melting temperature	24 °C
PCM equivalent capacity	600 W/Room

Energy absorption PCM

Melting temperature PCM

Energy desorption PCM

Comfort limit

30 July

31 July

Macro-encapsulated PCM in aluminium bags

Macro-encapsulated PCM

Passive heat removal

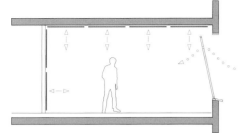

PCM in building materials

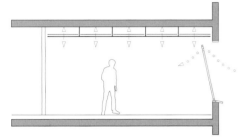

PCM in suspended ceiling

Active heat removal

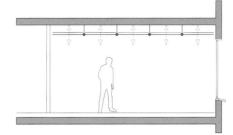

PCM in activated chilled panel sails

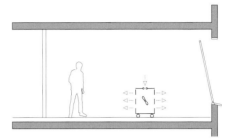

PCM in a cooling-cube

Fig. 4.21 Methods of influencing the thermal storage capacity of a room

	PCM in building materials	PCM in activated chilled panel sails	PCM in suspended ceiling	PCM in a cooling-cube	Comb. with under-floor heating, active	Gypsum boards, passive
New-build	+	+	+	–	+	+
Refurbishment	+	o	+	+	–	+
Offices	+	+	+	+	o	+
Residential	+	o	–	–	+	+
Central ventilation system	o	+	o	o	+	o
Window ventilation	+	–	+	+	o	+
High cooling loads	–	+	–	+	o	–
Low cooling loads	+	o	+	o	+	+
Comb. with solar heat	–	+	–	–	+	–

+ very suitable
o possible
– unsuitable

Tab. 4.6 Table showing suitability for use of PCM components

Macro-encapsulated PCM for heat storage in facade elements

PCM in facade elements

Solar screening

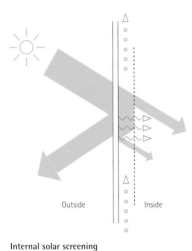

Internal solar screening

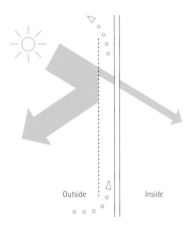

External solar screening

Fig. 4.22 **Position of solar screening**
With internal solar screening the absorbed radiation and a proportion of the reflected radiation is released as heat into the room. On the other hand, only the part of the solar radiation not reflected or absorbed by external solar screening contributes to heating up the room.

Solar screening is necessary to reduce the entry of radiation. The energy entering through a facade is determined by the shading factor F_c of the solar screening and the total solar energy transmittance g of the glazing. Attempts to reduce g-values are subject to functional and building-physical limits, whereas the F_c-value can be made very low. Adjustable solar screening permits the entry of solar radiation in winter, when it may be desirable. F_c and g are interrelated and affect the entry of daylight and the view out. Ideally solar screening should also be capable of redirecting or deflecting light and preventing glare. The effectiveness of solar screening depends to a large extent on its position. External screening can be between three and five times as efficient, although it is exposed to the weather and may have to be raised in windy conditions. Internal systems are less effective but they can be adjusted by the user and operate independently of the weather. The initial and maintenance costs are lower. Solar screening can also be installed in the glazing cavity between the panes. In this location the devices are very effective but may have a limited scope for adjustment and restrict visibility. When selecting the type of solar screening the designer must take into account the orientation and degree of transparency of the facade, its exposure to wind, daylighting requirements and visual comfort. The initial and maintenance costs are also important.

Physical aspects Solar screening generally operates using one of five physical processes: absorption, reflection, reduction, selection and transformation. Each of these principles has a different influence on the passage of diffused and direct solar radiation and on the heating up of the solar screening system. In the absorption process, light striking the solar screening is absorbed and converted into heat. Depending on the setting, the system

may block direct light alone or act on both direct and diffused light. With reflection, the system behaves like a mirror to reflect the light without heating up to any significant extent. This system can also reflect direct light alone or, when angled to close the louvres, both diffused and direct light. The system becomes an absorption system if the reflective properties are detrimentally affected by dirt or dust deposits. Reduction is based on decreasing the amount of surface area available for solar radiation to pass through, which also reduces the intensity of direct and diffused light to the same extent. Selection filters out certain bands of wavelengths of direct and diffused light. This allows the energy-rich fraction of the solar radiation to be excluded. However, there is normally some colour shift. With transformation, direct light is scattered and only diffused light penetrates the room. Some of the radiation is absorbed by the system, which leads to heating up of the solar screening.

External systems External solar screening is the most effective system because the solar radiation is blocked before it can reach the facade. However, initial and maintenance costs are higher because the system is exposed to weather and wind. In addition the controls will require a drive. In strong winds lamella systems have to be raised, and in this position can no longer provide solar screening, making additional glare protection necessary. Another way is to install moving elements that allow a clear zone to be maintained for visibility. External Venetian blinds made from aluminium, plastic or wood can achieve a shading factor F_c as low as 0.1. Disadvantages with respect to daylight use can be redressed by having differentially adjustable Venetian blinds in the skylight area. They can also redirect light. On southern facades the steep angle of incidence of the sun means that fixed systems, such as balconies, projections or loggia, can also be considered.

Vertical louvres

Horizontal louvres

Sliding shutters

Fixed solar screening

Internal systems Internal solar screening is protected from the weather, can be operated in all wind conditions and provides glare protection. The solar screening effect is considerably less than external systems. Internal solar screening can also be in the form of film roller blinds or highly reflective Venetian blinds. Solar protection films allow some visibility, with the effect that a reduced view out can be maintained. The protective effect is based on reflection and complements the absorption and reflection properties of the glazing. Internal systems can achieve F_c-values as low as 0.3; however in practice the quoted values are often exceeded because of dirt. Internal solar screening may heat up and act as a radiator, to the detriment of comfort.

Systems in the glazing cavity Movable systems within the glazing itself are highly efficient and not affected by wind. Solar screening systems within the glazing unit may be designed as fixed or moveable. Fixed systems, such as light-scattering layers, prints, textures or louvres reduce visibility and light entry. They are only suitable for locations where no view out is required. Moveable systems consisting of louvres in the glazing cavity can be manually or electrically operated and permit solar radiation conditions to be modified to suit user requirements. The louvres provide solar control and glare protection at the same time. If the drive motors for moveable solar screening in the glazing cavity fail it is often necessary to replace the whole glazing unit. Initial costs are also very high.

Reflective louvres in the glazing cavity of an insulating glazing unit can achieve, in combination with the glazing, a g_{tot}-value of 0.15. The g_{tot}-value depends on the solar angle of incidence.

Tab. 4.7 **Physical principles of solar screening systems**

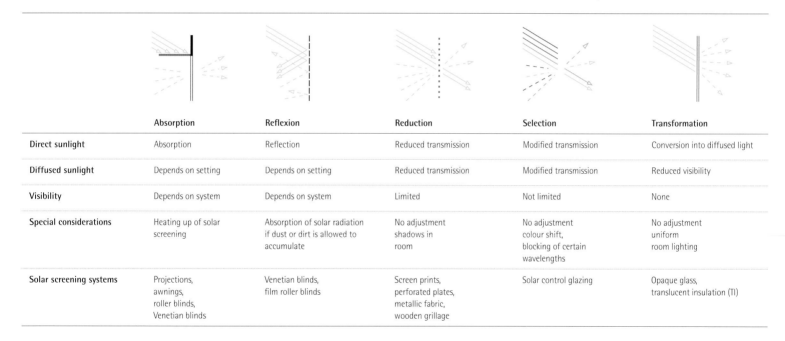

	Absorption	Reflexion	Reduction	Selection	Transformation
Direct sunlight	Absorption	Reflection	Reduced transmission	Modified transmission	Conversion into diffused light
Diffused sunlight	Depends on setting	Depends on setting	Reduced transmission	Modified transmission	Reduced visibility
Visibility	Depends on system	Depends on system	Limited	Not limited	None
Special considerations	Heating up of solar screening	Absorption of solar radiation if dust or dirt is allowed to accumulate	No adjustment shadows in room	No adjustment colour shift, blocking of certain wavelengths	No adjustment uniform room lighting
Solar screening systems	Projections, awnings, roller blinds, Venetian blinds	Venetian blinds, film roller blinds	Screen prints, perforated plates, metallic fabric, wooden grillage	Solar control glazing	Opaque glass, translucent insulation (TI)

Sliding shutters

Horizontal louvres

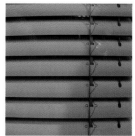

Internal louvres

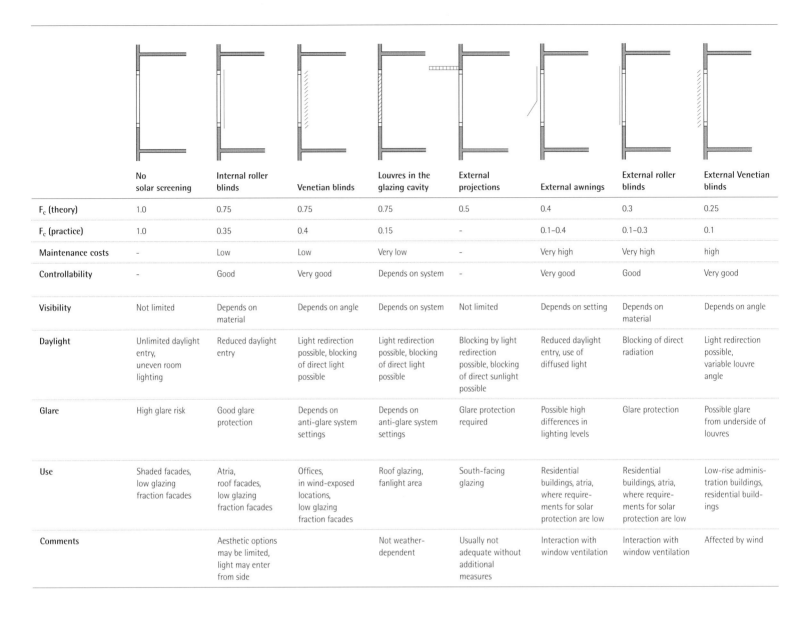

	No solar screening	Internal roller blinds	Venetian blinds	Louvres in the glazing cavity	External projections	External awnings	External roller blinds	External Venetian blinds
F_c (theory)	1.0	0.75	0.75	0.75	0.5	0.4	0.3	0.25
F_c (practice)	1.0	0.35	0.4	0.15	–	0.1–0.4	0.1–0.3	0.1
Maintenance costs	–	Low	Low	Very low	–	Very high	Very high	high
Controllability	–	Good	Very good	Depends on system	–	Very good	Good	Very good
Visibility	Not limited	Depends on material	Depends on angle	Depends on system	Not limited	Depends on setting	Depends on material	Depends on angle
Daylight	Unlimited daylight entry, uneven room lighting	Reduced daylight entry	Light redirection possible, blocking of direct light possible	Light redirection possible, blocking of direct light possible	Blocking by light redirection possible, blocking of direct sunlight possible	Reduced daylight entry, use of diffused light	Blocking of direct radiation	Light redirection possible, variable louvre angle
Glare	High glare risk	Good glare protection	Depends on anti-glare system settings	Depends on anti-glare system settings	Glare protection required	Possible high differences in lighting levels	Glare protection	Possible glare from underside of louvres
Use	Shaded facades, low glazing fraction facades	Atria, roof facades, low glazing fraction facades	Offices, in wind-exposed locations, low glazing fraction facades	Roof glazing, fanlight area	South-facing glazing	Residential buildings, atria, where requirements for solar protection are low	Residential buildings, atria, where requirements for solar protection are low	Low-rise administration buildings, residential buildings
Comments		Aesthetic options may be limited, light may enter from side		Not weather-dependent	Usually not adequate without additional measures	Interaction with window ventilation	Interaction with window ventilation	Affected by wind

Tab. 4.8 **Comparison of solar screening systems**

Fixed horizontal solar screening

Sliding shutters

External Venetian blinds

Glare protection Glare protection systems scatter direct light to create diffused light or reflect light outwards. Thus no direct sunlight reaches the working areas and great differences in lighting levels are avoided. The increasing number of computer monitors has raised the importance of visual comfort. Glare protection depends largely on the type of solar screening and the entry of daylight. The combination of external solar screening and internal anti-glare roller blinds offers the best solution for most of the year and times of day with respect to the entry of daylight and heat, glare and view out. The upper area of the glazing should still allow light to pass though it so that the room is not too dark. Therefore it is more satisfactory to have glare protection that operates progressively from the bottom up. Glare protection becomes particularly important in winter when the entry of solar radiation brings with it some desirable heat. Light entering the room from the side should be avoided because it leads to excessive luminance and may be accompanied by direct glare. If glare protection devices heat up too much they may radiate this heat into the room and reduce comfort for people in the area. Types of glare protection devices include translucent glazing, external or internal louvres, transparent and semi-transparent films or fabrics.

Internal Venetian blinds Highly reflective Venetian blinds on the room-side of glazing can provide optional glare protection. Ideally the upper areas of Venetian blinds should be designed to continue to allow daylight into the room via the ceiling. This ensures adequate brightness in the depth of the room and good luminance distribution. Some artificial light may be necessary to avoid rooms being too dark on days when there is insufficient daylight outside. Venetian blinds have the disadvantage for room users of losing their view out. Similar glare protection can also be obtained from vertical blinds.

Roller blinds Roller blinds made from reflective film or fabric greatly attenuate the light striking them. Their light transmittance is between 0 and 25%. The films are normally microperforated and therefore allow limited view out. They are generally highly reflective on the outside to prevent them from heating up excessively in sunlight. Fabrics heat up more than film because they are generally less reflective. The view out depends on the structure of the fabric.

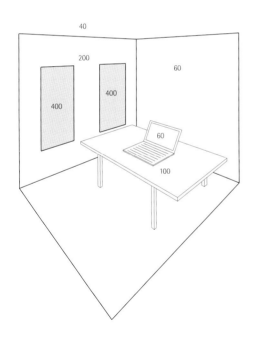

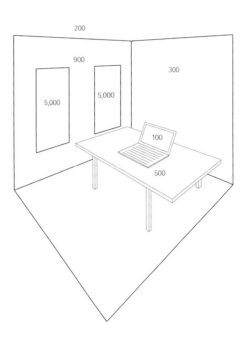

Fig. 4.23 **Typical luminance distribution in an office with film roller blinds as glare protection and in an office without glare protection** *(values in cd/m²)*

External screen   Internal louvres

Internal film

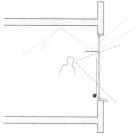

Light shelf

Light redirecting louvres

Prismatic panel

Fig. 4.24 **Forms of light redirection systems**
Light redirection systems can be placed in front of the facade or in the glazing cavity.

Natural light redirection systems

Good use of natural light cuts down the amount of electricity used to create artificial light, reduces cooling loads and leads to greater comfort. Natural light redirection systems produce uniform illumination and improve lighting conditions, particularly in the depth of the room. Lighting levels near windows are correspondingly reduced. This reduction hardly matters for the working areas near the windows. A well-designed natural light redirection system can reduce undesirable reflections and glare. These systems differ from one another in whether they direct diffused or direct light, transport light or are static or guided. Systems that change the path of direct light also do the same for indirect light from the part of the sky for which they have been designed. Depending on the system there may be synergy with solar protection. Light redirection systems can be attached inside or outside the facade. There are also systems that fit into the cavity of insulation glazing.

Functional principles All light redirection systems work by changing the course of direct or indirect outside light, or both, into the upper part of the room. The ceiling then distributes the light over the whole area of the room. For the best results from light redirection, the ceiling must be as light in colour as possible so that the light is not absorbed. Reflective surfaces such as aluminium or additional flat or curved reflectors can be attached to the ceiling. For most purposes, however, a white painted ceiling with a reflectance of 0.8–0.9 is adequate.

Controls Natural light redirection systems may be static or guided. Static systems usually redirect the diffused light from the zenith area of the sky. Mobile or guided systems require manual or automatic controls. Light-directing Venetian blinds or prismatic panels are guided to follow the course of the sun to provide optimum light redirection at all times of the year. Simple light redirection systems, such as two-part Venetian blinds in which the bottom provides shading whilst louvres at the top redirect light, can also be operated manually. Automatic guidance is advantageous for redirecting direct light because direct sunlight is always changing.

Direct light redirection systems Direct light redirection systems redirect light into the depth of the room. This method of using energy-rich bright sunlight can achieve good lighting conditions in the depth of the room. The best results are produced in combination with shading so that the risk of overheating in the room is reduced. With direct light redirection systems there is a higher risk of glare from the fanlight area than with a diffused light system. The possibility of overheating in rooms should be borne in mind with direct sunlight redirection. The risk is lower with low energy diffused light. A simple system is an external Venetian blind in which the angle of louvres in the top part of the blind can be separately adjusted.

Construction type	Principle	Efficiency of light redirection	Comment
Reflector principle	Reflection	Very good to good	Available in many versions
Prismatic system	Retro-reflection (direct), redirection (diffused or direct)	Good	Efficiency increased in combination with Venetian blinds
Holographic system	Retro-reflection (direct), redirection (diffused or direct)	Good	Almost no availability
Light diffusing system	Light diffusing	Low	No visibility

Tab. 4.9 **Overview of the effect and efficiency of light redirection systems**

Light deflection prism panels on the roof

Heliostats

Light shelf

Room lighting atmosphere with natural light redirection

The top part directs light; the bottom part provides shade. Fixed horizontal and guided louvres following the course of the sun can also perform these functions. Reflective horizontal surfaces in front of the facade in the fanlight area are able to throw light onto the ceiling and, when the sun is high, prevent glare when looking out from the area below them. They act in this way as solar screening in the summer half-year.

Systems in the glazing cavity can be designed so that they allow only the light from a certain part of the sky to enter the room. This allows the energy-rich radiation from the high sun to be blocked. Other systems, on the other hand, redirect light from the whole sky into the room.

Diffused light redirection systems Diffused light sky conditions tend to predominate in central Europe and natural light entering the room is often inadequate; light redirection systems offer a means of improving this situation. Diffused light is low in energy and reduces the risk of overheating in the room. Glare is also less likely with diffused light redirection. It is more difficult to redirect diffused light because it arrives from all directions. Therefore these systems are designed to concentrate on the zenith light, which is always more intensive. Diffused light redirection systems can improve the lighting conditions at northern facades or blocked-in facades oriented in other directions. They can act as solar screening on heavily insolated facades by cutting out direct sunlight.

Diffused light redirection systems are ideally attached in front of the facade or in the cavity of insulation glazing. Simple systems for noninsolated areas include reflective surfaces such as light shelves, which direct diffused zenith light into the room. Another possibility for redirecting zenith light is holographic optical elements (HOE).

Light transport systems Light transport systems reflect light several times. The light is "transported" for example by reflectors (heliostats), highly reflective ducts (solar pipes), anidolic systems or glass-fibre elements. They are mainly used in rooms that do not have a direct view out.

Light diffusing systems These systems do not redirect light in the accepted sense. They break up direct light into diffused light and thus provide a low glare option for people near the facade. With more intense direct sunlight even these systems can result in glare. Light diffusing systems are generally used in skylight areas because of the turbidity of their glass.

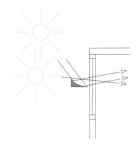

Fig. 4.25 **Reflector**
Light redirection by Venetian blinds, light shelves and heliostats relies on the principle of equal angles of incidence and reflection..

Fig. 4.26 **Prismatic panel**
Prismatic systems provide selective solar screening. Direct solar radiation within a certain range of angle is refracted and reflected. Zenith light is deflected into the room.

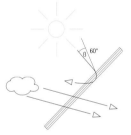

Fig. 4.27 **Hologram**
Holograms selectively deflect sunlight striking them or deflect it into defined areas within the building or block it. Holograms work by bending light. Special photographic techniques can minimise spectral scattering of the light so that the bent light appears white.

External prismatic panel

Perforated light redirection louvres

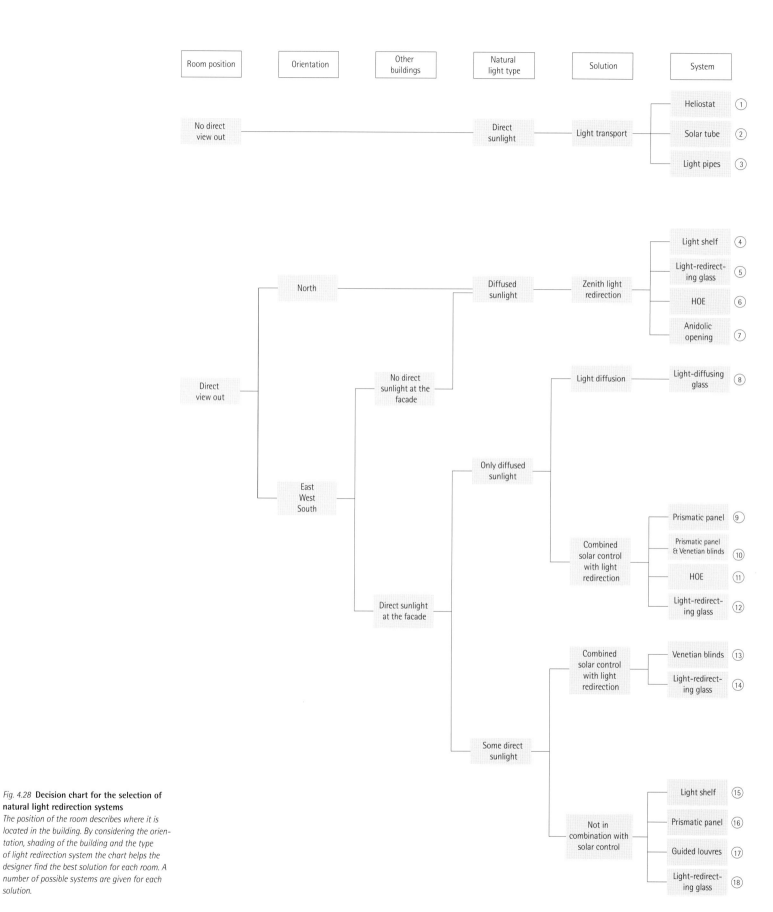

Room position	Orientation	Other buildings	Natural light type	Solution	System

No direct view out — Direct sunlight — Light transport — Heliostat ①
Solar tube ②
Light pipes ③

North — Diffused sunlight — Zenith light redirection — Light shelf ④
Light-redirecting glass ⑤
HOE ⑥
Anidolic opening ⑦

Direct view out

East West South — No direct sunlight at the facade

Only diffused sunlight — Light diffusion — Light-diffusing glass ⑧

Combined solar control with light redirection — Prismatic panel ⑨
Prismatic panel & Venetian blinds ⑩
HOE ⑪
Light-redirecting glass ⑫

Direct sunlight at the facade

Combined solar control with light redirection — Venetian blinds ⑬
Light-redirecting glass ⑭

Some direct sunlight

Not in combination with solar control — Light shelf ⑮
Prismatic panel ⑯
Guided louvres ⑰
Light-redirecting glass ⑱

Fig. 4.28 **Decision chart for the selection of natural light redirection systems**
The position of the room describes where it is located in the building. By considering the orientation, shading of the building and the type of light redirection system the chart helps the designer find the best solution for each room. A number of possible systems are given for each solution.

Mirror

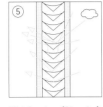

Highly reflective pipe

Fibre optic cable

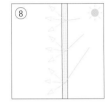

Aluminium light shelf

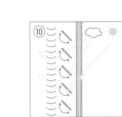

"Fish" system (Okasolar)

White light hologram

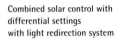

Anidolic opening

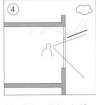

Opaque glass

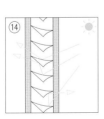

Solar control prisms

Solar control prisms and
reflective louvres

White light hologram;
cutting out direct light glare

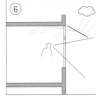

Reflective louvres

Combined solar control with
differential settings
with light redirection system

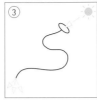

Solar screening,
with differential settings

Y-glass (Okasolar)

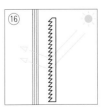

Aluminium light shelf

Direct light prisms

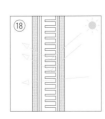

Fixed rotatable
horizontal louvres

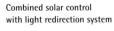

Laser-cut panel

Cold facade

Warm facade

Fig. 4.29 **Integration of photovoltaic modules into facades**

Photovoltaics

Solar cells are doped silicon semiconductors that create electricity when light strikes them. Between 20 and 40 individual cells are connected in series to form strings, which are embedded in 1.0 x 0.5 m modules. The voltage obtained from a single photovoltaic cell is approximately 0.6 volt and the power produced is proportional to the intensity of solar irradiance and the area of cells. For an irradiance of 900 W/m^2 a 10 x 10 cm cell supplies a current of about 3 amps. The best alignment of the modules depends on the orientation and the geographical latitude of their location. Photovoltaic systems can be designed to be installed away from their buildings in solar parks or incorporated into building roofs or facades to take advantage of economic and constructional synergies. Photovoltaic systems can operate autonomously or be connected to the national grid. Grid-connected systems use the public supply network as storage. If the solar electricity generated is more than that required by the building then the excess is fed into the grid. The in-

verter is the connection between the solar cells and the AC power grid.

Alignment and yield The annual global solar radiation, orientation and efficiency of the solar modules are the important factors in the generation of solar power. The annual incident global solar radiation falling on a horizontal surface on the ground is approximately 1200 kWh/m^{2}a. Alignment due south at an inclination of about 30° is recommended for higher yields, with this arrangement, for example at Munich, an irradiation of about 1300 kWh/m^{2}a can be assumed. This angle of inclination can normally only be achieved on sloping roofs. With a vertical south-facing facade the yield is still approximately 67%, whilst for a fully eastern or western orientation the figure is approximately 60%. Typical efficiencies are between 12 to 17% for crystalline and 5 to 8% for amorphous silica cells. Physics dictate that no further significant increases in efficiency can be expected. Efficiency reduces as temperature increases.

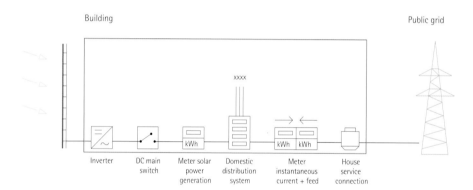

Fig. 4.30 **Idealised diagram of a photovoltaic system integrated into the public power grid**
When connected in parallel with the public power grid the energy created by solar generators is fed into the network. The solar inverter is the connection between the solar cells and the AC power grid. The solar inverter transforms the direct current from the modules into network-compatible 230 volt alternating current. Grid-connected systems use the public supply network as storage. If the electricity generated is more than that required by the building then the excess is fed into the grid. During the night and in periods of bad weather the building takes power from the grid.

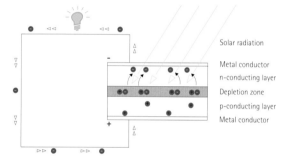

Fig. 4.31 **Functional principles of a solar cell**
Solar radiation striking the module creates two differently charged layers. The n-conducting layer has an increased number of electrons. The p-conducting layer has electron-holes. A boundary layer forms between the two layers. An electric field is created in this boundary layer, the depletion region. The solar energy releases electrons from their bonds in the atoms and the free electrons are moved by the electric field to the top side. Positively charged holes accumulate on the bottom side. A voltage builds up between the two sides. The excess electrons can flow through metal contacts on the top and bottom back to the bottom layer and fill the electron holes there.

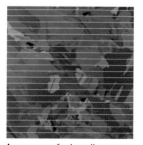

Appearance of solar cells

Solar modules are extremely sensitive to shade. The series arrangement of the solar cells means that the output of the whole module is determined by the cell with the lowest irradiance, so that even small shadows have a very negative effect. Central European locations have diffused light conditions for about 50% of the time and therefore sun-tracking control is normally not economically viable.

Integration into the facade Photovoltaic modules can be installed into cold or warm facades, glazing and roof coverings and designed to provide solar protection. Fully tempered glass provides the module with breakage and weather resistance. Integration into the building skin provides additional weather resistance, sound and thermal insulation and effective solar protection. Where there is a gap between the module and facade it can be used to preheat outside air for the supply air for room conditioning.

Cold facades are designed as rear-ventilated facades. Photovoltaic modules can be used to form the outside cladding, which is exposed to the weather. Modules can be integrated into mullion and transom construction or supported by point fixings. Warm facades have the modules integrated into their insulation glazing units. Semi-transparent modules are proving interesting. These modules reduce the amount of radiation entering the room yet maintain the view out.

In this situation the lack of rear ventilation causes the modules to heat up. Thin-film modules are therefore most suitable for warm facades as, in contrast to crystalline cells, their efficiency remains almost constant with increasing temperature. Thin-film solar modules manufactured from amorphous silicon can be processed into insulation-filled sandwich panels. These panels can be used to form the whole of a facade, for example on industrial buildings.

When working as shading elements with an optimum alignment to the sun and very good rear ventilation these photovoltaic modules can achieve particularly high yields. The systems can be fixed or moveable.

	Efficiency [%]
Monocrystalline silicon cells	15–17
Polycrystalline silicon cells	12–14
Amorphous silicon cells	5–8

Tab. 4.10 **Efficiencies of various cell types**

	Minimum yield [%]
Well-ventilated facade	approx. 4
Poorly ventilated facade	approx. 5
Integrated into facade, no rear-ventilation	approx. 9

Tab. 4.11 **Average estimated minimum yield for various arrangements of crystalline solar cells**

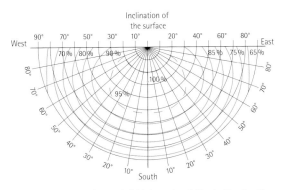

Fig. 4.32 **Reduction of annual yield shown in relation to the elevation angle and orientation of the PV system**
The values given correspond to a location at latitude 51 °N.

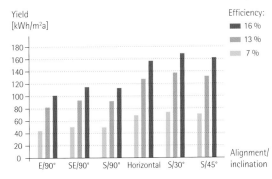

Fig. 4.33 **Annual yield of PV modules shown in relation to orientation and efficiency**
The yields assume a level of global solar radiation of 1050 kWh/m² and a location at a latitude of approximately 51 °N.

Facade-integrated PV modules

Residential Development, Hard
Prefabricated

Three five-storey blocks were constructed in a mixture of materials in Hard, Vorarlberg, Austria by the VOGEWOSI housing association.

The apartment blocks illustrate an interesting construction concept: Steel and concrete are used for the load-bearing members in the skeletal frame whilst all the non-load-bearing components are made of lightweight materials. This mixed form of construction exploits the advantages of the different materials, viz., the excellent load-bearing capacity of steel columns, the efficient sound insulation and thermal storage properties of concrete ceilings and the flexibility of lightweight internal walls. The facade is made up of prefabricated modular timber frame elements with an external skin of untreated larch. The reasons for adopting this form of construction were firstly considerations of architectural form and secondly the following advantages. The high degree of prefabrication results in a considerable shortening of construction time. The thermal insulation properties of the wall (U-value 0.15 W/m²K) relate to a wall thickness of 40 cm. The multiple layers making up the skin achieve a good level of sound insulation. In addition the untreated timber facade, which is protected by fire aprons, has a very long service life with no major maintenance being required for at least 50 years. The outer layer is easy to replace and presents no disposal difficulties.

The external wall construction follows the typical modern timber construction principle of providing separate functional layers for protection against wind and weather, thermal insulation, airtightness, moisture diffusion resistance, installation space and internal cladding. This differentiation offers the option of easy replacement of the external layers but requires high standards of design and construction at the interfaces with other components.

Horizontal sliding shutters of coated aluminium sheet are an important architectural design element in the facade but also provide optimum shading and flexible light control. The shutters on the south facade incorporate photovoltaics.

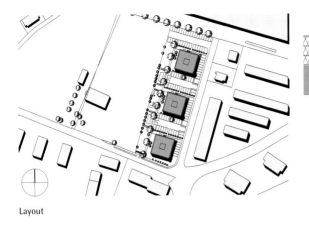

Layout

Plan

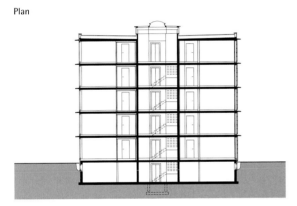

Section

Facade section at a window

Facade section at a timber element

Horizontal facade section

Fig. 4.34 **Layout**
The residential development is near the centre of the suburb and surrounded by multi-storey housing.

Fig. 4.35 **Plan**
The blocks have four apartments per floor in a space-saving arrangement with the wet cells located in the central zone.

Fig. 4.36 **Section**
The buildings are almost cubic in shape, which gives a very good surface to volume ratio.

Fig. 4.37 **Layout**
Facade section at a timber element
2 cm   vertical board
4 cm   horizontal battening
3 cm   vertical battening
1.6 cm DWD board
16 cm   wall panel 6/16
*   with insulation between*
1.2 cm chipboard
*   vapour barrier*
5 cm   horizontal battening
*   with insulation between*
1.5 cm plasterboard

Fig. 4.38 **wall construction**
Facade section at a window
Shutter 88/253 cm
Anti-fall laminated safety glass 12 mm
2-pane insulation glazing unit
(U-Wert 1.1 W/m²K)

Fig. 4.39 **Prefabrication**
Prefabricated timber frame wall elements are installed along with precast concrete fire apron units.

Fig. 4.40 **External view**

Completion: 2003
Use: Apartments
Client: Vorarlberger gemeinnützige Wohnungsbau-
u. Siedlungs GmbH, A-6850 Dornbirn
Architect: DI Hermann Kaufmann
and DI Werner Wertaschnigg
Building services: Kurt Prautsch, Schruns
Energy concept: DI Dr. Lothar Künz, Hard

Flight Test Facility, IBP Holzkirchen
Membrane structure

Pneumatically stabilised membrane cushion systems represent a particularly innovative form of lightweight structures and are increasingly catching the eye of the public. More and more leisure complexes are based on this principle, which allows the designer to create delicate yet long-span structures.

At the Fraunhofer-Institut für Bauphysik in Holzkirchen a trial membrane cushion roof was chosen for the new Flight Test Facility (FTF), which allowed the properties in terms of building physics of this very novel and forward-looking form of construction to be examined.

Building skin The hanger is approximately 30 m long and almost 30 m wide. Nine laminated timber arched beams span the 10 m high hall and the gaps between them are filled with a three-layer membrane cushion made from transparent ethylene-tetrafluorethylene. The cushions extend from the base of the hanger to the ridge and, at a pressure of 400 Pa, they are able to resist the loads imposed by the weather. An aluminium clamping profile secures the cushions to the timber substructure. The roof is completely constructed from ethylene-tetrafluorethylene (ETFE) cushions, as are even the smoke and heat extraction vents.

This material is particularly weatherproof and yet it has a high light transmittance, even for UV-light. Over 90% of the sunlight striking the membrane passes through it. The outer membrane is covered with small silver-coloured points in order to reduce the large amounts of solar energy entering the building in summer, without destroying the appearance of transparence. Although 65% of the whole membrane surface is covered in this way the membrane cushion is milky but transparent.

Building physics The high transparence, the low material thicknesses and the large but varying distance between the individual membrane layers provide this type of wall and roof system with special characteristics in terms of building physics, which can lead to problems if this is not allowed for in the engineering design. This is particularly important for thermal insulation in winter and summer, moisture protection, acoustic behaviour and room climate comfort. These aspects are therefore the subject of ongoing scientific research.

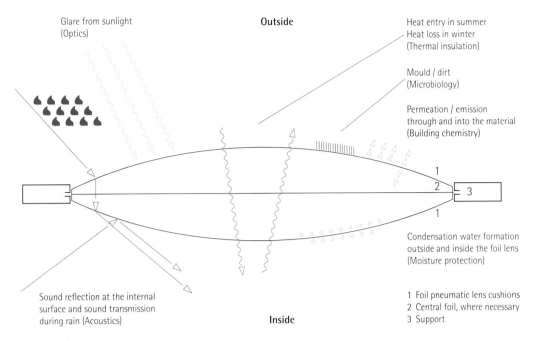

Glare from sunlight
(Optics)

Outside

Heat entry in summer
Heat loss in winter
(Thermal insulation)

Mould / dirt
(Microbiology)

Permeation / emission
through and into the material
(Building chemistry)

1
2   3
1

Condensation water formation
outside and inside the foil lens
(Moisture protection)

1 Foil pneumatic lens cushions
2 Central foil, where necessary
3 Support

Sound reflection at the internal
surface and sound transmission
during rain (Acoustics)

Inside

Building physics, special aspects

Fig. 4.41 **Building physics, special aspects**
*The small material thicknesses, the large cavities
between the membranes and the high light transparence result in considerable movement of heat,
through convection and radiation. The thermal
conductivity of the clamping profiles therefore
plays an important role.*
*The sound transmission and reflection properties
of these low-mass systems are of interest from
the point of view of acoustics. The noise generated
during periods of rain is particularly significant.
Secondary effects like condensation and mould
growth due to inadequate thermal design are
being investigated, as are the effects that permeation and emissions have on membranes.*

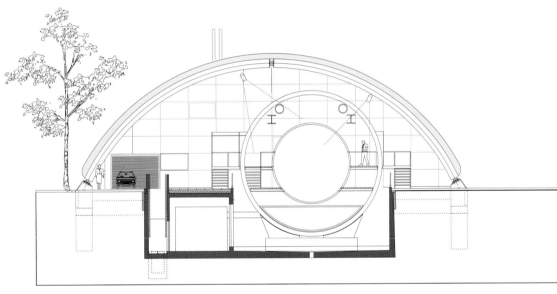

Section

Fig. 4.42 **Cross-section**
*The cross-section shows the FTF hanger looking
west. The vacuum ducts for the flight test facility (shown as round elements) are not centrally
placed in the hangar because of the demands on
space but are pushed into the northern part of
the hanger.*

Fig. 4.43 **External view of the FTF
hanger after completion**
*The gaps between the beams are filled with mem-
brane cushions. The facade surfaces at the gable
are made of unplastered cellular glass insulation.*

Fig. 4.44 **Internal view of the FTF hanger**
*Laminated timber structure of the flight test facil-
ity from the inside. In spite of the printed surface,
the impression from the inside of transparence
is not lost.*

Completion: 2005
Use: Membrane cushion trial roof (roof of the new
flight test hanger at the IBP)
Client: Fraunhofer-Gesellschaft zur Förderung
der angewandten Forschung e.V.
Architect: HENN Architekten
Timber structure: Wiehag
Membrane roof system: Covertex, Obing
Gable: Cellular glass insulation

Facade interactions

"The future of architecture is not architectural. It is not our inner knowledge that will resolve the crisis of architecture. The solution will resolve the crisis of architecture. The solution does not lie hidden in the codicils of Alberti, Piranesi, Lequeu or Ledoux. It is not important to know which traces to follow, which maestro to worship, which architecture to impose or which architects to banish. Architecture must go beyond its frontiers, give its elitist guardians a good shaking up and cease to be a privilege that no social revolution will ever abolish. The role of architects is to liberate their muse.

"For this reason they must express themselves in all media, but above all through construction: They must enter into harmony with a totally different culture environment and drink of the fountains of a whole civilisation. From now on, architecture must have significance. It must speak, relate, question, if necessary in detriment (and it often is) to technological purity, to constructed tradition, to conformity with references to cultural models (whether these be classical or modern in origin).

"Architecture must address the spirit rather than the eye: translate a living civilisation rather than a legacy. From this point of view the future of architecture is more literary than architectural, more linguistic, than formal. If architecture becomes transformed into this medium to convey ideas, to transmit meanings through space and volume, then the architect becomes a person who speaks (with construction as his language) to those who are going to live in the space and volumes that he defines. What he says, what he chooses to say, is at least as interesting as his form of saying it.

"The scope of architecture should be extended to include the definition of the vocabulary of new districts and the directions which urban modifications should take. In those places where city planning regulations are applied today, where technocratic rules govern, where the censorship of good taste is all powerful, architecture can spring up only by mistake. What to do then? Construct. In the most significant way. In 90% of the cases critical, provocative, denouncing, interrogating, ironic stances must be adopted. This way every building will raise a question as to what its nature should or could have been."

Jean Nouvel

Source: Excerpts from "Les Cahiers de la Recherche Architecturale", no. 6–7, 1980

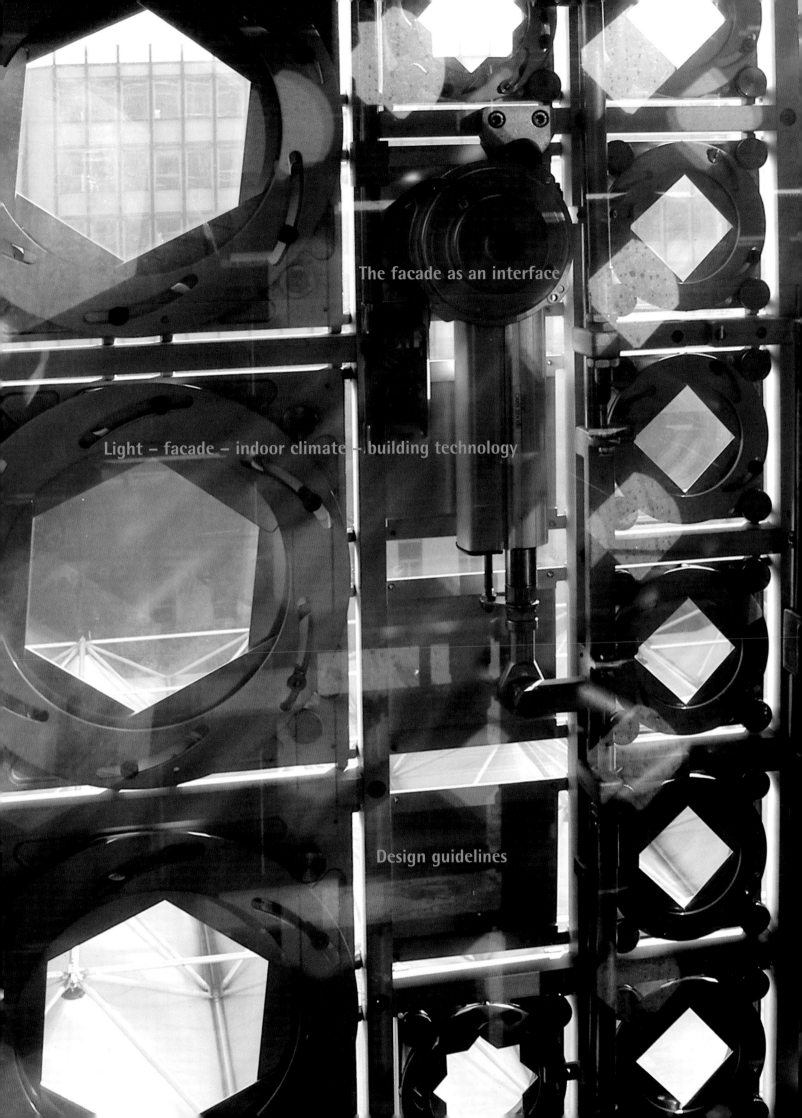

The facade as an interface

Light – facade – indoor climate – building technology

Design guidelines

The role of a facade with respect to energy and indoor climate is to bring indoor requirements into harmony to the greatest possible extent with the dynamically changing conditions outdoors. The better a facade performs this task, the smaller is the cost of the building services technology and energy required for room conditioning.

Outdoors
The situation outdoors is governed by solar radiation, outdoor air temperature, wind speed, noise load and the local microclimate. These factors interact greatly with one another and therefore the building concept always has to consider each one on its own merits.

Indoors
In order that the user inside the building feels comfortable, limits on temperature and air humidity must be set, good lighting and ventilation ensured and noise and pollutants minimised. In addition, room temperatures and daylight provision, solar radiation conditions and ventilation can be widely varied to suit the requirements of the user so that virtually all individual wishes can be fulfilled. The view out and with that the user's reference to the outside world are also important for a feeling of well-being.

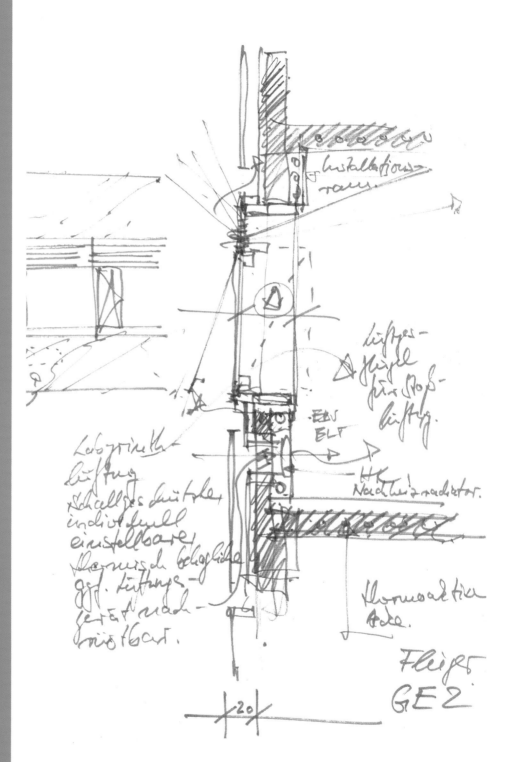

Sketch: Stefan Niese, 2006

The facade as an interface

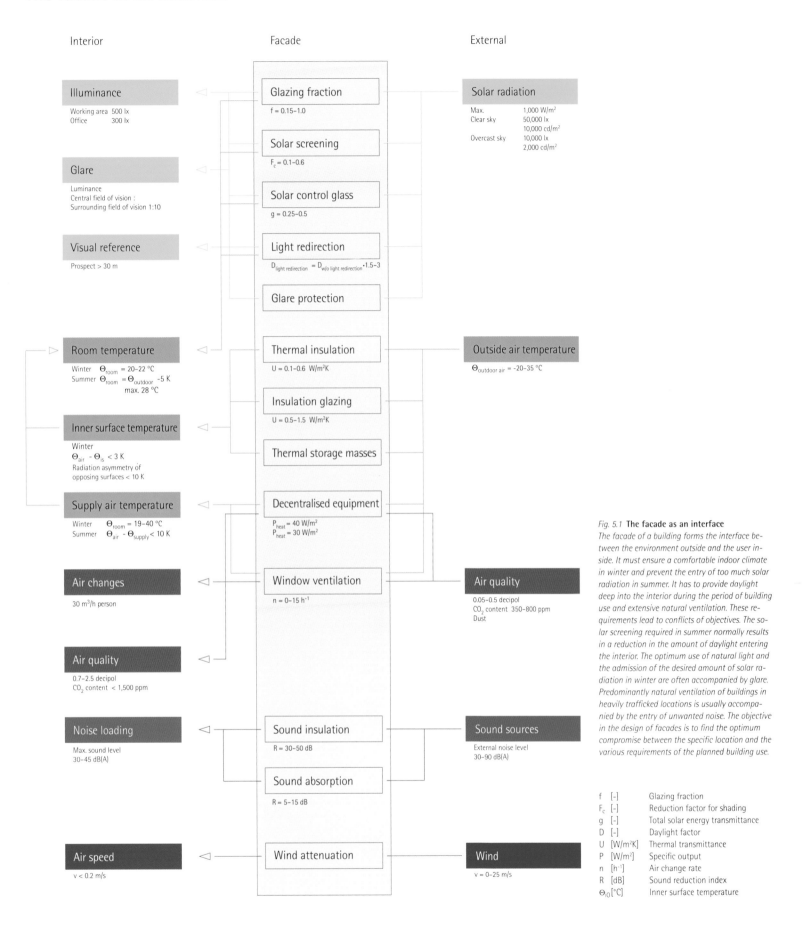

Interior

Illuminance
Working area 500 lx
Office 300 lx

Glare
Luminance
Central field of vision :
Surrounding field of vision 1:10

Visual reference
Prospect > 30 m

Room temperature
Winter Θ_{room} = 20–22 °C
Summer Θ_{room} = $\Theta_{outdoor}$ –5 K
max. 28 °C

Inner surface temperature
Winter
$\Theta_{air} - \Theta_{is} < 3$ K
Radiation asymmetry of
opposing surfaces < 10 K

Supply air temperature
Winter Θ_{room} = 19–40 °C
Summer $\Theta_{air} - \Theta_{supply} < 10$ K

Air changes
30 m³/h person

Air quality
0.7–2.5 decipol
CO_2 content < 1,500 ppm

Noise loading
Max. sound level
30–45 dB(A)

Air speed
v < 0.2 m/s

Facade

Glazing fraction
f = 0.15–1.0

Solar screening
F_c = 0.1–0.6

Solar control glass
g = 0.25–0.5

Light redirection
$D_{light\ redirection} = D_{w/o\ light\ redirection} \cdot 1.5–3$

Glare protection

Thermal insulation
U = 0.1–0.6 W/m²K

Insulation glazing
U = 0.5–1.5 W/m²K

Thermal storage masses

Decentralised equipment
P_{heat} = 40 W/m²
P_{heat} = 30 W/m²

Window ventilation
n = 0–15 h⁻¹

Sound insulation
R = 30–50 dB

Sound absorption
R = 5–15 dB

Wind attenuation

External

Solar radiation
Max. 1,000 W/m²
Clear sky 50,000 lx
10,000 cd/m²
Overcast sky 10,000 lx
2,000 cd/m²

Outside air temperature
$\Theta_{outdoor\ air}$ = –20–35 °C

Air quality
0.05–0.5 decipol
CO_2 content 350–800 ppm
Dust

Sound sources
External noise level
30–90 dB(A)

Wind
v = 0–25 m/s

Fig. 5.1 **The facade as an interface**
The facade of a building forms the interface between the environment outside and the user inside. It must ensure a comfortable indoor climate in winter and prevent the entry of too much solar radiation in summer. It has to provide daylight deep into the interior during the period of building use and extensive natural ventilation. These requirements lead to conflicts of objectives. The solar screening required in summer normally results in a reduction in the amount of daylight entering the interior. The optimum use of natural light and the admission of the desired amount of solar radiation in winter are often accompanied by glare. Predominantly natural ventilation of buildings in heavily trafficked locations is usually accompanied by the entry of unwanted noise. The objective in the design of facades is to find the optimum compromise between the specific location and the various requirements of the planned building use.

f	[–]	Glazing fraction
F_c	[–]	Reduction factor for shading
g	[–]	Total solar energy transmittance
D	[–]	Daylight factor
U	[W/m²K]	Thermal transmittance
P	[W/m²]	Specific output
n	[h⁻¹]	Air change rate
R	[dB]	Sound reduction index
Θ_{i0}	[°C]	Inner surface temperature

Outdoor conditions

Solar radiation

The inclination of the Earth's axis causes the apparent path of the sun to change throughout the year. As a result the solar angle of incidence and intensity of radiation on facades of any orientation also vary. The angle of azimuth is always the same for any particular time of day. Insolation is considerably less in winter than in summer. In winter, only the southern facade receives any significant solar radiation. In summer, the east and west facades receive high insolation. Considerably higher levels of insolation occur in September than in March. Even the north facade receives significant solar radiation in summer.

Data - reference climate, Germany

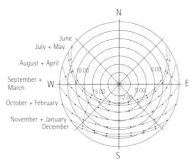

Sun-path diagram, latitude 51° north

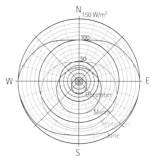

Average monthly insolation on a vertical surface

Temperature

Graph of outdoor air temperature over the year for the test reference year Würzburg

Outdoor air temperature depends on the amount of solar radiation and the temperature of the air masses moving into the area. Outdoor air temperature influences transmission and ventilation heat losses in winter, unwanted heat entry and the available cooling potential in summer.

During most of the year, outdoor air temperatures remain between –5 °C and 25 °C. Extremely low or high temperatures occur only for about 6% of the period of building use.

Night air temperatures in summer are important in improving thermal conditions in buildings with night cooling. The most unfavourable situation is hot days followed by high night air temperatures. This situation occurs on about fifteen days in summer.

Outdoor air temperatures are important for natural ventilation. If they are too low, it can result in comfort problems. If too high, heat builds up in the building. For about 64% of the period of building use it is perfectly possible to provide ventilation through the facade. If the way the supply air is introduced into the room is optimised then this period can be increased up to 90%. For 2% of the period of use, the building is too cold, whilst too much heat enters for 4% of the time.

Data - TRY Würzburg

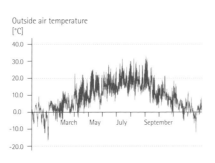

Graph of outdoor air temperature

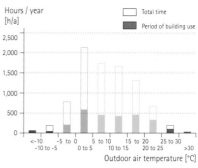

Frequency distribution of outdoor air temperatures

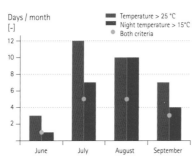

Analysis by day of temperature distribution in summer

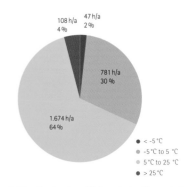

Possibility of natural ventilation during the period of building use

Sound

The noise load at the building location has a considerable influence on the ventilation and facade concepts. The noise load reduces with increasing distance to the source. For a point source this reduction is twice as much as for a linear source..

The following formula can be used for calculating the reduction of sound in free field conditions:
Linear sound source: $L_{P1} - L_{P2} = 10 \cdot \lg d/d_0$
Point sound source: $L_{P1} - L_{P2} = 20 \cdot \lg r/r_0$

L_{P1} Sound level of the sound source [dB(A)]
L_{P2} Sound level [dB(A)]
r,d Distance to sound source [m]
$r_0 = 0.282$ m, $d_0 = 0.282$ m

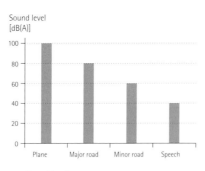

Sound level

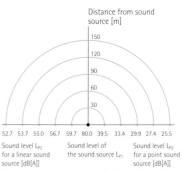

Sound propagation in free field conditions

Fig. 5.2 **Design-relevant factors in the outside environment**

Requirements for the conditions inside buildings

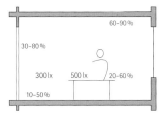

Illuminance and reflectivity

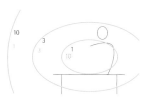

Luminance distribution

Light

The illuminance on and reflectivity of a surface determine its luminance. The required illuminance depends on the type of visual task. A value of 500 lx is recommended for offices. Luminance distributions of 10:3:1 for the visual task area, the immediate surroundings and the more distant field of vision respectively can help ensure high visual comfort.

DIN EN 12464-1, DIN 5035-7

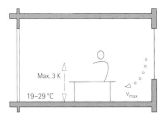

Floor temperature, vertical temperature gradient and air speed

	Winter	Summer
T_{op}	20–24 °C	23–26 °C
$v_{air, max}$	0.16 m/s	0.19 m/s

Room climate

Temperature

Floor temperature plays a significant role in thermal comfort. The temperature difference between the head and foot zones should not exceed 3 K. The room operating temperature and air speed are the decisive factors for thermal comfort indoors. Asymmetrical distribution of radiation temperature in the room due to excessive temperature differences of opposing surfaces can lead to discomfort. High temperature differences between air and surfaces can create draughts. Higher air temperatures can compensate for low surface temperatures to a certain extent.

DIN EN ISO 7730

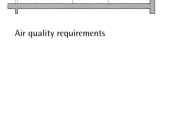

Air quality requirements

	olf	Air changes [h^{-1}]
Low odour load	4.4	1.5
Medium odour load	6.6	3.5
High odour load	8.8	6

Room volume: 67 m³

Air changes with different odour loadings

Ventilation

The required rate of air change for a room can be calculated from the odour loading of the room air. If a room has few polluting materials and a low proportion of smokers, it will require a lower rate of air change to produce good air quality. Other sources of pollutants include electrical equipment and ventilation systems.

Sound level and reverberation time T

	R [dB]	dB(A)
Window closed	30	50
Window ajar	15	65
Window open	5	75

Sound source: noisy street, 80 dB(A)

Sound reduction and sound level in a room

Sound

The sound level in the room must not interfere with communication or concentration. A value of 30–45 dB(A) is a desirable maximum in offices. Reverberation time is influenced by all the materials in the room and the room volume. From 40 dB(A), a difference of 10 dB(A) indicates a doubling or halving of sound volume. At less than 40 dB(A) even lower changes in sound level are perceived as a doubling of sound volume.

Fig. 5.3 Overview of indoor comfort criteria

Physical processes at facades and reference values

Transmission heat loss

Transmission heat loss is the energy loss due to heat conducted through the building skin. It is mainly determined by the thermal transmittances (U-values) of the individual components of the building exterior and the difference between indoor and outdoor temperatures. Transparent building components have composite U-values for the complete system of frame and glazed parts.

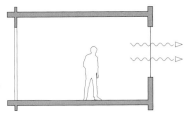

Transmission heat loss $Q_{Component}$

$$Q_{component} = A_{component} \cdot U_{component} \cdot \Delta\Theta \cdot t \qquad [Wh]$$

$A_{component}$ Area of component [m²]
$U_{component}$ U-value of component [W/m²K]
$\Delta\Theta$ Temperature difference indoor/outdoor [K]
t Time [h]

	U [W/m²K]
2-pane insulation glazing	1.4
3-pane insulation glazing	0.7
New build to EnEV (wall)	< 0.35
Low energy house (wall)	< 0.25
Passive house (wall)	< 0.15

Ventilation heat loss

Ventilation heat loss is the energy loss arising from ventilation in winter. It depends largely on air exchange and the difference between indoor and outdoor temperatures. In buildings with high rates of air change, ventilation heat loss is the biggest factor in total heat loss.

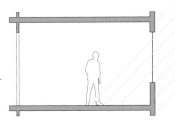

Ventilation heat loss $Q_{component}$

$$Q_{component} = V_{room} \cdot n \cdot C_{component} \cdot \Delta\Theta \cdot t \qquad [Wh]$$

V_{room} Room volume [m³]
$C_{component}$ Thermal capacity of air = 0.34 Wh/m³K
n Air change rate [h⁻¹]
$\Delta\Theta$ Temperature difference indoor/outdoor [K]
t Time [h]

	n [h⁻¹]
Windows and doors closed	0–0.5
Windows ajar	0.3–1.5
Windows half-open	5–10
Windows fully open	10–15
Opposing windows and doors open	> 40

Total solar energy transmittance

The total solar energy transmittance of a facade depends on the energy transmittance of the glazing, the glazing fraction and the reduction factor of the solar screening. The latter must be calculated specifically in each case for internal systems, as the energy transmittance depends on the reflectivity of the solar screening and glazing and the absorption properties of the glazing.

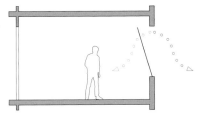

Total solar energy transmittance g_{tot}

$$g_{tot} = g \cdot F_c \cdot f \qquad [-]$$

g Solar energy transmittance glazing [-]
F_c Reduction factor of solar screening [-]
f Glazing fraction facade [-]

	g [-]
2-pane insulation glazing	0.6
3-pane insulation glazing	0.4
2-pane solar control glazing	0.3

	F_c [-]
Solar screening raised	1
External solar screening	0.1
External solar screening	0.5

Daylight factor

The daylight factor defines the ratio of the illuminance on a horizontal plane in the room and the illuminance on a horizontal plane in the open air under a completely overcast sky. A rough estimate of the room depth which could be provided with daylight from a side window is 1.5 times the window lintel height from the floor.

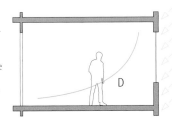

Daylight factor D

$$D = E_p / E_a \cdot 100 \qquad [\%]$$

E_p Illuminance in the room [lx]
E_a Illuminance in the open [lx]

Lighting depth in the room
$$\text{Lighting depth} = 1.5 \cdot h_{\text{lintel height}} \qquad [m]$$

$h_{\text{lintel height}}$ Height of underside of lintel above floor [m]

	D = 1 %	D = 5 %
Overcast sky (10,000 lx)	100 lx	500 lx

Boundary layer at the facade

In summer, depending on reflection conditions and colours, the temperature of a facade surface can rise to 40–80 °C. This rise in temperature heats the air directly in front of the facade and causes it to move upwards along the facade surface. Depending on wind conditions, this boundary layer may be several metres thick and 4–7 °C above the outdoor air temperature.

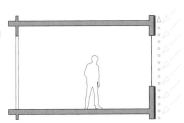

Temperature of boundary layer at the facade $\Theta_{\text{boundary layer}}$

$$\Theta_{\text{boundary layer}} = \Theta_a + 7\ ^\circ C \qquad [^\circ C]$$

Temperature of boundary layer at the facade in wind $\Theta_{\text{boundary layer, wind}}$

$$\Theta_{\text{boundary layer, wind}} = \Theta_a + 4\ ^\circ C \qquad [^\circ C]$$

Θ_a Outdoor air temperature [°C]

Inner surface temperature Θ_{i0}

$$\Theta_{i0} = \Theta_i - \Delta\Theta \cdot U_{wall} \cdot R_{si} \qquad [°C]$$

Θ_{i0} Inner surface temperature [°C]
Θ_i Room air temperature [°C]
$\Delta\Theta$ Temperature difference indoors-outdoors [°C]
U_{wall} U-value of wall [W/m²K]
R_{si} Thermal resistance, inner
     = 1.25 m²K/W

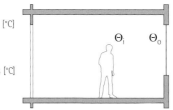

Inner surface temperature

The surface temperature at the internal wall surface depends on the U-value and the difference between the indoor and outdoor temperatures. The insolation and the absorption of the glazing also have to be taken into account in calculating the inner surface temperature of a window. In the wall area, insolation plays only a minor role.

	k [-]
Panel radiator	0.2
Radiator	0.4
Convector	0.8

Heating radiator output Q_{hr} to counteract the cold air drop (after Nowak)

$$Q_{HK} = \frac{A_{facade} \cdot U \cdot \Delta\Theta}{k} \qquad [W]$$

A_{facade} Facade area [m²]
U U-value facade, total [W/m²K]
$\Delta\Theta$ Temperature difference indoors/outdoors [K]
k Convection effect heating radiator [-]

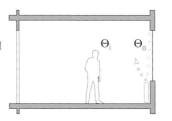

Cold air drop

When the temperatures of the outdoor air and the inner surface of the glazing are cold, the air near the window is rapidly cooled. This results in cold air drop at the window. This can be counteracted by placing a radiator close to the window, which prevents this local air circulation from taking place. The cold air does not reach the floor to cause discomfort.

Boundary conditions

Opening angle for open window	90°
Opening angle tilted-open window	1–7°

Reference values for air exchange due to thermal buoyancy with fully open windows

| $\Delta\Theta_{indoor-outdoor}$ | 20 K | ca. 1500 m³/h |
| $\Delta\Theta_{indoor-outdoor}$ | 5 K | ca. 700 m³/h |

with tilted-open windows

| $\Delta\Theta_{indoor-outdoor}$ | 20 K | ca. 40–130 m³/h |
| $\Delta\Theta_{indoor-outdoor}$ | 5 K | ca. 20–60 m³/h |

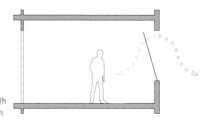

Air exchange produced by thermal buoyancy

When temperature differences exist between indoors and outdoors this sets up thermally induced air exchange through open windows. The rate of air change depends on the window height and width, opening angle, air flow properties of the window and the difference between indoor and outdoor temperatures.

Boundary conditions

Wind speed	1–4 m/s

Estimate of air exchange with tilted-open windows

| $\Delta\Theta_{indoor-outdoor}$ | 2–4 K | 50–110 m³/h |
| $\Delta\Theta_{indoor-outdoor}$ | 18–21 K | 100–140 m³/h |

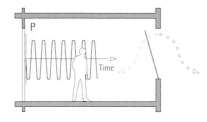

Air exchange due to wind

Wind-induced air exchange takes place in two ways. If air is able to flow through the building, air enters the room on the windward side, flows through the building via gaps or open doors and exits from the leeward side. Pump effects arising from pressure fluctuations caused by gusting wind produce wind-induced air exchange through an opening.

Typical sound insulation effect	[dB]
Aerated concrete 10 cm	41
Solid brick 24 cm	53
Heat insulation glass	30–35
Sound reduction glass	35–50

Sound level difference calculate according to standards D_N

$$D_N = L_a - L_i - 10\lg \cdot A/A_0 \qquad [dB]$$

L_0 Sound level outdoors [dB]
L_i Sound level indoors [dB]
A Equivalent absorption area [m²]
A_0 Reference absorption area [m²]

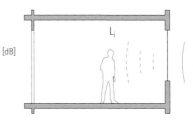

Sound insulation

The sound reduction index of a facade indicates how much sound the facade stops in the closed state. The weak spot in the facade in terms of sound insulation is normally the windows. The seals, window frames, fittings and installation details also affect the sound insulation properties of the facade.

Interactions

09:35

09:58

11:47

12:34

12:48

13:20   15:56   16:23   17:46   22:18

The starting point in the development of a building is the wishes and requirements of the client. The designer reacts to them in the design of the facade and the choice of room conditioning concept. These two aspects together influence the attainable room climate. Whilst the type of facade determines the daylighting conditions in the room, the space conditioning concept on the other hand influences the options for cooling systems. Thus there is an interaction of light, room climate and cooling systems and an interrelationship between cooling strategy and daylighting provision.

Early in the planning phase it is necessary to make a quick assessment of the interaction of facade and building services technology. Detailed calculations are not worthwhile at this stage because the boundary conditions are still imprecise and many options are still being considered. Therefore a parameter study has been carried out for many standard situations. The conclusions, which cover the aspects of light, facade, room climate and building technical services, can be used instead of some of the basic models in the concept phase. The results are presented initially for typical requirement profiles in effect chains, which can be used to assess the consequences of design requirements. All the results on light, room climate and energy are brought together in an overall matrix on three summary pages to allow the details of the interrelationships to be better analysed. The effects of design decisions are collected together into a set of comprehensive guidelines.

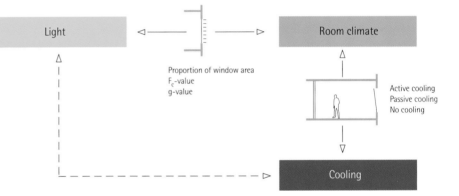

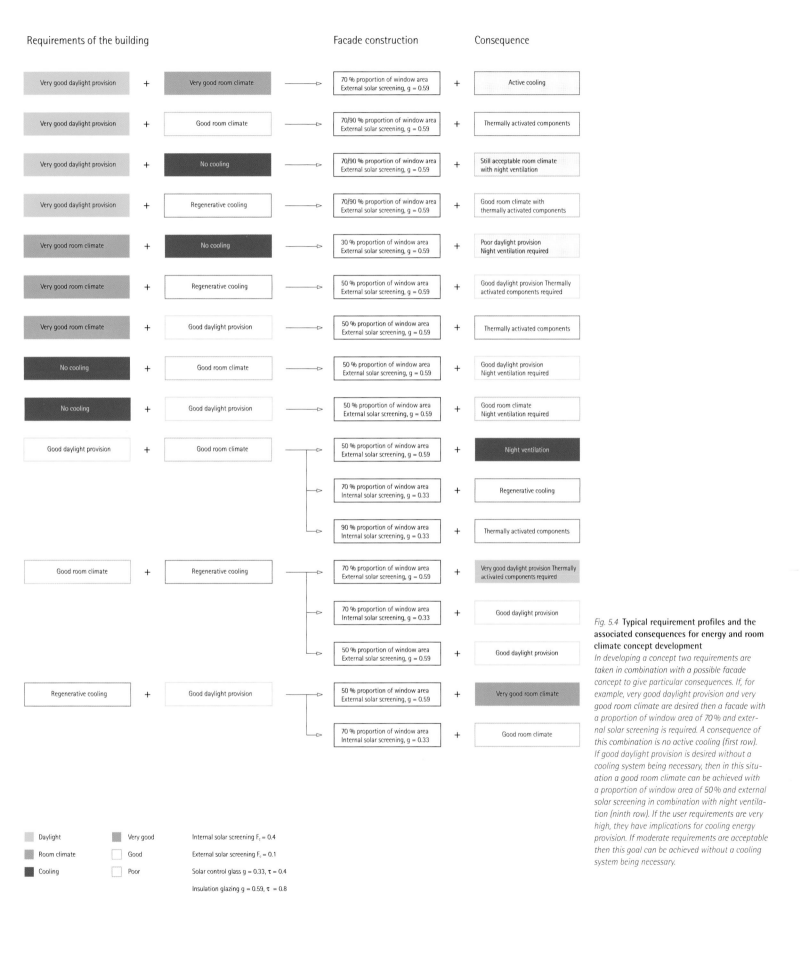

Requirements of the building

Facade construction

Consequence

Very good daylight provision	+ Very good room climate	→ 70 % proportion of window area / External solar screening, g = 0.59	+ Active cooling
Very good daylight provision	+ Good room climate	→ 70/90 % proportion of window area / External solar screening, g = 0.59	+ Thermally activated components
Very good daylight provision	+ No cooling	→ 70/90 % proportion of window area / External solar screening, g = 0.59	+ Still acceptable room climate with night ventilation
Very good daylight provision	+ Regenerative cooling	→ 70/90 % proportion of window area / External solar screening, g = 0.59	+ Good room climate with thermally activated components
Very good room climate	+ No cooling	→ 30 % proportion of window area / External solar screening, g = 0.59	+ Poor daylight provision / Night ventilation required
Very good room climate	+ Regenerative cooling	→ 50 % proportion of window area / External solar screening, g = 0.59	+ Good daylight provision Thermally activated components required
Very good room climate	+ Good daylight provision	→ 50 % proportion of window area / External solar screening, g = 0.59	+ Thermally activated components
No cooling	+ Good room climate	→ 50 % proportion of window area / External solar screening, g = 0.59	+ Good daylight provision / Night ventilation required
No cooling	+ Good daylight provision	→ 50 % proportion of window area / External solar screening, g = 0.59	+ Good room climate / Night ventilation required
Good daylight provision	+ Good room climate	→ 50 % proportion of window area / External solar screening, g = 0.59	+ Night ventilation
		→ 70 % proportion of window area / Internal solar screening, g = 0.33	+ Regenerative cooling
		→ 90 % proportion of window area / Internal solar screening, g = 0.33	+ Thermally activated components
Good room climate	+ Regenerative cooling	→ 70 % proportion of window area / External solar screening, g = 0.59	+ Very good daylight provision Thermally activated components required
		→ 70 % proportion of window area / Internal solar screening, g = 0.33	+ Good daylight provision
		→ 50 % proportion of window area / External solar screening, g = 0.59	+ Good daylight provision
Regenerative cooling	+ Good daylight provision	→ 50 % proportion of window area / External solar screening, g = 0.59	+ Very good room climate
		→ 70 % proportion of window area / Internal solar screening, g = 0.33	+ Good room climate

Fig. 5.4 **Typical requirement profiles and the associated consequences for energy and room climate concept development**
In developing a concept two requirements are taken in combination with a possible facade concept to give particular consequences. If, for example, very good daylight provision and very good room climate are desired then a facade with a proportion of window area of 70 % and external solar screening is required. A consequence of this combination is no active cooling (first row). If good daylight provision is desired without a cooling system being necessary, then in this situation a good room climate can be achieved with a proportion of window area of 50 % and external solar screening in combination with night ventilation (ninth row). If the user requirements are very high, they have implications for cooling energy provision. If moderate requirements are acceptable then this goal can be achieved without a cooling system being necessary.

Legend:
- Daylight
- Room climate
- Cooling
- Very good
- Good
- Poor
- Internal solar screening $F_c = 0.4$
- External solar screening $F_c = 0.1$
- Solar control glass $g = 0.33$, $\tau = 0.4$
- Insulation glazing $g = 0.59$, $\tau = 0.8$

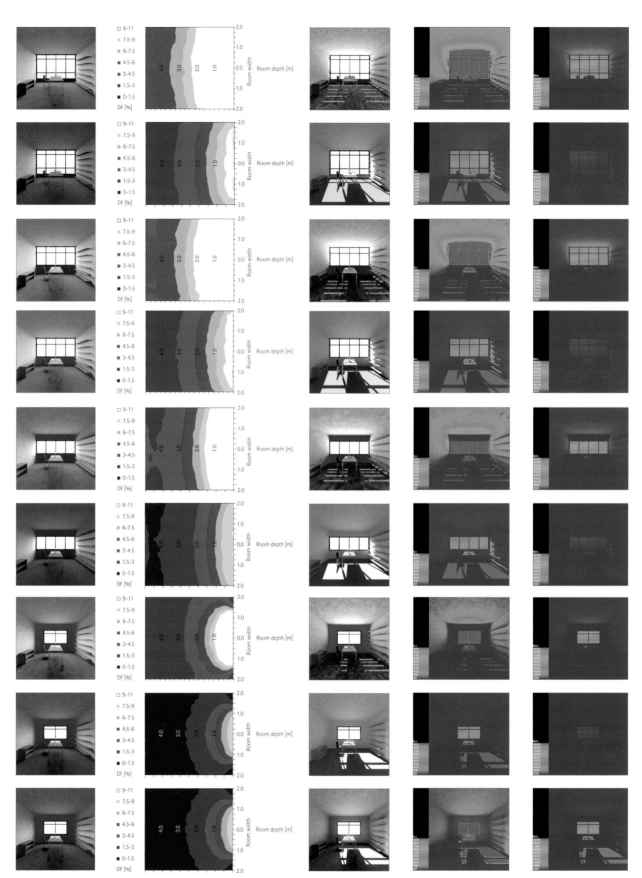

Fig. 5.5 **Interaction matrix for light, facade, room climate and building technology**
The matrix extends over pages 160–163. It can be read in both directions. For boundary conditions and explanations refer to pages 162 and 163.

Mood
Diffused sky
Solar screening open

Daylight factor

Mood with
sun, 21 March, 11:00 hrs
Solar screening closed

Illuminance distribution
with sun, 21 March, 11:00 hrs
Solar screening closed

Luminance distribution
with sun, 21 March, 11:00 hrs
Solar screening closed

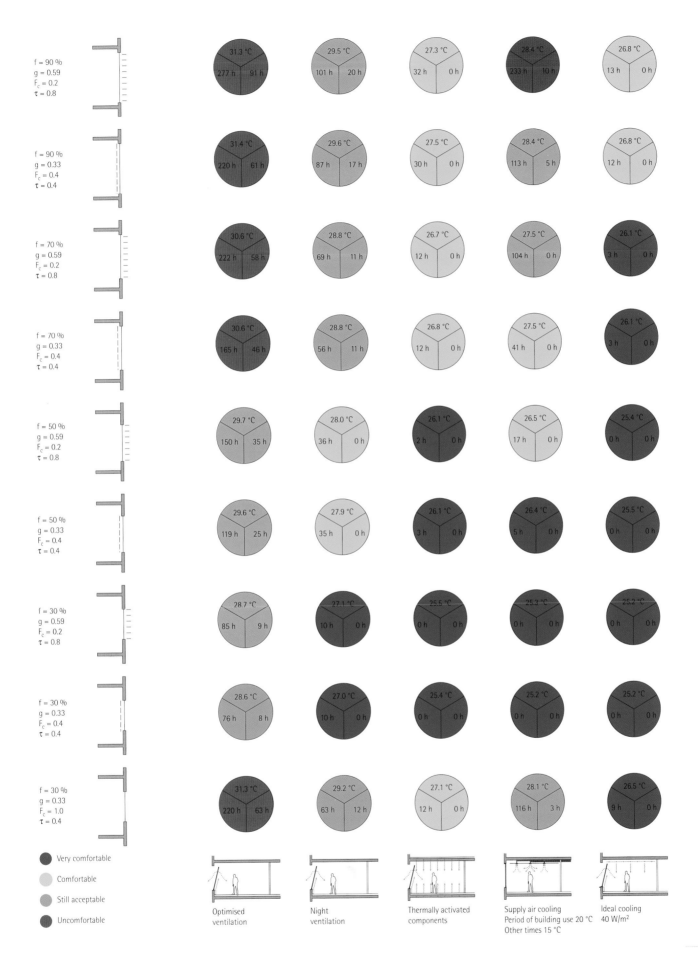

f = 90 %
g = 0.59
F_c = 0.2
τ = 0.8

f = 90 %
g = 0.33
F_c = 0.4
τ = 0.4

f = 70 %
g = 0.59
F_c = 0.2
τ = 0.8

f = 70 %
g = 0.33
F_c = 0.4
τ = 0.4

f = 50 %
g = 0.59
F_c = 0.2
τ = 0.8

f = 50 %
g = 0.33
F_c = 0.4
τ = 0.4

f = 30 %
g = 0.59
F_c = 0.2
τ = 0.8

f = 30 %
g = 0.33
F_c = 0.4
τ = 0.4

f = 30 %
g = 0.33
F_c = 1.0
τ = 0.4

Very comfortable

Comfortable

Still acceptable

Uncomfortable

Optimised
ventilation

Night
ventilation

Thermally activated
components

Supply air cooling
Period of building use 20 °C
Other times 15 °C

Ideal cooling
40 W/m²

Continued on page 163

Legend: Room climate during the period of building use (page 161)

Maximum room operating temperature

	27.1 °C
12 h	0 h

Hours/year $T_{op} > 26°C$ | Hours/year $T_{op} > 28°C$

- ● Very comfortable $T_{op > 26°C} < 10$ h/a
- ○ Comfortable $T_{op > 26°C} < 50$ h/a
- ◐ Still acceptable $T_{op > 26°C} < 150$ h/a
- ● Comfortable $T_{op > 26°C} < 150$ h/a

General thermal boundary conditions

Office area	22.5 m²
Orientation	South
Facade area	13.5 m²
Proportion of window area	30/50/70/90 %
Glazing	g = 0.60/0.33
	U = 1.1 W/m²K

Solar screening	
External, louvres	$F_c = 0.20$
Internal, film	$F_c = 0.40$

Ceilings	Lightweight, adiabatic
Loads	Solid, adiabatic
8:00–18:00 hrs	Weekdays
Cooling	2 pers. + 2 PCs
Climate	Varies
	Würzburg

Light-related boundary conditions

Reflectance	
Ceiling	80 %
Walls	80 %
Floor	20 %

Light transmittance	
Standard glass	$\tau = 0.8$
Solar control glass	$\tau = 0.4$
Location	Würzburg
Direct sun	21.03, 11:00 hrs
Diffused sky	21.03, 12:00 hrs

Variant with optimised ventilation

Ventilation	
Weekdays	
8:00–10:00 hrs	$n = 5.0$ h⁻¹
10:00–18:00 hrs	$n = 2.0$ h⁻¹
18:00–8:00 hrs	$n = 1.0$ h⁻¹
Weekends	$n = 1.0$ h⁻¹
Cooling	None

Variant with night ventilation

Ventilation	
Weekdays	
8:00–10:00 hrs	$n = 5.0$ h⁻¹
10:00–18:00 hrs	$n = 2.0$ h⁻¹
18:00–8:00 hrs	$n = 4.0$ h⁻¹
Weekends	$n = 1.0$ h⁻¹
Cooling	None

Variant with thermally activated components

Ventilation	
Weekdays	
8:00–18:00 hrs	$n = 2.0$ h⁻¹
18:00–8:00 hrs	$n = 1.0$ h⁻¹
Weekends	$n = 1.0$ h⁻¹
Thickness TAC	25 cm
Pipes	14/18 mm
Pipe centres	200 mm
Mass flow	15 kg/hm²
Inlet temperature	$T_{IT} = T_{outdoors}$
Through flow	22:00 – 6:00 Uhr

Variant with supply air cooling

Ventilation	
Weekdays	
8:00–18:00 hrs	$n = 2.0$ h⁻¹
18:00–8:00 hrs	$n = 1.0$ h⁻¹
Weekends	$n = 1.0$ h⁻¹
temperature	
Weekdays	
8:00–18:00 hrs	20 °C
18:00–8:00 hrs	15 °C
Weekends	15 °C

Variant with ideal cooling

Weekdays	
Weekends	
8:00–18:00 hrs	$n = 2.0$ h⁻¹
18:00–8:00 hrs	$n = 1.0$ h⁻¹
Weekends	$n = 1.0$ h⁻¹
Cooling	From $T_{room} > 25$ °C
Cooling output	max. 40 W/m²
Weekdays	
8:00–18:00 Uhr	On
18:00–8:00 Uhr	Off
Weekends	Off

Boundary conditions and specification of the room conditioning concepts for the interaction matrix for light, facade, room climate and technology on pages 160, 161 and 163 (Fig. 5.5).

Continued on page 161

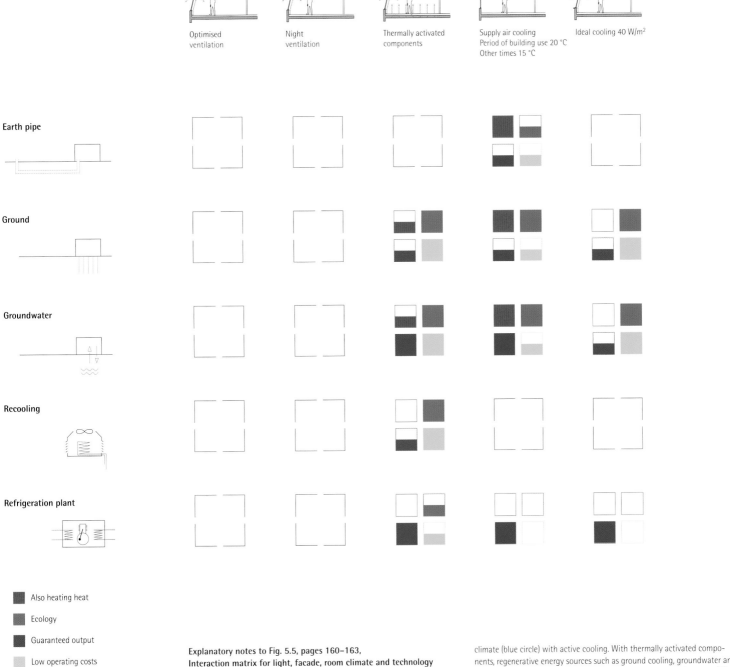

Optimised ventilation

Night ventilation

Thermally activated components

Supply air cooling
Period of building use 20 °C
Other times 15 °C

Ideal cooling 40 W/m²

Earth pipe

Ground

Groundwater

Recooling

Refrigeration plant

Also heating heat

Ecology

Guaranteed output

Low operating costs

Not possible

**Explanatory notes to Fig. 5.5, pages 160–163,
Interaction matrix for light, facade, room climate and technology**
The daylight conditions in the room are influenced by the proportion of window area and the light transmittance of the glazing. The facade and room conditioning concepts together determine the thermal conditions in summer. The room conditioning concept influences the possible cooling strategies and the required energy. The relationship between daylight entry, facade construction, room climate, room conditioning concept and possible cooling system can be read off the interaction matrix.

If, for example, very good daylight provision is desired, it can be achieved with a proportion of window area of 70% with conventional glazing. In combination with external solar screening, a good room climate (yellow circle) is achieved with thermally activated components, a very good room climate (blue circle) with active cooling. With thermally activated components, regenerative energy sources such as ground cooling, groundwater and night recooling are used. Regenerative cooling has low operating costs (filled yellow square) and is very ecological (filled green square). The output from groundwater cooling is always guaranteed to be available (filled blue square). With night recooling there is a dependency on night outdoor air temperature, ground cooling may become exhausted (half-filled blue square). Ground and groundwater can also be used for generating heat in winter by means of a heat pump (half-filled red square). To ensure a very good room climate with active cooling, a mechanical cooling system would be required. The output is guaranteed (filled blue square). Operating costs with this option are generally high (empty yellow square). The interrelationships also work in the opposite direction.

Proportion of window area

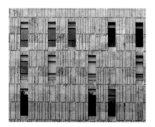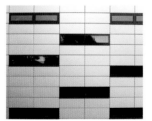

Proportion of window area 0–30% Proportion of window area 30–50%

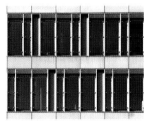

Proportion of window area 50-70 %

Proportion of window area 70-100 %

The first steps in the planning of buildings with optimised energy use and room climate must involve decisions on fundamental questions about the building concept, skin and technical services. These questions are interrelated and therefore cannot be answered in isolation, but must be considered as parts of an overall concept. The multiplicity of parameters and options generally prevent a detailed evaluation of these decisions on the initial concept. It is therefore helpful to assess each factor in the planning process in rough terms only, and above all recognising that a decision between two design options is of much more use than absolute quantifications at this stage. The following design guidelines have been drawn from the results of extensive modelling studies. The assumptions behind them have been chosen to allow the values to be applied to typical administration buildings. Most of the information is given in relative percentages to allow the designer to estimate the relevance of each theme.

Design guidelines

Building concept

To what extent can noise be avoided by the position and orientation of the building?

How does the building height affect the ventilation, fire safety and floor space requirements?

What influence has the building type on the surface area/volume ratio?

How does orientation affect heating energy demand, cooling energy demand and room climate?

What are the consequences of having corner rooms in terms of energy and room climate?

What are the advantages of through rooms in terms of energy and room climate?

How large are the potential benefits of PCM?

What influence has thermal storage mass on room climate?

Building skins

Which facade concept should be used for which outdoor situation?

How does the proportion of window area affect heating energy demand, cooling energy demand and room climate?

What influence has solar screening on room climate and cooling energy demand?

How does solar screening affect the maximum possible proportion of window area?

What influence has glazing quality on heating energy demand?

What is the relationship of insulation standard and internal loads in the context of heating energy demand?

How important is infiltration air change during overnight heat removal?

How much potential for room climatisation is there in night ventilation?

Building technical services

How large are the potential benefits of supply air preheating?

How large are the potential benefits of heat recovery?

How does the ventilation affect the room climate in summer?

How much potential for room climatisation is there in thermally activated components?

How should we design our buildings?

Orientation

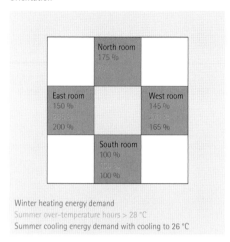

Winter heating energy demand
Summer over-temperature hours > 28 °C
Summer cooling energy demand with cooling to 26 °C

Orientation is influenced by the urban planning concept and the characteristics of the plot. In principle, the choice is between a north-south alignment, east-west alignment, a building of uniform height or a building with no predominant orientation. Orientation has considerable influence on the entry of solar radiation in summer and winter, the entry of noise and wind loading. The influence of orientation reduces with lower proportions of window area.

Building position

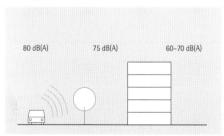

By arranging the occupied rooms on the side of the building facing away from the street the external noise load can be considerably reduced. Natural ventilation is easier to achieve. The construction of the facade can be simpler.

Building height

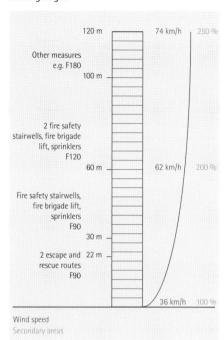

Wind speed
Secondary areas

The building height is influenced by the size of the plot, the general density of development and desired image to be created by the building. Building height affects wind loading, engineering complexity, fire safety concept, solar screening construction and the ventilation concept. The effects of building height are less with climatised buildings.

Building shape

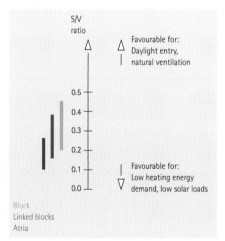

Block
Linked blocks
Atria

Building shape is influenced by the urban planning concept and the plot shape. Basic forms include individual and linked blocks as well as building types with features that bring light or air into their centres such as atria or internal courtyards. The building shape influences the surface area/volume ratio and interacts with the heating energy demand, entry of daylight and other solar radiation and the options for ventilation.

Facade concept

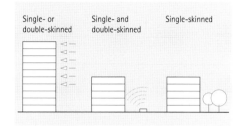

The facade concept is influenced by building height and noise loading. The concept may be single- or double-skinned or a combination of both. The type of facade has an effect on the construction of the solar screening and the possibility of natural ventilation.

Proportion of window area

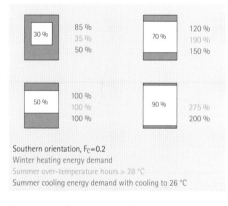

Southern orientation, F_C=0.2
Winter heating energy demand
Summer over-temperature hours > 28 °C
Summer cooling energy demand with cooling to 26 °C

The proportion of window area is influenced by the provision of daylight and our desire for transparence. Typical proportions of window area can lie between 30 and 90 %. The proportion of window area has effects on the entry of sunlight in summer, passive solar energy gain in winter and the provision of daylight. It interacts with the construction of solar screening, glazing quality and orientation.

Solar screening

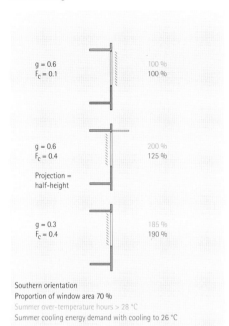

g = 0.6
F_c = 0.1
100 %
100 %

g = 0.6
F_c = 0.4
Projection =
half-height
200 %
125 %

g = 0.3
F_c = 0.4
185 %
190 %

Southern orientation
Proportion of window area 70 %
Summer over-temperature hours > 28 °C
Summer cooling energy demand with cooling to 26 °C

The construction of solar screening is largely determined by wind exposure and proportion of window area. The designer has the choice of external, internal solar screening or systems which lie in the glazing cavity. Between the systems themselves, there are differences in the amount of solar radiation admission, initial investment and maintenance costs. Daylight provision, visual comfort and view out are interrelated.
Solar screening control has a considerable influence on room climate in summer. Solar screening control can be activated by light entry or room temperature. Control based on light entry may still permit large amounts of diffused sunlight to enter the room. Room temperature controlled systems may result in the solar screening being closed even when there is no direct sunlight. This improves room climate in summer and ensures that solar screening is closed for fewer hours during the building period of use. The type of solar screening control is very significant for the north side of a building because there a system based on light entry would almost never be closed. The consequences would include relatively high room temperatures, even at the north facade.

Solar screening position

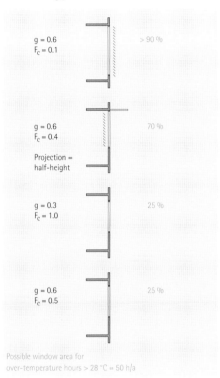

g = 0.6
F_c = 0.1
> 90 %

g = 0.6
F_c = 0.4
Projection =
half-height
70 %

g = 0.3
F_c = 1.0
25 %

g = 0.6
F_c = 0.5
25 %

Possible window area for
over-temperature hours > 28 °C = 50 h/a

The position of solar screening is determined by the wind loading, building orientation and proportion of window area. Internal fixed systems and those located in the glazing cavity are unaffected by the weather and can therefore be adopted for high-rise buildings. They are also associated with low maintenance costs. Fixed systems are only possible on southern-facing facades. The position of the solar screening determines the maximum possible proportion of window area.

Glazing quality

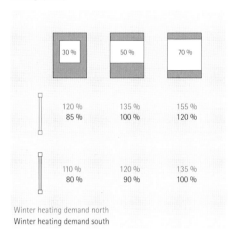

	30 %	50 %	70 %
	120 %	135 %	155 %
	85 %	100 %	120 %
	110 %	120 %	135 %
	80 %	90 %	100 %

Winter heating demand north
Winter heating demand south

The required glazing quality is influenced by the proportion of window area and thermal comfort. The designer has the choice of 2- and 3-pane insulation glazing, which offers different transmission heat losses, g-values and daylight entry. Glazing quality interacts with the room conditioning concept, in particular with respect to whether radiators are required at the facade.

Insulation standard

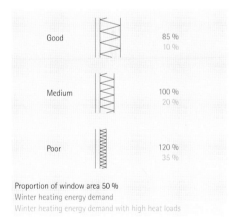

Good
85 %
10 %

Medium
100 %
20 %

Poor
120 %
35 %

Proportion of window area 50 %
Winter heating energy demand
Winter heating energy demand with high heat loads

The insulation standard is determined by the desired level of heat energy demand. The designer has a choice of 2- or 3-pane insulation glazing and insulation thicknesses from 10 to over 20 cm. The quality of the insulation has effects on the heat energy demand, heating system output, inner surface temperatures and therefore thermal comfort. It has some input into the room conditioning concept, because insulation quality has to be considered with internal heat loads. Even with high internal loads, thermal insulation has a relatively large influence but its absolute effect on heating energy demand is somewhat less.

Air change rate in winter

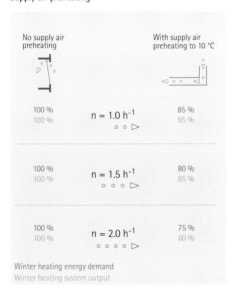

Winter heating energy demand
Winter heating system output

The necessary air change rate is determined by the size of the room, the number of occupants, emissions from equipment and building materials. The lowest possible rate of air exchange is preferred in the interests of energy efficiency, therefore emissions in the room should be minimised and supply air introduced into the room in as natural a state as possible. The rate of air change determines the heating energy demand and the heating system output and must take account of the internal heat loads. If the internal heat loads are high, then the significance of the air change rate reduces in relation to the heating energy demand and heating system output. The reason for this is that the increased rate of air change and internal heat loads normally occur at the same time and hence cancel one another out.

Supply air preheating

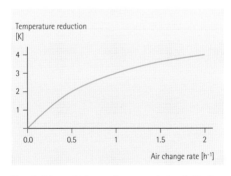

Winter heating energy demand
Winter heating system output

Preheating the supply air using energy from the local environment, e.g. through an earth pipe or groundwater register, can reduce ventilation heat loss. Supply air preheating to 10 °C reduces the effect of high air change rates. With supply air preheating, the required heating system output is hardly influenced by air changes.

Ventilation strategy in summer

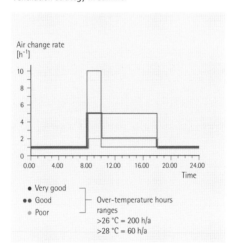

Ventilation in summer can remove heat from the room. It can also bring heat into the building if the outdoor temperature is higher than the room temperature. These effects are frequently overestimated; the amount of heat entering the building by ventilation is low because of the small temperature differences involved. With a suitable ventilation strategy the over-temperature hours in the lower temperature range can be reduced; the influence of the ventilation strategy is reduced in relation to high room temperatures.

Night ventilation

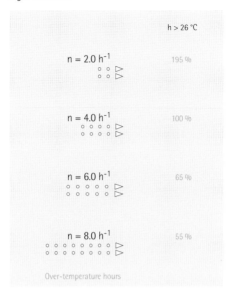

Over-temperature hours

Night ventilation can be used to remove heat from the building with cold night air. This represents a cost-effective cooling method with no energy costs. Efficient night ventilation requires thermal storage mass and an air exchange rate of $n = 4 \ h^{-1}$ or greater. The performance of night ventilation is influenced by climate; low night temperatures are favourable, as is, for example, a location at altitude. With medium-heavy construction there is usually an increase in daytime maximum temperatures of 2 to 3 K compared with heavy construction; for lightweight construction the figure would be 7 to 8 K.

Infiltration air changes at night

If small night ventilation openings cannot be installed in the facade, a basic level of air change should still be provided. Even low rates of air change of about $n = 1 \ h^{-1}$ can produce a considerable improvement of the room climate compared with a completely sealed building, provided a minimum amount of thermal storage mass is available.

Phase change materials (PCM)

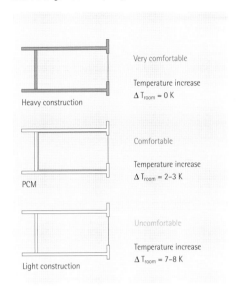

Very comfortable

Temperature increase
$\Delta T_{room} = 0$ K

Heavy construction

Comfortable

Temperature increase
$\Delta T_{room} = 2$–3 K

PCM

Uncomfortable

Temperature increase
$\Delta T_{room} = 7$–8 K

Light construction

Corner rooms

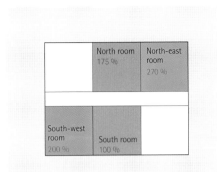

Winter heating energy demand
Uncomfortable in summer

Corner rooms with two glazed facade walls enjoy improved lighting in the depth of the room and the option of cross ventilation. The specific heat energy demand increases because of the higher external surface area. The considerably higher entry of solar radiation has an unfavourable effect on summer room climate conditions. Some means of limiting the entry of solar radiation should be seriously considered for corner rooms, otherwise people cannot be reasonably expected to use corner rooms without cooling.

PCM can take the place of conventional thermal storage masses. This is particularly important in buildings with high flexibility of use or refurbishment projects. Compared to conventional thermal storage mass, room users experience a steeper rise in temperature until the phase change point is reached. In comparison to lightweight construction, room climate is considerably improved. As with conventional thermal storage masses it is important to ensure that the heat is removed from the storage medium for the cycle to be repeated. This can be accomplished actively by means of a recirculatory water system or by increased rates of air change at night. The maximum daytime temperatures are 2 to 3 K higher compared to heavyweight construction. With lightweight construction, the temperatures would be 7 to 8 K higher, but the use of PCM can achieve room climates similar to those of medium-weight construction.

Night ventilation and thermal storage mass

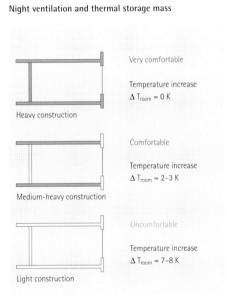

Very comfortable

Temperature increase
$\Delta T_{room} = 0$ K

Heavy construction

Comfortable

Temperature increase
$\Delta T_{room} = 2$–3 K

Medium-heavy construction

Uncomfortable

Temperature increase
$\Delta T_{room} = 7$–8 K

Light construction

Controllable thermally activated storage masses have a considerable influence on the cooling potential of night cooling. Good night ventilation requires at least medium-weight construction. Lightweight construction cannot create comfortable conditions even with high rates of air change. In combination with high rates of air change, heavyweight construction with exposed ceilings and solid internal walls can achieve very good room climate in summer.

Through rooms

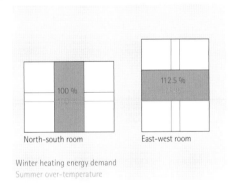

North-south room   East-west room

Winter heating energy demand
Summer over-temperature

With light entering from two opposite sides, the various spatial characteristics of through rooms, particularly with a north-south orientation, produce less extreme conditions. The heating energy demand given here is the average for all the individual orientations. Through rooms have advantages in terms of room climate. Compared to non-through rooms, conditions are improved, in particular for through rooms with an east-west orientation.

Thermally activated components

	☾	☾ ☀
0 K	TAC off	0 K
-2.5 K	IT = 20 °C	-3.0 K
-3.0 K	IT = 18 °C	-4.0 K
-4.5 K	IT = 16 °C	-5.5 K

Night through-ventilation
Continuous through-ventilation

Thermally activated components represent a very effective method of conditioning room climate. Ceilings with water circulating though them can be operated continuously or just during the night. The inlet temperatures are generally between 16 and 20 °C. Their performance depends on the period of operation and the permitted water temperature levels. In combination with good solar screening, thermally activated components can ensure that room temperatures exceed 26°C for very few hours during the period of use.

Solar radiation penetration

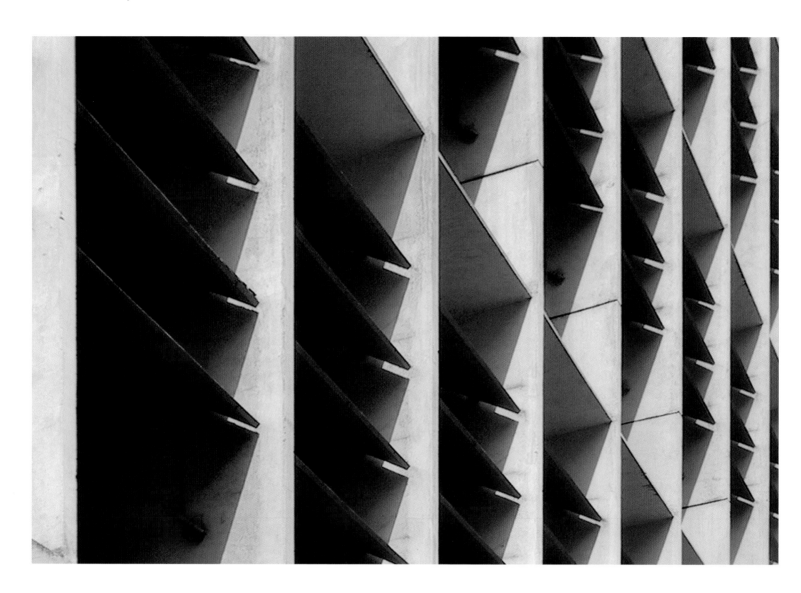

External solar screening   Solar screening in the facade cavity

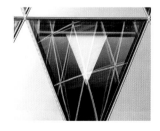

Internal solar screening   Solar control glass

TIME [HR]	Q_heiz W/m²	Q_inf W/m²	Q_vent W/m²	Q_conv W/m²	Q_rad W/m²	Q_soltr W/m²	Q_ W	Q_lat W/m²	Q_tabsfl W/m²	Q_tabs W/m²
1.00	0.000	0.000	0.000	0.000	0.000	0.000	0.00	0.000	0.000	0.000
2.00	16.153	-9.830	0.000	0.000	0.000	0.000	0.0	0.000	0.000	2.374
3.00	17.209	-9.824	0.000	0.000	0.000	0.000	0.0	0.000	0.000	2.537
4.00	17.725	-9.773	0.000	0.000	0.000	0.000	0.0	0.000	0.000	2.566
5.00	18.059	-9.735	0.000	0.000	0.000	0.000	0.0	0.000	0.000	2.551
6.00	18.475	-9.798	0.000	0.000	0.000	0.000	0.0	0.000	0.000	2.548
7.00	18.879	-9.875	0.000	0.000	0.000	0.000	0.0	0.000	0.000	2.544
8.00	19.215	-9.925	0.000	0.000	0.000	0.000	0.0	0.000	0.000	2.530
9.00	31.927	-39.904	0.000	16.444	2.667	0.813	0.	0.000	0.000	2.247
10.00	30.120	-40.006	0.000	16.444	2.667	4.469	0.	0.000	0.000	1.560
11.00	28.227	-39.498	0.000	16.444	2.667	6.094	0.	0.000	0.000	1.109
12.00	27.651	-38.889	0.000	16.444	2.667	4.794	0.	0.000	0.000	1.169
13.00	26.839	-38.381	0.000	16.444	2.667	5.038	0.	0.000	0.000	1.069
14.00	27.073	-38.540	0.000	16.444	2.667	4.713	0.	0.000	0.000	1.104
15.00	28.188	-39.077	0.000	16.444	2.667	3.656	0.	0.000	0.000	1.302
16.00	29.966	-39.803	0.000	16.444	2.667	2.031	0.	0.000	0.000	1.639
17.00	31.926	-40.466	0.000	16.444	2.667	0.244	0.	0.000	0.000	2.025
18.00	32.748	-40.683	0.000	16.444	2.667	0.000	0	0.000	0.000	2.136
19.00	19.557	-10.100	0.000	0.000	0.000	0.000	0.0	0.000	0.000	2.254
20.00	19.636	-9.875	0.000	0.000	0.000	0.000	0.0	0.000	0.000	2.200
21.00	19.461	-9.621	0.000	0.000	0.000	0.000	0.0	0.000	0.000	2.099
22.00	19.242	-9.395	0.000	0.000	0.000	0.000	0.0	0.000	0.000	1.996
23.00	19.271	-9.336	0.000	0.000	0.000	0.000	0.0	0.000	0.000	1.937
24.00	19.675	-9.494	0.000	0.000	0.000	0.000	0.0	0.000	0.000	1.942
25.00	20.145	-9.680	0.000	0.000	0.000	0.000	0.0	0.000	0.000	1.958
26.00	20.477	-9.786	0.000	0.000	0.000	0.000	0.0	0.000	0.000	1.950
27.00	20.634	-9.798	0.000	0.000	0.000	0.000	0.0	0.000	0.000	1.912
28.00	20.751	-9.798	0.000	0.000	0.000	0.000	0.0	0.000	0.000	1.866
29.00	20.855	-9.798	0.000	0.000	0.000	0.000	0.0	0.000	0.000	1.820
30.00	20.974	-9.811	0.000	0.000	0.000	0.000	0.0	0.000	0.000	1.777
31.00	21.247	-9.913	0.000	0.000	0.000	0.000	0.0	0.000	0.000	1.760
32.00	21.688	-10.103	0.000	0.000	0.000	0.000	0.	0.000	0.000	1.772
33.00	35.696	-41.224	0.000	16.444	2.667	0.488	0	0.000	0.000	1.578

Requirements

Interaction and effects of the various requirements and conditions in the design process.
The starting point in the design of any building is to examine its usage requirements and conditions imposed by its location. They have a crucial influence on the subsequent design stages and affect the energy use, indoor climate, function and economic viability of a building. Whilst requirements can be varied to a certain extent, they can have considerable consequences. Therefore they should be identified and established very carefully.

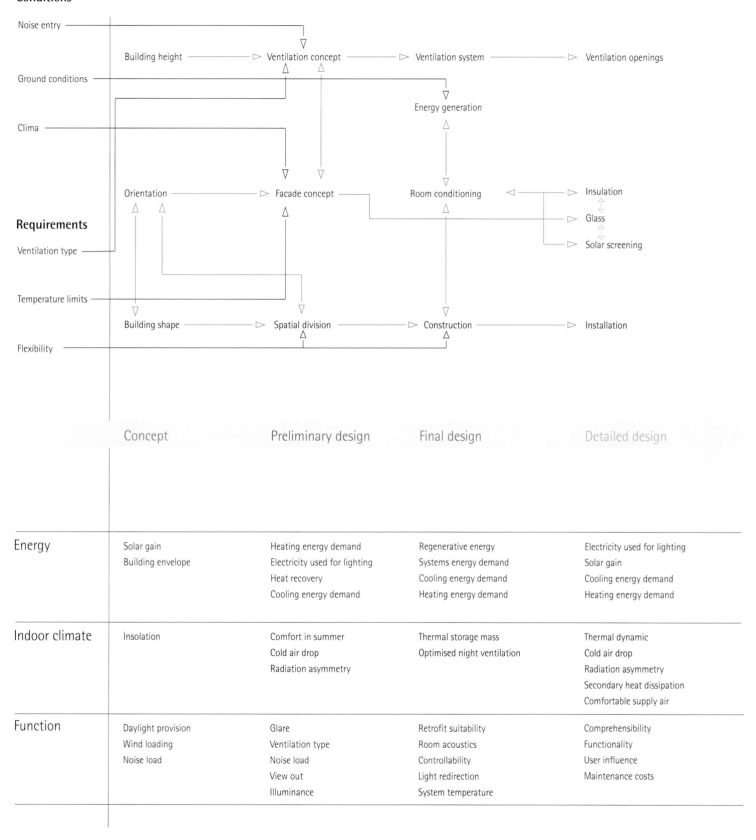

	Concept	Preliminary design	Final design	Detailed design
Energy	Solar gain	Heating energy demand	Regenerative energy	Electricity used for lighting
	Building envelope	Electricity used for lighting	Systems energy demand	Solar gain
		Heat recovery	Cooling energy demand	Cooling energy demand
		Cooling energy demand	Heating energy demand	Heating energy demand
Indoor climate	Insolation	Comfort in summer	Thermal storage mass	Thermal dynamic
		Cold air drop	Optimised night ventilation	Cold air drop
		Radiation asymmetry		Radiation asymmetry
				Secondary heat dissipation
				Comfortable supply air
Function	Daylight provision	Glare	Retrofit suitability	Comprehensibility
	Wind loading	Ventilation type	Room acoustics	Functionality
	Noise load	Noise load	Controllability	User influence
		View out	Light redirection	Maintenance costs
		Illuminance	System temperature	

Definitions

General

SI units

The name "Système International d'Unités" (International System of Units) and its abbreviation SI were chosen by the 11th General Conference on Weights and Measures (CGPM) in 1960. SI base units are units from which all the other units in the system are derived. The base units are: length (metre), mass (kilogram), time (second), electrical current (ampere), thermodynamic temperature (Kelvin), amount of substance (mole) and light intensity (candela). Derived SI units are coherent, that is to say, they are calculated from the base units using the rules of multiplication and division and no numerical factors other then 1.

Density ρ [kg/m³, kg/dm³]

Density ρ is the ratio of the mass m to the volume V of a portion of substance. A portion of substance is a specific volume of matter (solid, liquid, gas), which may consist of one or more substances or defined components of substances.

$\rho = m/V$

m   Mass [kg]
V   Volume [m³, dm³]

Pressure p [Pa]

The physical quantity pressure p is the ratio of the normal force F_N acting on a surface to the area A of this surface.

$p = F_N/A$

F_N Normal force [N]
A   Area [m²]

Force F [N]

The force F is the product of the mass m of a body and the acceleration a, which the mass experiences or would experience as a result of the force F.

$F = m \cdot a$

m   Mass [kg]
a   Acceleration [m/s²]

Mass m [kg]

The mass m describes the property of a body which results in inertia effects in response to a change in its motion or in the attraction forces between it and another body.

Light

Absorptance α [–]

The absorptance a is the ratio of the absorbed radiation energy or the luminous flux to the incident radiation energy or luminous flux under the same specified conditions.

General colour rendering index CIE 1974 Ra [–]

The general colour rendering index Ra is the average of the special colour rendering indices CIE 1974 for a standardised set of eight test colours.

Illuminance E [lx]

The illuminance E at a point on a surface is the ratio of the luminous flux dΦ, incident upon an element containing the point on the surface and the area dA of this element.

$E = d\Phi/dA$

Φ Luminous flux
A   Area [m²]

Colour temperature T_c [K]

The colour temperature T_c is the temperature to which a black body source would have to be heated to produce light of the same visual colour.

Colour rendering

Colour rendering is the effect of a light source on the colour appearance of objects it illuminates compared to the appearance of the same object under a reference source.

Global solar radiation

Global radiation is the sum of direct and diffused sunlight.

Diffused sunlight

Diffused sunlight is the part of sunlight that reaches the Earth after being scattered by air molecules, aerosols and cloud particles or other particles.

Direct sunlight

Direct sunlight is the part of extraterrestrial sunlight that reaches the Earth's surface as parallel rays after selective attenuation in the atmosphere.

Luminance L [cd/m²]

The luminance L in a given direction and at a given point in a real or imaginary surface is defined by the formula:

$L = d\Phi/(dA \cdot \cos\Theta \cdot d\Omega)$

dΦ The luminous flux which passes in an elementary bundle through the specified point and is propagated in a solid angle element dΩ, which contains the specified direction [lm]
dA   Cross-sectional area of this bundle, which contains the specified point [m²]
Θ Angle between the normal to the cross-sectional surface and direction of the bundle [sr]

Light intensity I [cd]

The light intensity I is the ratio of the luminous flux dΦ, that is emitted from a light source into a solid angle element dΩ according to the CIE standard photometric curves.

$I = d\Phi/d\Omega$

Φ Luminous flux [lm]
Ω Solid angle [sr]

Luminous flux Φ [lm]

The luminous flux Φ is the value obtained by weighting the effect of the radiation from a radiation flux Φ_e according to the CIE standard photometric curves.

Reflectance ρ [–]

The reflectance ρ is the ratio of the reflected radiation flux or the reflected luminous flux to the incident radiation flux or incident luminous flux under the same conditions (for radiation with a given spectral distribution, polarisation and geometric distribution).

Daylight factor D [–]

The daylight factor D is the ratio of the illuminance at a point on a given plane created by direct or indirect sunlight with assumed or known luminance distribution to the horizontal illuminance for an unobstructed sky hemisphere.
The proportions of direct sunlight for both illuminances are not taken into account.

Transmittance τ [–]

The transmittance τ is the ratio of the transmitted radiation flux or the transmitted luminous flux to the incident radiation flux or incident luminous flux under the same conditions (for radiation with a given spectral distribution, polarisation and geometric distribution).

Heat

Celsius temperature θ [°C]
The Celsius temperature θ represents the difference between a given (thermodynamic) temperature T and the fixed reference temperature T_0.
$\theta = T - T_0$
T	Thermodynamic temperature [K]
T_0	Reference temperature $T_0 = 273.15$ K

Total solar energy transmittance of the glazing g [–]
The total solar energy transmittance of the glazing g is the sum of the direct solar energy transmittance τ_e and the secondary internal heat transfer factor qi of the glazing. The latter is caused by the heat transport due to convection and longwave IR radiation from the proportion of the incident radiation absorbed by the glazing.
$g = \tau_e + q_i$
τ_e	Direct solar energy transmittance
q_i	Secondary heat given off by the glazing into the room

Total energy transmittance gtotal g_{total} [–]
The total energy transmittance g_{total} is calculated from the total energy transmittance of the glazing and the reduction factor due to the solar screening.
$g_{total} = g \cdot F_c$
g	Total energy transmittance of the glazing [-]
F_c	Reduction factor of the solar screening system [-]

Coefficient of longitudinal thermal expansion α [mm/mK]
The coefficient of longitudinal thermal expansion α indicates the amount a 1 m-long piece of material expands or contracts in length when heated or cooled through 1 K.

Thermodynamic temperature T [K]
The temperature or thermodynamic temperature T of an object is a fundamental unit with the base unit [K]. The thermodynamic temperature T is the physical unit upon which the laws of thermodynamics are based.

Thermal transmittance U (U–Wert) [W/m²K]
The thermal transmittance U is a measure of the amount of heat flowing in one second through a 1 m² area of a building component under steady state conditions subject to a temperature difference of 1 K. It is the inverse of the heat transfer resistance R_T.
$U = 1/R_T = 1/(R_{si} + \Sigma (d/\lambda) + R_{se})$
R_T	Heat transfer resistance [m²K/W]
R_{si}	Heat transfer resistance internal [m²K/W]
R_{se}	Heat transfer resistance external [m²K/W]
d	Thickness of the material [m]
λ	Thermal conductivity of the material [W/mK]

Heat transfer resistance R_T [m²K/W]
The heat transfer resistance R_T describes the resistance in the direction of heat flow of a flat component composed of thermally homogenous layers including its interior and exterior heat transfer resistance. The heat transfer resistance R_T of a building component consisting of n layers is calculated according to the following equation:
$R_T = R_{si} + R_1 + R_2 + R_3 + ... R_n + R_{se}$
R_{si}	Heat transfer resistance, interior [m²K/W]
$R_1, R_2...R_n$	Characteristic values of the heat transfer resistance of each layer [m²K/W]
R_{se}	Heat transfer resistance, exterior [m²K/W]

Coefficient of heat penetration b [J/m²Ks$^{1/2}$]
The coefficient of heat penetration b is the square root of the product of the thermal conductivity, density and specific heat capacity. This property is determined under nonsteady state conditions. It can be measured or calculated from separately measured values. In addition to other properties, the coefficient of heat penetration is responsible for the reaction of a surface temperature to a change of heat flux density at the surface. The smaller the coefficient of heat penetration of the material, the stronger the temperature reacts to changes in heat flux at the surface.

$b = \sqrt{(\lambda \cdot \rho \cdot c)}$
λ	Thermal conductivity [W/mK]
ρ	Density [kg/m³]
c	Specific heat capacity [J/kgK]

Heat capacity C [J/K]
The heat capacity C is defined by the following equation:
$C = dQ/dT$
Q	Heat energy [J]
T	Temperature [K]

Specific heat capacity c [J/kgK]
The specific heat capacity c of a material is the heat required to raise the temperature of 1 kg mass of the material by 1 K. In general c increases with increasing temperature.
$c = C/m$
C	Heat capacity [J/K]
m	Mass [kg]

Thermal conductivity λ [W/mK]
The thermal conductivity λ is the heat flux Φ transmitted through a component layer d with an area of 1 m² and thickness 1 m under a temperature difference of 1 K. The thermal conductivity of construction materials mainly depends on their bulk density but also on their moisture content and temperature.

Heat storage capacity Q_{sp} [kJ]
The heat storage capacity Q_{sp} is the heat stored in a material when it undergoes an increase in temperature of 1 K. A material with a higher specific heat capacity stores more heat than one with a lower specific heat capacity. The stored heat increases with mass and temperature difference to the surroundings.
$Q_{SP} = c \cdot m \cdot dT$
c	Specific heat capacity [J/kgK]
m	Mass [kg]
T	Temperature [K]

Heat storage coefficient W [kJ/m²K]
The heat storage coefficient W is the amount of heat stored in 1 m² of a component if the temperature difference between the interior and exterior sides is 1 K. A component with a higher heat storage coefficient can store more heat than one with a lower coefficient. The heat storage coefficient W is particularly useful for expressing the storage capacity of flat components. In practice the storage capacity of an external component is only usable down to a certain depth.
$W = c \cdot \rho \cdot d$
c	Specific heat capacity [J/kgK]
ρ	Density [kg/m³]
d	Thickness of the component [m]

Volumetric heat capacity coefficient S [kJ/m³K]
The volumetric heat capacity coefficient S is the amount of heat required to raise the temperature of 1 m³ of a material by 1 K. A heavier material generally has a higher volumetric heat capacity coefficient.
$S = c \cdot \rho$
c	Specific heat capacity [J/kgK]
ρ	Density [kg/m³]

Heat flux Φ [W]
The heat flux Φ is a measure of the amount of heat transmitted over a certain period of time.
$\Phi = dQ/dt$
Q	Heat energy [J]
t	Time [s]

Heat flux density q [W/m²]
The heat flux density q is the heat flux per unit area of surface.
$q = d\Phi/dA$
Φ	Heat flux [W]
A	Area [m²]

Heat transfer coefficient h [W/m²K]
The heat transfer coefficient h is the amount of heat transferred in 1 second between 1 m² of the surface of a component and the adjacent air when the temperature difference between the two is 1 K.

Heat transfer resistance R_{se} and. R_{si} [m²K/W]
The exterior heat transfer resistance R_{se} is the inverse of the exterior heat transfer coefficient h_e.
$R_{se} = 1/h_e$
h_e Exterior heat transfer coefficient [W/m²K]
The interior heat transfer resistance R_{si} is the inverse of the interior heat transfer coefficient h_i.
$R_{si} = 1/h_i$
h_i Interior heat transfer coefficient [W/m²K]
The values given below may be used for flat surfaces if no specific information on the boundary conditions is available. The procedures given in DIN EN ISO 6946 Appendix A must be used for nonflat surfaces or if there are special boundary conditions.
$R_{se} = 0.04$ m²K/W
$R_{si} = 0.10$ m²K/W (with the heat flowing upwards)
$R_{si} = 0.13$ m²K/W (with the heat flowing horizontally) and ± 30° to the horizontal)
$R_{si} = 0.17$ m²K/W (with the heat flowing downwards)

Wind

Gust speed $\hat{v}$ [m/s]
The gust speed is the highest monthly wind speed observed during the monitoring period.

Dynamic wind pressure q [kN/m²]
The dynamic wind pressure q for a particular wind speed v is:
$q = (\rho/2) \cdot v^2$
v   Wind speed [m/s]
ρ Density of air [kg/m³]
      Unless there are any overriding factors a value of $\rho = 1.25$ kg/m³ may be adopted. This value arises from an atmospheric pressure of 1.013 hPa and a temperature of 10 °C at sea level.
Where:
$q = v^2/1,600$

Reference wind speed v_r [m/s]
The reference wind speed v_r is the wind speed assumed to apply at a height of 10 m above ground level in open countryside without any close obstructions.

Wind pressure w_e [Pa]
The wind pressure w_e is the wind pressure that acts on the external surface of a building.
$w_e = c_{pe} \cdot q(z_e)$
c_{pe} Aerodynamic factor for the external pressure in accordance with DIN 1055-4 [-]
z_e Reference height in accordance with DIN 1055-4 [m]
q   Dynamic wind pressure [kN/m²]

Wind pressure w_i [Pa]
The wind pressure wi is the wind pressure that acts on a surface inside a building.
$w_i = c_{pi} \cdot q(z_i)$
c_{pi} Aerodynamic factor for the internal pressure in accordance with DIN 1055-4 [-]
z_i Reference height in accordance with DIN 1055-4 [m]
q   Dynamic wind pressure [kN/m²]
The internal pressure in a building depends on the size and position of the openings in the external skin. It acts on all the enclosing surfaces of an internal space at the same time and with the same preceding sign (positive or suction pressure). The loading from wind pressure is the resultant of the internal and external pressures. If the internal pressure has a relieving effect on a response from the structure then it must be ignored and taken as zero.

Sound

Sound absorption coefficient α [-]
The sound absorption coefficient α is the ratio of the dissipated and transmitted sound energy to the incident sound energy. The nonreflected fraction a at the wall surface (considered as a separating wall) is taken as being "absorbed". In other areas of physics often only the dissipated fraction is described as the "absorbed fraction".

$\alpha = \delta + \tau$
δ Sound dissipation coefficient [-]
τ Sound transmission coefficient [-]

Equivalent sound absorption area A [m²]
The equivalent sound absorption area A is the area with a sound absorption coefficient $\alpha = 1$ that would absorb the same proportion of sound energy as the whole surface of the room and the objects and people in it.

Sound dissipation coefficient δ [-]
The sound dissipation coefficient d is the ratio of the dissipated sound energy to the incident sound energy.

Reverberation time T_{60} [s]
The reverberation time T_{60} is the period of time between the sound stopping and the time when the average sound energy density in an enclosed room decreases to one millionth (i.e., by 60 dB) of the value immediately before the sound stopped.

Phase velocity c [m/s]
The phase velocity c is the propagation velocity of the phase of a sound wave.
$c = \lambda \cdot f$
λ Wave length [m]
f   Frequency [Hz]

Sound reflection coefficient ρ [-]
The sound reflection coefficient d is ratio of the reflected sound energy to the incident sound energy.

Sound reduction index R [dB]
The sound reduction index is a measure of the sound reduction effect of building components. For the value between two spaces, R is calculated from the sound level difference D, the equivalent absorption area A of the receiving space and the test area S of the component.
$R = D + 10 \lg (S/A)$
D   Sound level difference [dB]
S   Test area of the component [m²]
A   Equivalent absorption area of the receiving space [m²]

Sound pressure p [Pa]
The sound pressure p is the alternating pressure which is created by the sound wave in gases or liquids and which is superimposed on the static pressure (e.g., on the atmospheric pressure).
$p = u \cdot \rho \cdot c$
ρ Density of the medium [kg/m³]
u   Seed of sound [m/s]
c   Phase velocity [m/s]

Sound pressure level L_P [dB]
The sound pressure level L_p is 10 times the logarithm of the ratio of the square of the sound pressure p to the square of the specified reference sound pressure p_0.
$L_p = 10 \lg (p/p_0)^2$
p   Sound pressure [Pa]
p_0 Reference value for airborne sound $p_0 = 20 \, \mu Pa$

Sound power P [W]
The sound power P is the power emitted, transmitted or received in the form of sound waves.

Sound level difference D D [dB]
The sound level difference is the difference between the sound level L_1 in the sending space and the sound level L_2 in the receiving space.
$D = L_1 - L_2$
L_1 Sound level in the emitting space [dB]
L_2 Sound level in the receiving space [dB]
This difference depends on how much sound is absorbed by the enclosing surfaces and the objects in the receiving space. In order to eliminate these influences, the equivalent absorption area A can be calculated and related to an agreed reference absorption area A_0 to produce the standard sound level difference D_n.
$D_n = D - 10 \lg (A/A_0)$
A   Equivalent absorption area of the receiving space [m²]
A_0 Reference absorption area of the receiving space [m²]
      $A_0 = 10$ m² unless a more accurate figure is available.

Sound transmission coefficient τ [K]
The sound transmission coefficient τ is the ratio of the transmitted sound energy to the incident sound energy.
$\delta + \rho + \tau = 1$
δ Sound dissipation coefficient [-]
ρ Sound reflection coefficient [-]
For an amount of incident sound energy 1 striking a wall, a proportion ρ is reflected, δ is lost in the wall and τ is transmitted into the adjoining space.

Wave length λ [m]
The wave length λ is the distance between two consecutive points in the direction of propagation of a sinusoidal wave separated by a 2π phase difference at a particular time of observation.

Moisture

Relative humidity φ [–]
The relative humidity φ is the ratio of the partial pressure of water vapour to the saturation vapour pressure at the temperature θ. The value is always by definition a value between 0 and 1 and may be given as a percentage.

$\varphi = p_D/p_S$

p_D Partial pressure of water vapour [hPa]
p_S Saturation vapour pressure [hPa]

Water vapour diffusion-equivalent air film thickness s_d [m]
The water vapour diffusion-equivalent air film thickness s_d is the thickness of a layer of still air which would have the same water vapour diffusion resistance as the component layer or component composed of a number of layers under consideration. It indicates the resistance to the diffusion of water vapour. The water vapour diffusion-equivalent air film thickness can be a property of a layer or a component. Definition for a layer in a component:

$s_d = \mu \cdot d$

μ Water vapour diffusion resistance factor [-]
d Thickness of the component [m]

The water vapour diffusion-equivalent air film thicknesses of the individual layers in multilayered flat components can be added together to give the figure for the whole component.
Layer open to diffusion:
Layer with $s_d \leq 0.5$ m
Diffusion-inhibiting layer:
Layer with 0.5 m < s_d < 1,500 m
Diffusion-blocking layer:
Layer with $s_d \geq 1,500$ m

Water vapour diffusion resistance factor m [-]
The water vapour diffusion resistance factor m is a material property. It is the product of the water vapour diffusion coefficient in air and the water vapour diffusion coefficient in a material. It indicates how much the water vapour diffusion resistance of the material under consideration is greater than that of a layer of still air of the same thickness at the same temperature.

Water vapour pressure p [Pa]
The water vapour pressure p is the pressure created by the water vapour contained in the air. The water vapour pressure depends on the temperature and relative humidity of the air. The water vapour pressure at a given temperature and relative humidity is described as the water vapour partial pressure or the partial pressure of water vapour p_D. At the same temperature, the maximum possible water vapour pressure ($\varphi = 1$ bzw. 100 %) is described as the saturation vapour pressure p_s.

Water content of air x [g/kg]
The water content x is usually described as the absolute humidity x of the air. If x kg of water vapour is added to each kg of dry air, then the mass of the resulting mixture is (1 + x) kg. This mixture would be described as having an absolute humidity of x kg of water per kg of dry air. The absolute humidity of saturated air ($\varphi = 1$ bzw. 100 %) is x_s.

$x = p_D/p_L$

p_D Partial pressure of water vapour (absolute) [hPa]
p_L Partial pressure of dry air (absolute) [hPa] [hPa]

EnEV – energy saving regulations

A/V$_e$- ratio [m^{-1}]
The surface area to volume ratio A/V$_e$ of a building is the ratio of the heat-transmitting enclosing surface to the heated building volume.

A Heat-transmitting enclosing surface area of a building calculated in accordance with DIN EN ISO 13789 Annex B [m^2]
The surfaces referred to here comprise the external skin of the enclosed heated zone
V_e Heated building volume [m^3]
The volume enclosed by A

Annual primary energy demand Q_p [kWh/a]
$Q_p = (Q_h + Q_W) \cdot e_P$

Q_h Annual heating energy demand [kWh/a]
Q_W Hot water energy demand [kWh/a]
e_P Installation energy use index assessed in accordance with DIN 4701-10 [-]

Hot water energy demand Q_W [kWh/a]
$Q_W = 12.5 \cdot A_N$

A_N Usable floor area [m^2]

Simplified procedure for residential buildings with a proportion of window area of less than 30 %
Annual heating energy demand Q_h [kWh/a]

$Q_h = 66 \cdot (H_T + H_V) - 0.95 \cdot (Q_S + Q_i)$

66 A factor which takes into account the average degree day figure and night reduction [kKh/a]
H_T Specific transmission heat loss [W/K]
H_V Specific ventilation heat loss [W/K]
0.95 Reduction factor for the degree of utilisation of heat gain [-]
Q_S Solar gain [kWh/a]
Q_i Internal gain [kWh/a]

Specific transmission heat loss H_T [W/K]
$H_T = \sum (F_{xcomponent} \cdot U_{component} \cdot A_{component}) + 0.05 \cdot A_{totalt}$

$F_{component}$ Temperature correction factor for components [-]
$U_{component}$ U-value of component [W/m^{2}K]
$A_{component}$ Area of the component [m^2]
0.05 Factor taking into account heat bridges in accordance with examples in DIN 4108 [-]
A_{total} Total heat transfer area [m^2]

Specific ventilation heat loss H_V [W/K]
$H_V = 0.19 \cdot V_e$ without airtightness test
$H_V = 0.163 \cdot V_e$ with airtightness test
V_e Heated gross volume [m^3]

Solar gain Q_S [kWh/a]
$Q_S = (0.567 \cdot I_{s,j} \cdot g_{window} \cdot A_{window})$

0.567 Reduction factor for proportion of window frame area, partial shading, dirt, etc. [-]
$I_{s,j}$ Available solar energy during the time considered, e.g., heating period, depending on the orientation [kWh/m^{2}a]
g_{window} Total energy transmittance of the glazing [-]
A_{window} Usable floor area [m^2]

Internal gain Q_i [kWh/a]
$Q_i = 22 \cdot A_N$

22 A factor which takes into account the number of heating days per year and internal loads in residential buildings [kWh/m^{2}a]
A_N Usable floor area [m^2]

Material properties

Material group or use	ρ [kg/m³]	λ [W/mK]	c_p [J/kgK]	μ moist/dry	b_p [J/(m²Ks$^{1/2}$)]	S [kJ/m³K]
Concrete						
Concrete, medium density	2,000	1.35	1,000	60/100	1,643	2,000
Concrete high density	2,400	2	1,000	80/30	2,191	2,400
Concrete, reinforced (with 1% steel)	2,300	2.3	1,000	80/130	2,300	2,300
Concrete, with pumice aggregate	500–1,300	0.12–0.47	1,000	40/50	245–782	500–1,300
Concrete, with nonporous aggregate / artificial stone	1,600–2,400	0.81–1.40	1,000	120/150	1,138–1,833	1,600–2,400
Concrete, with expanded clay aggregate	400–700	0.13–0.23	1,000	4/6	228–401	400–700
Concrete, aerated	300–1,000	0.11–0.31	1,000	6/10	182–557	300–1,000
Concrete, with lightweight aggregate	500–2,000	0.22–1.20	1,000	10/15	332–1,549	500–2,000
Stone and masonry						
Natural stone, crystalline	2,800	3.5	1,000	10,000	3,130	2,800
Natural stone, sedimentary	2,600	2.3	1,000	2/250	2,445	2,600
Natural stone, lightweight sedimentary	1,500	0.85	1,000	20/30	1,129	1,500
Granite	2,500–2,700	2.8	1,000	10,000	2,646–2,750	2,500–2,700
Marble	2,800	3.5	1,000	10,000	3,130	2,800
Slate	2,000–2,800	2.2	1,000	800/1,000	2,098–2,482	2,000–2,800
Limestone	1,600–2,600	0.85–2.3	1,000	20–200/30–250	1,166–2,445	1,600–2,600
Sandstone, (quartzite)	2,600	2.3	1,000	30/40	2,445	2,600
Solid brick, (fired clay)	1,000–2,400	0.50–1.4	1,000	10/16	707–1,833	1,000–2,400
Wood						
Construction timber	700	0.18	1,600	50/200	449	1,120
Plywood	300–1,000	0.09–0.24	1,600	50–110/150–250	208–620	480–1,600
Chipboard, cement-bound	1,200	0.23	1,500	30/50	643	1,800
Chipboard	300–900	0.10–0.18	1,700	10–20/50	226–525	510–1,530
OSB board	650	0.13	1,700	30/50	379	1,105
Wood-fibre board, including MDF	250–800	0.07–0.18	1,700	2–20/5–10	172–495	425–1,360
Metals						
Aluminium	2,800	160	880	∞	19,855	2,464
Copper	8,900	380	380	∞	35,849	3,382
Cast iron	7500	50	450	∞	12,990	3,375
Lead	11,300	35	130	∞	7,170	1,469
Steel	7,800	50	450	∞	13,248	3,510
Steel, stainless	7,900	17	460	∞	7,860	3,634
Zinc	7,200	110	380	∞	17,348	2,736
Solid plastics						
Acrylic plastics	1,050	0.2	1,500	10,000	561	1,575
Polycarbonate	1,200	0.2	1,200	5,000	537	1,440

Material group or use	ρ [kg/m³]	λ [W/mK]	c_p [J/kgK]	μ moist/dry	b_p [J/(m²Ks^{1/2})]	S [kJ/m³K]
Polytetrafluorethylene plastics (PTFE) (Teflon)	2,200	0.25	1,000	10,000	742	2,200
Polyvinylchloride (PVC)	1,390	0.17	900	50,000	461	1,251
Polyamide (Nylon)	1,150	0.25	1,600	50,000	678	1,840
Polyethylene, high density	980	0.5	1,800	100,000	939	1,764
Polystyrene	1,050	0.16	1,300	100,000	467	1,365
Polyurethane (PU)	1,200	0.25	1,800	6,000	735	2,160
Silicone without filler	1,200	0.35	1,000	5,000	648	1,200
Urethane / polyurethane foam	1,300	0.21	1,800	60	701	2,340
Plasters and mortars						
Gypsum insulating plaster	600	0.18	1,000	6/10	329	600
Gypsum plaster	1,000–1,300	0.40–0.57	1,000	6/10	632–861	1,000–1,300
Cement, sand	1,800	1	1,000	6/10	1,342	1,800
Mortar (masonry mortar and render)	250–2,000	0.21–1.4	1,000	10/20	229–1,673	250–2,000
Thermal insulation						
Rigid polystyrene foam, expanded	10–50	0.030–0.050	1,450	60	21–60	15–73
Rigid polystyrene foam, extruded	20–65	0.026–0.040	1,450	150	27–61	29–94
Rigid polyurethane foam	28–55	0.020–0.040	1,400	60	28–55	39–77
Mineral wool	10–200	0.030–0.050	1,030	1	18–101	10–206
Foam glass	100–150	0.038–0.055	1,000	∞	62–91	100–150
Perlite boards	140–240	0.045–0.065	900	5	75–118	126–216
Cork, expanded	90–140	0.040–0.055	1,560	5/10	75–110	140–218
Wood wool lightweight boards	250–450	0.060–0.10	1,470	3/5	148 – 257	368 – 662
Wood fibre insulation boards	150–250	0.035–0.060	1,400	5/10	86–145	210–350
Polyurethane spray foam	30–50	0.025–0.035	1,400	60	32–49	42–70
Mineral wool, loose	15–60	0.030–0.050	1,030	1	22–56	15–62
Cellulose fibres, loose	20–60	0.035–0.045	1,600	2	33–66	32–96
Expanded perlite fill	30–150	0.06	900	2	40–90	27–135
Expanded clay fill	200–400	0.10–0.16	1,000	2	141–253	200–400
Polystyrene particle fill	10–30	0.040–0.060	1,400	2	24–50	14–42
Miscellaneous						
Bitumen	1,050	0.17	1,000	50,000	422	1,050
Gypsum	600–1,500	0.18–0.56	1,000	4/10	329–917	600–1,500
Gypsum plasterboards	900	0.25	1,000	4/10	474	900
Glass, float glass	2,500	1	750	∞	1,369	1,875
Ceramic / porcelain boards	2,300	1.3	840	∞	1,585	1,932
Plastic boards	1,000	0.2	1,000	10,000	447	1,000
Air, dry	1,23	0.025	1,008	1	6	1,24
Water at 0 °C	1,000	0.6	4,190	–	1,586	4,190
Water, ice at 0 °C	900	2.2	2,000	–	1,990	1,800

Parameters and units

Basic and derived units	Symbol	SI unit	Symbol	Relationships
Length	l	Metre	m	1 m = 100 cm = 1,000 mm
Area	A	Square metre	m^2	$1\ m^2 = 1\ m \cdot 1\ m$
Volume	V	Cubic metre	m^3	$1\ m^3 = 1\ m \cdot 1\ m \cdot 1\ m$
Time	t	Second	s	1 s = 1/60 min = 1/3,600 h
Velocity	v	Metre per second	m/s	m/s = 3.6 km/h
Volumetric flow	$\dot{V}$	Cubic metre per second	m^3/s	$1\ m^3/s = 1,000\ l/s$
Density	ρ	Kilogram per m^3	kg/m^3	$1\ kg/m^3 = 1\ mg/cm^3$
Pressure	p	Pascal	Pa	$1\ Pa = 1\ N/m^2$
Force	F	Newton	N	$1\ N = 1\ kg \cdot m/s^2$
Mass	m	Kilogram	kg	1 kg = 1.000 g
Energy, work	W	Joule	J	1 J = 1 Ws = 1 Nm
Power	P	Watt	W	1 W = 1 VA = 1 J/s = 1 Nm/s
Illuminance	E	Lux	lx	$1\ lx = 1\ lm/m^2$
Luminance	L	Candela per m^2	cd/m^2	$1\ cd/m^2 = 104\ cd/cm^2 = 104\ sb$
Light intensity	I	Candela	cd	1 lm/sr
Luminous flux	Φ	Lumen	lm	$1\ lm = 1\ cd \cdot sr$
Coeff. of long. thermal expansion	α	Millimetre	mm	$1\ mm = 1 \cdot 10^{-3}\ m$
Thermodynamic temperature	T	Kelvin	K	0 K = -273.15 °C
Celsius temperature	θ	Degree Celsius	°C	0 °C = +273.15 K
Thermal transmittance (ISO 6946)	U	Watt per ($m^2 \cdot$ Kelvin)	$W/(m^2 \cdot K)$	
Thermal resistance (ISO 6946)	R_T	($m^2 \cdot$ Kelvin) per Watt	$m^2 \cdot K/W$	
Thermal transmittance	Λ	Watt per ($m^2 \cdot$ Kelvin)	$W/(m^2 \cdot K)$	
Thermal resistance	R	($m^2 \cdot$ Kelvin) per watt	$m^2 \cdot K/W$	
Coefficient of heat penetration	b	Joule per ($m^2 \cdot$ Kelvin $\cdot\ s^{1/2}$)	$J/(m^2 \cdot K \cdot s^{1/2})$	
Heat capacity	C	Joule per Kelvin	J/K	
Specific heat capacity	c	Joule per (kg $\cdot$ K)	$J/(kg \cdot K)$	$1\ J/(kg \cdot K) = 1 \cdot 10^{-3}\ kJ/(kg \cdot K) = 0.28 \cdot 10^{-6}\ kWh/(kg \cdot K)$
Heat energy	Q	Joule, kilowatt hour	J, kWh	1 kWh = 3,600 kJ
Thermal conductivity	λ	Watt per (m $\cdot$ Kelvin)	$W/(m \cdot K)$	
Heat storage capacity	Q_{SP}	Kilojoule	kJ	1 kJ = 1,000 J = 0.28 Wh
Heat storage coefficient	W	Kilojoule per ($m^2 \cdot$ Kelvin)	$kJ/m^2 \cdot K$	
Volumetric heat capacity	S	Kilojoule per ($m^3 \cdot$ Kelvin)	$kJ/m^3 \cdot K$	
Heat flux	Φ	Watt	W	1 W = 1 J/s = 1 Nm/s
Heat flux density	q	Watt per m^2	W/m^2	
Heat transfer coefficient	h	Watt per ($m^2 \cdot$ Kelvin)	$W/(m^2 \cdot K)$	
Exterior heat transfer resistance	R_{se}	($m^2 \cdot$ Kelvin) per Watt	$m^2 \cdot K/W$	
Interior heat transfer resistance	R_{si}	($m^2 \cdot$ Kelvin) per Watt	$m^2 \cdot K/W$	

Boundary conditions for all simulations

Thermal simulations
The thermal simulations were carried out using the TRNSYS computer program. The models were based in a typical standard office room in order to be able to make statements about the interactions between energy and building climate. The room dimensions represent the most unfavourable case; with larger room depths the thermal conditions are normally more favourable. Occupancy rates and internal heat loads were based on typical office use. The results are not transferable to situations with very high internal loads from IT or very high occupancy. Usually only one or two parameters were varied so that comparability of results could be retained between different options. Typical usage was assumed.

Daylight simulations
The daylight simulations were carried out using the Radiance computer program. The room dimensions are the same as those selected for the thermal simulations. Typical reflectivities were selected for the standard case. The characteristics of the glazing are the same as those selected for the thermal simulations to enable the interactions between indoor climate and daylight to be clearly readable.

Room model

Room dims. L/B/H	5.0/4.5/3.0 m
Area	22.5 m²
Volume	67.5 m³

Internal loads
PCs	2 x 230 W
Persons	2 x 75 W

Period of building use	8:00-18:00 hrs

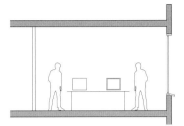

Construction

Ceiling, thermal storage mass not effective
Solid ceiling with double floor and suspended ceiling with sound absorber

Thickness	280 mm
U-value	0.37 W/m²K
Effective thermal storage mass	c_{eff} = 0.8 Wh/m²K
Reflectivity of ceiling	80 %
Reflectivity of floor	20 %

Ceiling, thermal storage mass effective
Solid slabs with screed, without cladding

Thickness	260 mm
U-value	0.83 W/m²K
Effective thermal storage mass	c_{eff} = 103.9 Wh/m²K
Reflectivity of ceiling	40 %
Reflectivity of floor	10 %

Internal wall, heavy

Thickness	180 mm
U-value	2.67 W/m²K
Effective thermal storage mass	c_{eff} = 51.7 Wh/m²K
Reflectance	40 %

Internal wall, light

Thickness	125 mm
U-value	0.35 W/m²K
Effective thermal storage mass	c_{eff} = 3.3 Wh/m²K
Reflectance	80 %

External wall

Thickness	190 mm
U-value	0.29 W/m²K
Effective thermal storage mass	c_{eff} = 11.6 Wh/m²K
Reflectance	80 %

Facade

Glazing types

	U-value [W/m²K]	g-value [-]	τ-value [-]
2-pane insulation glazing, argon	1.4	0.6	0.8
2-pane insulation glazing, krypton	1.1	0.6	0.8
3-pane insulation glazing, krypton	0.7	0.4	0.7
Solar control glass	1.1	0.33	0.4

 30 %
 50 %
 70 %
 90 %

Solar screening control

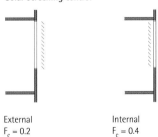

External	Internal
F_c = 0.2	F_c = 0.4

Sonnenschutzsteuerung

Temperature-controlled	Closed at T_{room} > 24 °C
Light-controlled	Closed at I_{room} > 180 W/m²

Ventilation

Ventilation strategies summer day

Air changes n [h⁻¹]

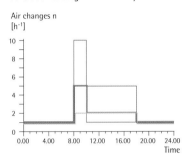

Ventilation strategies night ventilation

Air changes n [h⁻¹]

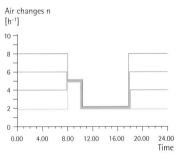

Ventilation strategies winter day

Air changes n [h⁻¹]

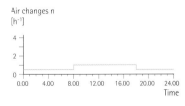

Boundary conditions for pages 15–16

Room and climate

Office area	22.5 m²
Orientation	West
Facade area	13.5 m²
Proportion of window area	Varies
U-value glazing	1.3 W/m²K
g-value	0.6
F_c-value	0.2
Solar screening	Outside
Solar screening control	Closed at $I_{Fa} > 180$ W/m²
U-value external wall	0.30 W/m²K
Internal walls	Lightweight, adiabatic
Ceilings	Solid, adiabatic
Loads 8:00–18:00 hrs	Weekdays 2 pers. + 2 PCs
Lighting	None
Climate	Manama, Singapore, Rio de Janeiro, Sydney, New York, Shanghai, Kapstadt, Mexico City

Room conditioning

Natural ventilation + night ventilation

Ventilation	Weekdays
8:00–18:00 hrs	$n = 2\ h^{-1}$
18:00–8:00 hrs	$n = 4\ h^{-1}$
Weekends	$n = 1\ h^{-1}$
Cooling	None

Natural ventilation + thermally activated components

Ventilation	Weekdays
8:00–18:00 hrs	$n = 2\ h^{-1}$
18:00–8:00 hrs	$n = 1\ h^{-1}$
Weekends	$n = 1\ h^{-1}$
Inlet temp. TAC	Wet bulb temp.
Weekends	TAC off

Supply air cooling

Mech. ventilation	Weekdays
8:00–18:00 hrs	$n = 2\ h^{-1}$
18:00–8:00 hrs	$n = 1\ h^{-1}$
Weekends	$n = 1\ h^{-1}$
Supply air temperature	
Period of building use	20 °C
Other times	15 °C

Supply air cooling + thermally activated components

Mech. ventilation	Weekdays
8:00–18:00 hrs	$n = 2\ h^{-1}$ T=20 °C
18:00–8:00 hrs	$n = 1\ h^{-1}$ T=15 °C
Weekends	$n = 1\ h^{-1}$ T=15 °C
Inlet temp. TAC	20 °C
Weekends	TAC off

Ideal cooling

Mech. ventilation	Weekdays
8:00–18:00 hrs	$n = 2\ h^{-1}$ T=20 °C
18:00–8:00 hrs	$n = 1\ h^{-1}$ T=15 °C
Weekends	$n = 1\ h^{-1}$ T=15 °C
Active cooling (cooled ceiling)	at $T_{room} > 25$ °C max. 60 W/m²

Bibliography

General literature

Behling, S., Behling, St., Schindler, B.: Sol Power. Die Evolution der solaren Architektur. Munich/New York 1996.

Bischof, W., Bullinger-Naber, M., Kruppa, B.: Expositionen und gesundheitliche Beeinträchtigungen in Bürogebäuden. Results of the ProKlimA Project. 2003.

BKI Baukosten 2001, Part 2: Kostenkennwerte für Bauelemente. Stuttgart 2001/2002.

CCI: Urteil mit enormer Tragweite – Im Büro gilt die 26°C-Grenze. CCI-Print 7/2003.
Compagno, A.: Intelligente Glasfassaden. Material, Anwendung, Gestaltung. 5th revised and updated edition. Berlin 2002.

Daniels, K.: The Technology of Ecological Building. Basic Principles and Measures, Examples and Ideas. Basel/Boston/Berlin 1997.

Daniels, K.: Low-Tech Light-Tech High-Tech. Building in the Information Age. Basel 1998.

Daniels, K.: Advanced Building Systems. A Technical Guide for Architects and Engineers. Basel 2003.

Danner, D., Dassler, F.H., Krause, J.R.: Die klimaaktive Fassade. Edition -Intelligente Architektur. Leinfelden-Echterdingen 1999.

Eisele, J., Kloft, E. (eds.): High-Rise Manual. Typology and Design, Construction and Technology. Basel 2003.

Flagge, I., Herzog, T.: Architektur und Technologie. Munich 2001.

Frank, W.: Raumklima und thermische Behaglichkeit. Berichte aus der Bauforschung. Berlin 1975.

Hausladen, G. (ed.): Innovative Gebäude-, Technik- und -Energiekonzepte. Munich 2001.

Hausladen, G., de Saldanha, M., Liedl, P., Sager C.: ClimateDesign. Basel 2005.

Hausladen, G., de Saldanha, M., Nowak, W., Liedl, P.: Einführung in die Bau-klimatik. Klima und Energiekonzepte für Gebäude. Munich 2003.

Hausladen, G., de Saldanha, M., Sager, C., Liedl, P.: Climadesign, Messe-München Publikationen. Munich 2003.

Hegger, M., Auch-Schwelk, V., Fuchs, M., Rosenkranz, T.: Construction Materials Manual. Edition DETAIL. Munich 2005.

Heisel, J.: Planungsatlas. Berlin 2004.

Herzog, T.: Solar Energy in Architecture and Urban Planning. Munich 1996.

Herzog, T., Krippner, R., Lang, W.: Facade Construction Manual. Edition DETAIL. Munich 2004.

Hinrichs, D.U., Heusler, W.: Fassaden-Gebäudehüllen für das 21. Jahrhundert. 2., erweiterte Ausgabe. Basel 2006.

Hohmann, R., Setzer, M.J.: Bauphysikalische Formeln und -Tabellen. Wärmeschutz, Feuchteschutz, Schallschutz. Düsseldorf 1993.

Klotz, H.: Von der Urhütte zum Wolkenkratzer. Geschichte der gebauten Umwelt. Munich 1991.

Knissel, J.: Energieeffiziente Büro- und Verwaltungsgebäude. Institut Wohnen und Umwelt. Darmstadt 1999.

Müller, W., Vogel, G.: dtv-Atlas Baukunst. Vols. 1 and 2, 11th Edition. Munich 1997.

Neufert, P. and C., Neff, L., Franken, C.: Neufert Bauentwurfslehre. 37th Edition Brunswick/Wiesbaden 2002.

Soft Success Factors, Empirische Studie im Verbundforschungsprojekt-OFFICE 21.

Pisthol, W.: Handbuch der Gebäudetechnik. Planungsgrundlagen und Beispiele. Vols.1 and 2. Düsseldorf 2005.

Pültz, G.: Bauklimatischer Entwurf für moderne Glasarchitektur. Passive Maßnahmen der Energieeinsparung, Angewandte Bauphysik. Berlin 2002.

Recknagel, H., Sprenger, E., Schramek, R.: Taschenbuch für Heizung + Klimatechnik 03/04. Munich 2003.

RWE: Bau-Handbuch. Frankfurt am Main 2004.

Schempp, D. et al.: Solares Bauen. Cologne 1992.

Schittich, C.: Solar Architecture. Strategies, Visions, Concepts. Edition DETAIL. Basel/Boston/Berlin 2003.

Schittich, C., Staib, G., Balkow, D., Schuler, M., Sobek, W.: Glass Construction Manual. Edition DETAIL. Basel 1999.

Spath, D., Kern, P.: Zukunftsoffensive OFFICE 21 – Mehr Leistung in innovativen Arbeitswelten. Cologne 2004.

Voss, K., Löhnert, G., Herkel, S., Wagner, A., Wambsganß, M.: Bürogebäude mit Zukunft. Cologne 2005.

Wellpott E.: Technischer Ausbau von Gebäuden. 8th Edition. Stuttgart 2005.

Wormuth, R., Schneider, K.J.: Baulexikon. Berlin 2000.

Wyon. D.P.: The effects of indoor climate on productivity and performance.

Zimmermann, M.: Handbuch der passiven Kühlung. EMPA. Dübendorf 1999.

Chapter 2: Facade functions

Bartenbach, C.: Tagesbelichtung von Arbeitsräumen. Lichttechnische und wahrnehmungspsychologische Aspekte. Munich 2002.

BINE Informationsdienst, profi info I/00: Tageslichtnutzung in Gebäuden. Fachinformationszentrum Karlsruhe 2001.

BINE Informationsdienst, themen info I/03: Passive Kühlung mit Nachtlüftung. Fachinformationszentrum Karlsruhe 2003.

Blaich, J. et al., EMPA-Akademie: Die Gebäudehülle. -Konstruktive, -bauphysikalische und umweltrelevante Aspekte. Stuttgart 2000.

Blum, H.-J., Compagno, A., Fitzner, K., Heusler, W., Hortmanns, M., Hosser, D., Müller, H., Nolte, C., Schwarzkopf, D., Sedlacek, G., Thiel, D., Ziller, C.: Doppelfassaden. Berlin 2001.

Brandi, U., Geissmar-Brandi, C.: Lichtbuch. Die Praxis der Lichtplanung. Basel/Boston/Berlin 2001.

Davies, M.: Eine Wand für alle Jahreszeiten: die intelligente Umwelt erschaffen. In: Arch+ Nr. 104, 7/1990.

Eicke-Henning, W.: Glasarchitektur – Lehren aus einem Großversuch. 2004.

Eicke-Henning, W.: Schwitzen im Glaskasten. In: Deutsche Bauzeitung 5/2004.

Feist, W.: Grundlagen der Gestaltung von Passivhäusern. Darmstadt 2001.

Gertis, K., Hauser, G.: Energieeinsparung durch Stoßlüftung? In: HLH 30 No. 3/1979.

Glück, B.: Wärmetechnisches Raummodell. Heidelberg 1997.

Hauser, G.: Sommerliches Temperaturverhalten von Einzelbüros. In: TAB 10 12/1979, pp. 1015–1019.

Hauser, G., Heibel, B.: Thermische Wirkung einer zusammengesetzten Sonnenschutzvorrichtung. In: Ingenieur-Hochbau. Reports from research and practice. Commemorative publication for the 60th birthday of Prof. Dr. Erich Cziesielski. Düsseldorf 1998.

Hauser, G., Heibel, B.: Bemessungsgrundlagen für Zuluftfassaden. Bauphysik 20 3/1998, pp. 74–79.

Hauser, G., Heibel, B.: Modellierung und Quantifizierung der Wirkung von Sonnenschutzvorrichtungen über die Sommerperiode. DFG-Priority Research Programme "Bauphysik der Außenwände", Final Report, pp. 109–130. Stuttgart 2000.

Hauser, G., Otto, F.: Einfluss der Wärmespeicherfähigkeit auf Heizwärmebedarf und sommerliches Wärmeverhalten. In: db 134 4/2000, pp. 113–118.

Heusler, W., Scholz, C.: Tageslichtsysteme – Aktuelle Entwicklungen und Tendenzen. In: Bauphysik 15 6/1993, pp. 173–178.

Ihle, C., Bader, R., Golla, M.: Tabellenbuch. Sanitär, Heizung, Lüftung. 4th Edition. Troisdorf 2002.

Interpane Glas Industrie AG: Gestalten mit Glas. 6th Edition. Lauenförde 2002.

Lohmeyer, G. C. O.: Praktische Bauphysik. Eine Einführung mit Berechnungsbeispielen. 4th Edition. Stuttgart/Leipzig/Wiesbaden 2001.

Maas, A.: Experimentelle Quantifizierung des Luftwechsels bei Fensterlüftung. Dissertation Universität Gesamthochschule Kassel. 1995.

Maas, A., Schmidt, D., Hauser, G.: Experimentelle Untersuchungen zum Luftaustausch bei Querlüftung. In: TAB 30 11/1999, pp. 57–64.

Oesterle, E., Lutz, M., Lieb, R.-D., Heusler, W.: Doppelschalige Fassaden. Ganzheitliche Planung, Konstruktion, Bauphysik, Aerophysik, Raumkonditionierung, Wirtschaftlichkeit. Munich 1999.

Pernpeintner, A.: Der Wind als Faktor in der Gebäudeplanung. In: Climadesign. Messe-München Publikationen. Munich 2003.

Richter, W.: Handbuch der thermischen Behaglichkeit – Heizperiode. Dortmund/Berlin/Dresden 2003.

Rouvel, L., Kolmetz, S.: Thermische Bewertung von Gebäuden unter sommerlichen Randbedingungen. In: Gesundheitsingenieur 2/1997, pp. 65–120.

Schittich, C. (ed.): Building Skins: Concepts, Layers, Materials. Edition DETAIL. Basel/Boston/Berlin 2001.

Szerman, M.: Auswirkungen der Tageslichtnutzung auf das energetische -Verhalten von Bürogebäuden. Dissertation. Universität Stuttgart. 1994.

Testreferenzjahre für Deutschland (TRY). Deutscher Wetterdienst (www.dwd.de/TRY). Offenbach 2004.

WAREMA Sonnenschutztechnik. Product catalogue 2005.

Ziller, C., Sedlacek, G., Ruscheweyh, H., Oesterle E.; Lieb, R.D.: Natürliche Belüftung eines Hochhauses mit Doppelfassade. In: Ki 8/1996.

Chapter 3: Facade concepts

Auer, F., Hausladen, G.: Konzeptstudie Langenscheidt Hochhaus. unpublished 2001.

BINE Informationsdienst, project info 01/04: Mehr als Fassade. Fachinformationszentrum Karlsruhe 2004.

BINE Informationsdienst, project info 07/01: Energiesparendes modulares -Fassadensystem. Fachinformationszentrum Karlsruhe 2004.

Bundesamt für Energie, Bern (Pub.): Lüftung von großen Räumen – Handbuch für Planer. Dübendorf 1998.

Compagno, A.: Die Intelligente Fassade – High-Tech für ein klimagerechtes Bauen. 1993.

Döge, K.; Franzke, U.: Zusammenwirken von Außenklima, Doppelfassade und Raumklima. In: TAB 1/1998, pp. 41–46.

Gertis, K.: Sind neuere Fassadenentwicklungen sinnvoll? Teil 2: Glas-Doppelfassaden (GDF). In: Bauphysik 21 2/1999, pp. 54–66.

Hall, M.: Untersuchungen zum thermisch bedingten Luftwechselpotenzial von Kippfenstern. Dissertation Universität Kassel 2004.

Hauser, G.: Energetische Wirkung einer durchströmten Glasfassade. In: TAB 19 4/1989, pp. 329–338.

Hellwig, R.: Natürlich behaglich. Natürliche Lüftung und Behaglichkeit – Gegensätze? In: Gesundheitsingenieur 125, 5/2004.

Herzog, T.: Nachhaltige Höhe – Deutsche Messe AG Hannover, Verwaltungsgelände. Munich/London/New York 2000.

Heusler, W., Compagno, A.: Mehrschalige Fassaden. Eine Gegenüberstellung verschiedener zweischaliger Fassadensysteme. In: DBZ 6/1998. pp. 131–138.

Klauck, B.: Zur Konstruktion der energetisch optimierten Glasfassaden. In: Bauwelt 43/1996 and 44/1996, pp. 2456–2461.

Kornadt, O., Lehmann, L., Zapp F.J.: Doppelfassaden: Nutzen und Kosten. In: Bauphysik 21, 1/1999, pp. 10–19.

Lang, W.: Typologie Mehrschaliger Fassaden. Dissertation TU Munich. 2000.

Sedlacek, G., Ziller, C.: Strömungstechnische Untersuchungen von Doppelfassaden. In: Tagungsband zum Internationalen Bauphysikkongress 1997, pp. 127–137.

Trieb, O.: e-on Weiden. In: Xia intelligente architektur 07/09. 2005.

Ziller, C.: Modellversuche und Berechnungen zur Optimierung der natürlichen Lüftung durch Doppelfassaden. Dissertation at the RWTH Aachen. Lehrstuhl für Stahlbau u. Windingenieurtechnik. 1999.

Chapter 4: Facade technologies

BASF Product brochure: Micronal PCM, Smartboard. Ludwigshafen 2006.

BINE Projekt-info Service No. 9/October 95: Tageslichtlenksysteme mit holographisch-optischen Elementen. Karlsruhe 1995.

BINE Informationsdienst, Projekt-info 02/2000: Raumluftkonditionierung mit Erdwärmetauschern. Fachinformationszentrum Karlsruhe 2000.

BINE Informationsdienst, Projekt-info 05/2000: Kraft-Wärme-Kopplung mit Brennstoffzellen. Fachinformationszentrum Karlsruhe 2000.

BINE Informationsdienst, Projekt-info 14/2001: Neue Wärmepumpen-Konzepte für energieeffiziente Gebäude. Fachinformationszentrum Karlsruhe 2001.

BINE Informationsdienst, Projekt-info I/02: Schaltbare und regelbare Verglasungen. Fachinformationszentrum Karlsruhe 2002.

BINE Informationsdienst, Projekt-info 4/01: Vakuumdämmung. Fachinformationszentrum Karlsruhe 2002.

BINE Informationsdienst, Themeninfo IV/02: Latentwärmespeicher. Fachinformationszentrum Karlsruhe 2002.

BINE Informationsdienst, Projekt-info 06/02: Latentwärmespeicher in Baustoffen. Fachinformationszentrum Karlsruhe 2002.

BINE Informationsdienst, Projekt-info 03/2003: Performance von Photovoltaik-Anlagen. Fachinformationszentrum Karlsruhe 2003.

BINE Informationsdienst, basisEnergie 3: Photovoltaik. Fachinformationszentrum Karlsruhe 2003.

BINE Informationsdienst, basisEnergie 4: Thermische Nutzung der Solarenergie. Fachinformationszentrum Karlsruhe 2003.

Buntkiel-Kuck, K.: Tageslichtlenksysteme. In: Baumeister-Sonderheft 4/1993, pp. 14–15.

Burg, M., Dietrich, U., Kischkoweit-Lopin, M., Müller, H., Siedentop, G.: Lichtlenkende Hologramme in Fassaden. In: Baumeister-Sonderheft 4/1993, pp. 4–8.

Dörken Product brochure: Delta – Cool 24. Herdecke 2006.

Hullmann, H.: Photovoltaik in Gebäuden. Handbuch für Architekten und Ingenieure. Stuttgart 2000.

Kaltenbach, F.: PCM Latent Thermal Storage Media – Heating and Cooling without Energy Consumption? In: DETAIL 6/2005, pp. 660–665.

Kerschberger, A., Platzer, W., Weidlich, B.: TWD, Transparente Wärmedämmung. Produkte, Projekte, Planungshinweise. Wiesbaden/Berlin 1998.

Müller, F.O.: Holografisch-optische Elemente. In: Das Bauzentrum 5/1995, pp. 31–33.

Nickel, J.: Heizen und Kühlen mit Decken. In: TAB 5/1997, pp. 41–44.

Olesen, B.W.: Flächenheizung und Kühlung. Einsatzbereiche für Fußboden-, Wand-, und Deckensysteme. Velta GmbH, Norderstedt 1997.

Schossig, P., Henning, H.M., Raicu, A., Haussmann, T.: Mikroverkapselte Phasenwechselmaterialien in Wandverbundsystemen zur Komfortsteigerung und Energieeinsparung. 12. Symposium Thermische Solarenergie. OTTI Technologie-Kolleg, Symposium Proceedings pp. 169–173. Staffelstein 2002.

Schwab, H., Heinemann, U., Fricke, J.: Vacuum Insulation Panels – a Highly Efficient Insulation System for the Future. In: DETAIL 7/2001, pp. 1301–1304.

Strieder, B.: Passive Klimatisierung von Containerbauten durch den Einsatz von PCM. ZAE Symposium 2004. Wärme- und Kältespeicherung durch Phasenwechselmaterialien. Garching 2004.

Willems, M.: Vakuumdämmung. In: Bauphysik Kalender. Berlin 2004.

Wirth, H., Horn, R.: Entwicklung von selbstregulierenden Sonnenschutzgläsern. 8th Symposium Innovative Lichttechnik in Gebäuden. OTTI Technologie-Kolleg, Symposium Proceedings pp. 124-128. Staffelstein 24/25.01.2002.

Guidelines and standards

Workplace Regulation 5: Ventilation.

Workplace Regulation 6/1 and 3: Room temperatures.

Workplace Regulation 7/1: Visual relationships with the outside world.
DIN 1055-4: Action on structures - Part 4: Wind loads. Berlin 2005.

DIN 12524: Building materials and products - Hygrothermal properties - Tabulated design values. Berlin 2000.

DIN 18041: Acoustic quality in small to medium-sized rooms. Berlin 2004.

DIN 18599: Energy efficiency of buildings – Calculation of the net, final and primary energy demand for heating, cooling, ventilation, domestic hot water and lighting. Berlin 2005.

DIN 1946-6: Ventilation and air conditioning - Part 6: Ventilation for residential buildings. Requirements, performance, acceptance.
(VDI ventilation code of practice). Berlin 1998.

DIN 33403: Climate at the workplace and in its environments. Berlin 2000.

DIN 4108: Thermal insulation and energy economy of buildings. Berlin 2004.

DIN 4109: Sound insulation in buildings. Berlin 1989.

DIN 4543-1: Office workplaces - Part 1: Space for the arrangement and use of office furniture. Berlin 1994.

DIN 4701-10: Energy efficiency of heating and ventilation systems in buildings. Berlin 2003.

DIN 4710: Statistics on German meteorological data for calculating the energy requirements for heating and air conditioning equipment. Berlin 2003.

DIN 5034: Daylight in interiors. Berlin 2005.

DIN 5035: Artificial lighting. Berlin 2006.

DIN 5039: Light, lamps, luminaires. Berlin 1995.

DIN 5040: Luminaires for lighting purposes. Berlin 1999.

DIN EN 12464: Light and lighting - Lighting of workplaces. Berlin 2003.

DIN EN 12524: Building materials and products - Hygrothermal properties - Tabulated design values. Berlin 2000.

DIN EN 12665: Light and lighting – Basic terms and criteria for specifying lighting requirements. Berlin 2002.

DIN EN 410: Glass in building - Determination of luminous and solar characteristics of glazing. Berlin 1998.

DIN EN 673: Glass in building - Determination of thermal transmittance (U value). Berlin 2003.

DIN EN ISO 10077: Thermal performance of windows, doors and shutters – Calculation of thermal transmittance. Berlin 2004.

DIN EN ISO 15927: Hygrothermal performance of buildings – Calculation and presentation of climatic data. Berlin 2004.

DIN EN ISO 6946: Building components – Thermal resistance and thermal transmittance – Calculation method. Berlin 2005 (Draft).

DIN EN ISO 7345: Thermal insulation. Berlin 1996.

DIN EN ISO 8996: Ergonomics of the thermal environment – Determination of metabolic rate. Berlin 2005.

DIN EN ISO 9241: Ergonomic requirements for office work with visual display terminals. Berlin 2002.

VDI 2050, Sheet 1: Central heating installations – Central heating installations in buildings - Engineering principles for planning and design. Berlin 1995.

VDI 2067, Sheet 1 Draft: Economic efficiency of building installations – Fundamentals and economic calculation. Berlin 1999.

VDI 2067, Sheet 3: Economy calculation of heat-providing installations; air conditioning installations. Berlin 1983.

VDI 2078: Cooling load calculation of air-conditioned rooms. Berlin 1998.

VDI 2714: Outdoor sound propagation. Berlin 1988.

VDI 2719: Sound insulation of windows and their auxiliary equipment. Düsseldorf 1987.

VDI 3803: Air-conditioning systems – Structural and technical requirements. Berlin 1986.

VDI 3807: Characteristic values of energy consumption in buildings. Sheets 1 and 2. Berlin 1994.

VDI 4600: Cumulative energy demand – Terms, definitions, methods of calculation. Berlin 1997.

VDI 6030: Designing free heating surfaces - Fundamentals and design of heating appliances. Berlin 2002.

Internet

www.baunetz.de
www.bauphysik.de
www.bine.fiz-karlsruhe.de
www.bph.hbt.arch.ethz.de
www.bpy.uni-kassel.de/solaropt
www.climadesign.de
www.eclim.de
www.erneuerbare-energien.de
www.impulsprogramm.de
www.iwu.de
www.okalux.de
www.solarbau.de
www.trox.de
www.waermedaemmstoffe.com
www.warema.de

Index

Authors

Gerhard Hausladen
Prof. Dr.-Ing.
07.10.1947
Mechanical Engineering, TU München
Lst. für Bauklimatik
und Haustechnik, TU München
Ingenieurbüro Hausladen,
Building technology, building
physics, energy concepts, climate
design

Michael de Saldanha
Dr.-Ing.
05.04.1966
Architecture, GH Kassel
Lst. für Bauklimatik und
Haustechnik, TU München
Climate design

Petra Liedl
Dipl.-Ing.
21.07.1976
Architecture, TU München
Lst. für Bauklimatik und
Haustechnik, TU München
Climate design

Hermann Kaufmann
Prof. Dipl.-Ing.
11.06.1955
Architecture, TH Innsbruck,
TU Vienna
Specialism: timber construction,
TU München
Architekturbüro DI Kaufmann
Timber construction

Gerd Hauser
Prof. Dr.-Ing.
08.03.1948
Mechanical Engineering,
TU München
Lst. für Bauphysik, TU München
Fraunhofer-Inst. für Bauphysik,
Chair Thermal and energetic
behaviour of buildings, energy
concepts

Klaus Fitzner
Prof. a. D. Dr.-Ing.
11.08.1937
Mechanical Engineering,
TU München
Hermann-Rietschel-Institut,
TU Berlin
Klimakonzept IG
Heating and climate engineering,
room air flow, air quality

Christian Bartenbach
Prof. Dipl.-Ing.
14.05.1930
Graduate Engineer
Lichtakademie Bartenbach, Aldrans, A
Bartenbach LichtLabor, Company founder
Natural and artificial lighting,
research and development

Winfried Nerdinger
Prof. Dr.-Ing.
24.08.1944
Architecture, TU München
Architecture Museum,
TU München
History and theory of 18th–20th
century architecture

Winfried Heusler
Dr.-Ing.
20.09.1955
Mechanical Engineering,
TU München
SCHÜCO International KG
Direktor Project Engineering
Innovative solutions for complex
facade projects

Friedemann Jung
Dipl.-Ing.
06.11.1979
Architecture, TU München
Lst. für Bauklimatik und
Haustechnik, TU München
Climate design

Michael Kehr
cand. arch.
28.09.1981
Architecture, TU München
Lst. für Bauklimatik und
Haustechnik, TU München
Climate design

Christiane Kirschbaum
Dipl.-Ing.
17.12.1979
Architecture, TU München
Lst. für Bauklimatik und
Haustechnik, TU München
Climate design

Alexandra Liedl
Dipl.-Psych.
07.09.1979
Psychology, FSU Jena
Intercultural matters

Moritz Selinger
Dipl.-Ing.
26.11.1979
Architecture, TU München
Lst. für Bauklimatik und
Haustechnik, TU München
Climate design

Michael Smola
Dipl.-Ing.
20.01.1979
Architecture, TU München
Lst. für Bauklimatik und
Haustechnik, TU München
Climate design

Josef Bauer
14.04.1965
Utilities Engineer, Regensburg
Ingenieurbüro Hausladen,
Director
Room climate, energy concept
development

Cornelia Jacobsen
Dipl.-Ing. (FH)
19.06.1970
Physical Technology, FH München
Ingenieurbüro Hausladen,
Energy Design Manager
Energy concepts,
Facade consultancy

Oliver Trieb
Dipl.-Ing. (FH)
24.06.1965
Mechanical Engineering,
Neubiberg
Ingenieurbüro Hausladen,
Senior Manager Utility
engineering, energy concepts,
building technical services,
residential buildings

Illustration credits

The authors and publisher would like to thank all those who have helped to make this book a reality by providing illustrations, granting permission for reproducing them, or giving advice. All the drawings in this book have been produced in-house. Photographs for which no photographer is named have been obtained from the departmental library. Despite intensive efforts we were not able to determine the owners of some of the illustrations. The copyrights of these images are nevertheless preserved. Where this has occurred we would welcome the relevant information. The numbering refers to the number of the figure in the book or the page number.

02 Facade functions

Auer+Weber+Assoziierte: p. 27
Scheffler + Partner Architekten: p. 36,
    Figs. 2.14, 2.16, 2.17, 2.18
Lang Hugger Rampp Architekten GmbH: p. 50, 51,
    Figs. 2.35, 2.36, 2.38
Bartenbach Lichtlabor GmbH: p. 51, Fig. 2.37
Auer+Weber+Assoziierte: p. 64, 65, Figs. 2.56–2.60
Robert Müller, Bartenbach Lichtlabor GmbH: p. 82, 83,
    Figs. 2.73, 2.74, 2.75

03 Facade concepts

Matthias Kestel: p. 85
Jens Passoth: p. 92, Figs. 3.8, 3.9
Allmann Sattler Wappner Architekten GmbH:
    Figs. 3.5, 3.6, 3.7
Prof. Dr.-Ing. Wienands: p. 116, Figs. 3.35, 3.36, 3.39, 3.40
Ingenieurbüro für Bauklimatik Hausladen & Meyer, Kassel:
    p. 116, Figs. 3.37, 3.38

04 Facade technology

Development and projects: Bartenbach Lichtlabor GmbH
(Development and projects) Peter Bartenbach (photos):
    p. 138, p. 139 all Figs. bottom
Ferit Kuyas: p. 142 bottom left
Ben Wiesenfarth: p. 142 bottom right
Jens Passoth: p. 143 bottom left
Volker Bitzer: p. 143 bottom centre
Bruno Klomfar: p. 144, Figs. 4.39, 4.40
Architekturbüro DI Hermann Kaufmann ZT GmbH:
    Figs. 4.34, 4.35, 4.36, 4.37, 4.38
A. Kaufmann, Fraunhofer IBP Holzkirchen: p. 146,
    Figs. 4.41, 4.43, 4.44
Henn Architekten: Fig. 4.42

05 Facade interactions

Stefan Niese, Auer+Weber+Assoziierte: S. 150

All drawings have been created based on the documents made available by the participating architectural offices.

Acknowledgements

Our particular thanks are due to all architects, companies and institutions that have made images and drawings available to use or provided us with specialised advice and through their efforts have made a crucial contribution to the creation of this book.

- Albert Speer & Partner GmbH, Frankfurt
- Allmann Sattler Wappner Architekten GmbH, Munich
- ArchitekturBüro DI Hermann Kaufmann ZT GmbH,
  Schwarzach, A
- Auer+Weber+Assoziierte, Munich
- Bartenbach Lichtlabor, Aldrans, A
- Fraunhofer-Institut für Bauphysik, Holzkirchen
- Henn Architekten, Munich
- Scheffler + Partner Architekten, Frankfurt
- Stefan Forster Architekten, Frankfurt
- Steidle + Partner, Munich

We would also like to extend our thanks to the authors of our third-party contributions whose specialised knowledge of current issues has extended the coverage of the book into many new aspects.

- Prof. Dipl.-Ing. Hermann Kaufmann
- Prof. Dr.-Ing. Gerd Hauser
- Prof. Dr.-Ing. Klaus Fitzner
- Prof. Ing. Christian Bartenbach
- Prof. Dr.-Ing. Winfried Nerdinger
- Dr.-Ing. Winfried Heusler

We are grateful to HOCHTIEF Construction AG for its extensive support and close cooperation.

We would also like to thank the following people and organisations:

- Bettina Rühm, our Editor, for her outstanding work. The consistency of style and clarity of the contributions to this book owe a great deal to her rich flow of ideas and suggestions.

- Callwey Verlag, in particular Dr. Marcella Baur-Callwey, Ursula Kilguß and Caroline Keller, who were responsible for the contentual and technical aspects of the "ClimateSkin" project and Dr. Stefan Granzow for getting the book underway.

- prosa Architektur & Grafik, in particular Ellen Kloft and Sven Kling, who handled the extensive graphics and typesetting work in this book with great patience and commitment.

- Elisabeth Peter for her active support on the PC.

- Christian Huber for his advice on the theme of insulation.

- Felix Lausch for his creative contribution in Dresden.

- Mira Müller

We have greatly enjoyed working with everyone involved with this book.

Without all these people providing their valuable assistance behind the scenes, a project of this complexity would not have been possible.

Publisher's imprint

This book was prepared at the Institut für Entwerfen und Bautechnik, Fakultät für Architektur, Lehrstuhl für Bauklimatik und Haustechnik, Technische Universität München.

Translation into English: Raymond Peat, Aberdeenshire, UK
English copy editing: John O'Toole, New York

Library of Congress Control Number: 2007942749

Bibliographic information published by the German National Library
The German National Library lists this publication in the Deutsche Nationalbibliografie; detailed bibliographic data are available on the Internet at http://dnb.d-nb.de.

© German edition 2006 ClimaSkin by Verlag D.W. Callwey GmbH & Co. KG, München.
2008 Licence granted to Birkhäuser Verlag AG
Basel · Boston · Berlin
P.O. Box 133, CH-4010 Basel, Switzerland
Part of Springer Science+Business Media

Printed on acid-free paper produced from chlorine-free pulp.
TCF ∞
Printed in Germany

ISBN: 978-3-7643-7725-0

9 8 7 6 5 4 3 2 1   www.birkhauser.ch